THE APARTMENT VEGETARIAN COOKBOOK

LINDSAY MILLER

Peace Press
1978

Peace Press, Inc.
3828 Willat Avenue
Culver City, California 90230

9 8 7 6 5 4 3

Cover painting and illustrations by Theresa Abramian.
Typesetting by Gutenberg 2000, Santa Monica, California.
Printed in the United States of America by Peace Press.

Library of Congress Cataloging in Publication Data

Miller, Lindsay, 1950-
      The apartment vegetarian cookbook.

      Bibliography: p.
      Includes index.
      1. Vegetarian cookery. I. Title.
TX837.M57   641.5′636   78-19250
ISBN 0-915238-26-8

ACKNOWLEDGMENTS

I am grateful to all the people at Peace Press who put so much work into publishing this book, and especially to Dorothy Schuler whose prompt correspondence and answers to my questions were so helpful. Thanks also to the people at Carnegie Library in Pittsburgh who so willingly went searching whenever I needed help tracking down information.

Many thanks to all the friends and acquaintances whose advice and encouragement were such a lift during times when the writing and experimenting seemed to drag interminably and my confidence had settled into a real rut.

Finally, I want to thank my family for their support, and for allowing me to use them as guinea pigs in all my cooking experiments. The recipes wouldn't have been possible without them.

CONTENTS

INTRODUCTION

This book is intended for new vegetarians, old vegetarians, semi-vegetarians, and anyone else who would like to decrease his consumption of flesh foods without sacrificing good nutrition. It is especially for those vegetarians who live alone, with one roommate, or in a houseful of meat-eaters. It is for mothers who suddenly find themselves with a teenaged "vegie" in the family and are sure that their "baby" is going to succumb to malnutrition.

There are a number of good vegetarian cookbooks on the market. Unfortunately, most of them contain recipes for a large number of people (6 or 8). If you only want a meal for one or two you're stuck doing a lot of arithmetic to reduce the quantities to the size you can use. Even then you're never sure if the dish is going to come out seasoned the way it's supposed to be, and dealing with measurements like one-sixteenth of a teaspoon can get to be a hassle. The recipes in this book will solve these problems as they are tailored for feeding two (and sometimes company), and I have already done all the arithmetic for you.

If you are a beginner at cooking you will, I hope, be pleased to discover that I've included thorough instructions for all the cooking methods used in the recipes. When I began cooking it was a pretty hit-or-miss operation. Although the discovering process was fun, at times I really did wish that I'd had the information I needed at my fingertips, rather than having to search through book after book to find what I was looking for. I've tried to pass on my useful discoveries to you.

The protein concepts presented here are closely based on those in *Diet for a Small Planet*, by Frances Moore Lappé. Getting enough high-quality protein in a non-meat diet can appear to be a mind boggling endeavor, which it needn't be. I've based my work on Ms. Lappé's discoveries because they seem to be the most complete and least confusing basis for getting high quality protein in a vegetarian diet.

I hope that you'll find this book to be a useful tool in your kitchen, and that you'll find at least half as much enjoyment in cooking and eating the dishes as I have found in devising them for you.

FOOD FROM THE EARTH

At one time humanity was intimately involved with the production of food. People planted, tended, harvested, preserved, and cooked their own food and bartered for the few necessities they could not produce. With the advent of modern technology this simple system began to change, at times for the better (modern transportation makes it possible for northerners to enjoy fresh fruits and vegetables year-round), but often for the worse. Technology has "improved" foods to the point that the list of ingredients on many food packages is mainly a list of chemicals used to flavor, color, and preserve foods which are processed — until they have no color, flavor, or food value left to preserve.

"Natural" foods are those which are eaten as they grow on the earth. This means whole grains, dry legumes, fresh fruits and vegetables, naturally produced meat and dairy products, and herbs and spices, without added chemicals and preservatives. Of course there is room for some leeway in this — if you can't get fresh vegetables, I'm sure canned vegetables are better than none at all.

The first time I picked up a natural foods cookbook I was bewildered by all the "new" foods with names I'd never heard of — bulgar, wheat berries, millet (that's birdseed isn't it?) — the list went on and on. But although these foods were new to *me*, they are staple foods in many areas of the world. I began to discover that by switching to natural, vegetarian foods I wasn't limiting myself to a lifetime of plain brown rice and soybeans. Instead I had stepped into a much broader realm of eating than the chemicalized one left behind. There were centuries of eating traditions behind me and a lifetime of discovery and experimentation ahead.

Today many of us live in cities and towns, far removed, it seems, from the great natural cycles which preserve the earth and support her inhabitants. Fortunately we still have the option of strengthening our ties with the earth by eating directly from her bounty rather than from a test tube.

THE WHYS AND WHEREFORES OF VEGETARIAN EATING

Many people become vegetarians after seeing a movie like *Bambi* or *The Yearling* — they swear off meat "for life." I must confess that my own interest in eliminating meat from my diet began in much the same way. But as I investigated the subject, I began to discover that there are many other reasons for eliminating, or at least reducing, the amount of meat in the daily diet.

ECOLOGICAL EATING

Ecological considerations are first on the list of reasons to reduce meat consumption. After centuries of raping the earth to satisfy its own greed humanity is finally beginning to realize that the earth's resources are finite. We simply cannot go on indefinitely in the pattern of mining the earth, taking what we want from it, and discarding what is extra or unwanted. Unfortunately most meat producers are still guilty of the wasting and discarding method of production.

Certain livestock, such as cattle, have the ability to produce protein (milk and meat) without eating protein. This makes it possible to transform humanly inedible plants into high quality protein by passing them through a cow. This sounds wonderful, and it would be if the process stopped there. High-grade meat commands high prices and the grade depends on the amount of marbling (internal fat) in the meat — the more marbling, the higher the grade. To increase marbling the animal is fattened on high protein grains and legumes, most of which are humanly edible as protein sources. Instead of using the cow's protein-producing capacity the meat producers squander it, largely eliminating low-quality feeds. The net result is a considerable gain in meat fat content, little gain in meat protein content, and a considerable loss in total protein; 95 percent of the protein fed to the cattle is lost for human use.

If the earth's protein-producing capacity were unlimited this amount of waste might make some sort of sense. Unfortunately, only a relatively small proportion of the earth's surface is suitable for crop production. While Americans waste protein in producing meat many people in other countries cannot get enough protein to maintain health. By changing our methods of meat production and by eating less meat we could free huge amounts of vegetable protein for direct human consumption.

If the world population continues to grow, a point will come when the earth will no longer be able to support its population. The recommended solution is birth control, which would work quite well in stable, developed countries where people feel fairly secure. However, in developing or poverty-stricken countries the only security is the family unit. Couples have many children to insure themselves against hunger — more children means more people to produce food by farming. If enough food were available the population growth might diminish, as people in underdeveloped countries would not need to have as many children. More food *could* be supplied by diverting high protein feeds to direct human consumption.

HEALTHFUL EATING

On the average vegetarians seem to live longer, healthier lives than meat-eaters. This is partly due to the fact that most vegetarians are more nutrition conscious than the average person. But there are differences in the foods themselves which tend to make a vegetarian diet more healthful.

There is no food value in meat which cannot be found in equal or greater amounts in non-meat foods. In the average western diet, high in meat and low in fruits and vegetables, most of the vitamins and minerals come from the fruits and vegetables. Protein is abundant in plant sources such as grains, legumes, seeds, and vegetables, and non-meat animal products like milk and eggs. Only vitamin B-12 is absent from most plant foods, and it can easily be supplied by milk rather than meat.

Far from being essential, meat, especially in large amounts, can actually be harmful. All meats contain saturated fats and cholesterol, which, if eaten in excess, can lead to such serious conditions as high blood pressure, hardening of the arteries (one cause of senility), heart disease, heart attacks, and strokes. By reducing or eliminating meat we would drastically reduce our intake of harmful saturated fats.

Even in a "perfect world" meat-eating would present the saturated fat problem. In our far from perfect world the fat content in meat provides additional problems. To increase fat production in an animal it is not only fed a grain diet, but also injected with synthetic hormones — some are known carcinogens. The hormones are deposited in the fat and various organs of the animal; so when we eat meat we are ingesting hormones too.

Animal fats are also repositories for pesticide residues. The pesticide residue in plants is fairly small, but when an animal consumes plants it is also consuming pesticides. The food eventually passes out of the animal's system. But the pesticide remains, gradually building up until the pesticide concentration in the animal is much higher than in the plants. When a person eats meat the same process occurs, but much more pesticide is being ingested and retained. It is impossible to totally eliminate pesticide intake, but by eating mainly plants we can reduce it greatly. (Note: Since most of the pesticide residue in milk occurs in the butterfat, low-fat milk products can be used freely without too much worry.)

ECONOMICAL EATING

One trip to the meat counter of the local supermarket is enough to make many people at least consider the economic benefits of giving up meat. Meat prices are high. Since the American population has been so well programmed into believing that meat is indespensible people may balk at the prices, but they usually end up paying them. Scores of healthy vegetarians can attest to the fact that meat does not deserve its terrific reputation. In fact, until quite recently most of the earth's population considered meat a luxury to be consumed by the rich but only sparingly by the common person.

Many people frown on meatless diets because they think vegetarians eat nothing but lettuce, with an occasional helping of "something weird" like seaweed. Any diet as limited as that would be sure to eventually result in some kind of deficiency. It is possible to combine non-meat foods to produce high-protein, nutritious meals. The economic boon with non-meat foods is that they are all fairly inexpensive. A pound of soybeans contains more protein than a pound of meat and the soybeans cost less than fifty cents per pound.

ORGANIC GROWING

The best way to be certain of the source of natural foods is to grow your own. Although few of us have the land necessary to grow all of our own food, all of us have the facilities to grow at least some of it. A flowerpot is all that's needed to get started. Modern agribusiness (what a word to apply to farming!) is locked in a cycle of chemical dependence. Pesticides encourage the breeding of pesticide resistant insects, and chemical fertilizers do nothing to rebuild depleted soil. As pests grow stronger and the soil grows weaker it becomes necessary to use stronger and stronger chemicals to continue to grow crops in the same area. In addition, the chemicals contribute to pollution and upset the natural balance by poisoning wildlife, not to mention people.

There is a way out of this cycle. Organic growers concentrate on building healthy soil, trusting that good soil will grow healthy plants, and expecting healthy plants to produce good food. The organic grower builds his soil by tilling natural rock fertilizers and organic wastes into the soil. These materials decompose, adding nutrients to the soil and providing food for the many organisms that build the soil. Left to itself, nature would work the same cycle: organisms grow, die, and decompose to provide food for the next generation.

I recommend the organic method, no matter how limited your garden. It is ecologically sound and very inexpensive. Save all your kitchen wastes and compost them. If you have no room for a compost pile bury the garbage between the garden rows and let the earthworms compost it for you. Or you can put kitchen wastes in a blender with a little water and "buzz" them until finely ground. Water and feed your plants with the mixture. For most satisfactory results, it is best to ask your nursery for seed and plant varieties suited to your gardening situation.

SURVIVAL COOKING

For any type of survival cooking situation, be it a weather emergency, a move to a wilderness cabin, or a backpacking trip, natural foods make sense. They are light, compact, and require no energy for storage (as do frozen foods). In their dry state whole grains and legumes can be stored for a year or more without significant loss of food value. In the event of isolation or a power outage people dependent on two weekly trips to the supermarket or stored frozen foods are in trouble. People with a supply of dry natural foods can cook good, nutritious meals, even over a wood fire if necessary. Dry foods can be supplemented with fruits and vegetables such as apples, potatoes, onions, carrots, and winter squash, which store well without refrigeration. For fresh greens, and their vitamin content, you can grow sprouts from small amounts of dry foods.

Some types of survival situations, like being snowed in, can actually be fun — a time to do mental and physical battle with the situation or to just curl up by the fire and read a good book. Secure in the knowledge that your natural foods are there to take care of your nutritional needs you can banish worries and enjoy the situation for what it's worth.

GOOD FOOD, GOOD NUTRITION

All living organisms must "eat" to survive. Plants eat by taking up nutrients through roots and leaves and, with the help of light, converting nutrients into usable forms for growth, maturation, and procreation. Animals eat by chewing, swallowing, and digesting. The nutrients in animal foods are used for the same purposes as in plants: growth (including the replacement of worn out cells), maturation and procreation (undernourished animals may have difficulty conceiving and bearing healthy young).In order for animal bodies, including our own, to operate at their best it is necessary that they be fed the right kinds of food in order to have the proper balance of nutrients, i.e., vitamins, minerals, fats, carbohydrates, and proteins. If a wide variety of whole, natural foods are eaten and a little wisdom applied in serving and cooking, deficiencies should not be a problem.

VITAMINS AND MINERALS

By weight and bulk the various vitamins and minerals comprise a very small part of our diets, but our bodies need those small amounts to function properly. A deficiency or lack of a vitamin or mineral can cause any number of problems, ranging from greying hair through various forms of mental illness.

Necessary vitamins and minerals can be found in abundance in fresh foods, but they are easily lost or destroyed through improper cooking and handling. Fresh foods, such as vegetables and dairy products, should be stored in the refrigerator until they are ready to be eaten or cooked. Heat (even room temperature) and light can destroy vitamins. Wash vegetables quickly and do not let them soak in large amounts of water. Soaking leaches out vitamins and minerals which then go down the drain with the soaking water. Eat vegetables raw as often as possible; when you cook them do so quickly and carefully. In most cases, avoid peeling or paring vegetables before eating them.

Choosing and handling your foods carefully should eliminate any need for vitamin or mineral supplement pills. If you should decide to take some kind of supplement, please be sure to take it with food. Vitamins cannot keep you healthy by themselves as their value comes from the way they interact and work in conjunction with foods. Mother Nature's vitamins all occur in foods because they are most useful in foods; you will never find them growing in isolation on a vitamin plant. Don't make the mistake of thinking that as long as you take enough vitamin pills you will stay well no matter how poorly you eat. You will only be wasting your money and ruining your health. Brewer's yeast, raw (untoasted) wheat germ, and wheat germ oil are excellent natural food supplements; they provide minerals and the B-complex and E vitamins that are easily destroyed in foods by careless handling.

THE BIG THREE

In addition to small amounts of vitamins, minerals, and other trace components, foods provide carbohydrates, fats, and proteins which are used in different ways to fuel and rebuild our bodies. For the average person the daily calorie intake should consist of roughly 60 percent carbohydrate calories, less than 25 percent fat calories, and at least 15 percent protein calories. Of course these percentages vary with the individual and partially depend on physical activity and metabolism efficiency. Carbohydrates, fats, and proteins occur in combinations in foods; so if you are eating a variety of foods, while keeping an eye on protein and fat intake, the percentages should even out. You don't even have to keep computerized tables on everything you eat.

CARBOHYDRATES

Carbohydrates are starches and sugars. They provide fuel and energy and are found in foods of plant origin and dairy products. There is some overlap, but generally starches occur in grains, root vegetables, and legumes. Sugars are found in fruits, vegetables, milk, and such foods as honey and maple syrup.

Simple sugars, such as those in fruits and honey, are easily digested, while more complex sugars and starches must be converted into simple sugars before the body can use them. The conversion process usually begins in the mouth where the saliva reduces the starches to simple sugars; so always chew well to give this process time to work. By cooking we can give the body a head start on changing starches to sugars, and indeed, most starchy foods would be unpalatable without cooking or baking. I for one cannot imagine eating raw flours, uncooked dry grains, or uncooked dry legumes. Combined with other foods and cooked, they become the basis for any number of delicious dishes.

In recent years carbohydrates have been considered the bad guy in the battle for weight control. In large part this reputation for being fattening has come about because of the way in which carbohydrates are consumed, i.e., mainly in white sugar, white flour, and polished rice. Primitive peoples who eat large amounts of carbohydrates in whole grains and vegetables remain slim, but gain weight if put on a "civilized" diet containing white sugar and flour. Food fiber content, of course, has a great deal to do with this effect; whole grains are rich in fiber while white flour has had its fiber content removed. In addition, devitalized foods, especially white sugar, seem to have an almost addictive effect upon the body. People with weight problems, except in rare cases of glandular imbalance, generally have cravings for white bread, sweet rolls, cake, cookies, and candy, rather than for healthful foods like fruits and vegetables. If this sounds like you, try substituting whole grains and honey for your usual devitalized grains and white sugar. It won't solve all your problems, but it should help. And don't think of carbohydrates as "the enemy" as they are an important part of the daily diet. Just be sure for your health's sake (slim health) to eat carbohydrates in nutritious foods, not junk foods.

FATS

Fats provide the body with slow-release fuel, insulation from heat and cold, lubrication (especially for the skin), and a medium for the absorption of the fat soluble vitamins A, D, and E. The calories in fats are very concentrated. One table-spoon of oil or butter has about 100 calories, so it doesn't take much fat to fill the daily requirement. Watch out for "hidden fats," such as those in nuts, dairy products, and cooking oils, which can go completely unnoticed while still contributing to fat intake.

Fats are "saturated" or "unsaturated." For an over-simplified illustration, picture a fat molecule as a chain with hydrogen atoms as some of its links. In saturated fats all of the hydrogen atoms are present in the molecule; in unsaturated fats one or more of the hydrogen atoms is missing. These empty links can be filled by hydrogen atoms absorbed from the molecule's surroundings. In the human body this absorbing action results in a lowering of cholesterol (a saturated fat) and an acceleration of the movement of fats through the system. Unsaturated fats don't settle in lumpy bulges on hips, thighs, and the tummy as do saturated fats.

Obviously then, we should try to ingest more unsaturated than saturated fats. Saturated fats are found in animal prod-ucts, including milk, cheese, and eggs, coconut oil, and any vegetable oil product whose lable says it is "hydrogenated" or "partially hydrogenated." Unsaturated fats are found in veg-etable oils such as safflower oil, corn oil, and soybean oil. Try to include at least one or two tablespoons of unsaturated oils in your daily diet. If you have been on a severely fat restricted diet and have failed to lose weight you may find that daily *adding* the 100 calories in a tablespoon of unsaturated oil may actually help you to reduce. Read labels carefully though; if a product says it contains vegetable oil chances are it is highly saturated coconut oil rather than the unsaturated oil you are looking for.

When cooking with fats be careful not to let them get too hot. You can add a teaspoon or two of water to keep the heat down. For frying and greasing baking pans it may be better to use a saturated fat such as butter, hydrogenated soy margarine, or shortening because of the high heats involved. Saturated fats are more stable under high heats; unsaturated fats *may* break down into undesirable forms when they get too hot. Use the unsaturated oils for cooler cooking methods and especially in salad dressings for fresh raw vegetables.

PROTEINS

Protein is used for building the structural framework of the body and for replacing worn out cells. The production of cells which make up this framework (bone, blood, and muscle) is not possible without sufficient protein intake. Protein is also necessary for regulating metabolism, maintaining a neutral pH balance in the body, and forming antibodies for protection against infection and disease.

COMPLETE AND INCOMPLETE PROTEIN

Proteins are made up of 22 amino acids. Eight of these, the Essential Amino Acids (EAA's), the body is unable to synthesize from other materials. They must be replenished daily by eating protein rich foods. Unfortunately, there is a hitch to this process as the body will use only one amino acid pattern completely. All of the EAA's must be present in the correct proportions, at the same time, in order for the body to use them efficiently. If there is a shortage of one of the EAA's, the other amino acids can be used as protein only in proportion to this reduced amount of the one lacking amino acid. For example, if you consumed a dish which provided 100 percent of your daily need of seven of the EAA's, but only 10 percent of the remaining EAA, your body would assume that you had fed it only 10 percent of *all* the EAA's. The rest of the amino acids would then be converted to carbohydrate or passed out of the body as wastes.

The fact that the body is able to use only one amino acid pattern completely has lead to the concept of "complete" and "incomplete" proteins. Actually we should speak of "more nearly complete" proteins, as there is no naturally occurring food protein which is 100 percent utilizable in the human body. So called complete proteins are those in which a high percentage of the protein, usually 60 percent or more, is usable by the human body. In "incomplete" proteins less than 60 percent can be used because of one or more amino acid deficiencies. The percentage of usable protein in a food is called Net Protein Utilization, or NPU. Complete proteins, those with an NPU higher than 60, are found in eggs (NPU of 94 — nearly perfect!), milk products, fish, brown rice, poultry, meats, wheat germ, oats, and soybeans. Incomplete proteins are found in whole grains, nuts and seeds, dried legumes, brewer's yeast, and fresh vegetables.

Since food proteins vary in how well the body can use them, getting enough protein in the daily diet becomes not just a matter of protein quantity, but also of protein quality. We will want to look for protein foods with a high NPU. Meat has a fairly high NPU, but at 67 it's not nearly as high as one would think considering its reputation for indispensability in the human diet. If we wish to reduce or eliminate flesh foods in the diet we can still choose complete proteins from eggs, milk products, brown rice, wheat germ, oats, and soybeans.

PROTEIN COMPLEMENTARITY

In addition to choosing foods with an intrinsic high NPU we can actually put high quality protein into our diets by using foods with lower NPU's. Low NPU foods can be combined so that the amino acid weaknesses in each are matched by strengths in the other. The resulting combined NPU is higher than the individual NPU. This is called protein complementarity because the strengths in one protein complement (or complete) the weaknesses in the other. For instance, whole wheat is strong in its amounts of the amino acid tryptophan and the sulfur containing amino acids, but weak in isoleucine and lysine. Beans are strong in isoleucine and lysine, but weak in tryptophan and the sulfur containing amino acids. Thus, the amino acid strengths and weaknesses in beans and wheat match up; if they are eaten together the body actually has about 33 percent more usable protein than if the two foods were eaten separately.*

Generally, milk protein will complement the protein in legumes, whole grains, and seeds. Legumes and grains complement each other, as do legumes and seeds, and in certain combinations, grains and seeds. Remember though, you must eat these food combinations at the same meal in order to exploit their complementary effect. Having beans for lunch and whole wheat for dinner will not result in their complementing each other. All of the amino acids have to be present at the same time in order for them to function as complete protein.

QUANTITY OF DAILY PROTEIN NEED

To maintain health we must daily eat enough high NPU protein to fulfill our individual needs. But how much is

*Lappé, Frances Moore, *Diet for a Small Planet*, Ballantine Books, N.Y., 1971, p. 52.

enough? Protein content of foods is measured in grams. Most protein charts list foods according to the total number of grams of protein which they contain, no matter what the NPU of that protein might be. For the purposes of this book we will think in terms of usable protein — the number of grams of protein in a food which are actually available to the body for use as protein.

The number of grams of usable protein in a food depends upon the NPU of that protein. For example, one cup of milk contains nine grams of total protein. But since the NPU of milk is 82, the number of grams of protein which the body can actually use is reduced to seven $(9 \times .82 = 7.38)$. One-half cup of dry beans has about 24 grams of total protein, but with an NPU of only 43, only 10 grams are available as usable protein $(24 \times .43 = 10.32)$.*

The average person requires about 0.28 grams of usable protein per pound of body weight each day. To find your approximate daily protein need multiply your weight by 0.28. If you weigh 130 pounds you will need 36.4 grams of usable protein each day, unless you are pregnant or nursing a baby, in which case you will need 30 percent to 70 percent more. For convenience, recipes in this book which provide significant amounts of protein have that protein content expressed in usable grams.

One hint for being sure to get enough usable protein in your diet is to have a glass of milk with each meal. You need the calcium from the milk anyway, and the protein in the milk will complement any extra incomplete protein in the main part of the meal.

Now that we've talked about getting enough protein, there is another side to the story. The body will use protein *as* protein only in the amount it needs to fill its needs. Any extra protein is then changed to carbohydrate to be used as fuel. Aside from wasting the protein, this is also very hard on the system. The internal organs must work overtime to convert the protein to carbohydrate. Kidney problems can be one result of an over-intake of protein. So please avoid those "all protein" reducing diets. You'll lose weight — but you may end up with worse problems.

In general you can tell if you are getting enough protein by observing your body and its general condition. If you are healthy and have a good energy level, your hair and nails are in

---

*Lappé, *Small Planet*, pp. 74, 78

fairly good condition, and abrasions on your skin heal fairly quickly, chances are you are getting enough protein. If you are having problems with any of these you will want to increase your protein intake. Remember, protein requirements vary with the individual. People who are very active or under a great deal of pressure may require more protein than the average person. Some people's bodies are so efficient that they require very little protein each day. *You* are the only one who can really determine how well your body is faring on what you are feeding it. So observe carefully and adjust your diet according to what you discover.

A HEALTHY FOOD REGIMEN

Since everyone differs in his daily requirements of the different nutrients, I will make suggestions rather than formulate hard and fast nutritional laws. People seem to function best if they eat at least certain minimum amounts of the following:
Dairy products — Try to have a *minimum* of two cups of milk or yogurt each day. Milk provides calcium, much of which is lost in the making of cheese, so don't try to use cheese as your only milk product. The chocolate in chocolate milk inhibits the body's absorption of calcium, so learn to drink the real thing. Two cups of milk will also provide about ⅓ of your daily protein need.

Fruits and Vegetables — I can't encourage you enough to eat as many of these as you can. Have *at least* two servings of each every day. That's a glass of orange juice for breakfast, an apple for lunch, and a steamed vegetable and a salad for dinner. It isn't all that much when you think about it.

Whole grains — Have 1-2 cups of cooked whole grains (⅓-⅔ c. raw) or 2-6 slices of whole grain bread daily. Whole grains are an excellent source of food fiber as well as proteins and carbohydrates.

Protein — Fill out your daily protein quota by adding extra dairy products (more milk, cheese, eggs) and by eating complementary combinations of other protein foods.

Liquids — Drink 5 or more cups of water or other liquids daily in addition to your milk.

If you are trying to lose weight you should stick pretty closely to these suggestions. Choose low calorie protein foods like skim milk and cottage cheese and eat lots of vegetables. Raw vegetables fill the stomach but add few calories. Don't eliminate all whole grains and vegetable fats. Your body needs the fiber from the grains and we have already seen that unsaturated fats may actually help you to lose weight (*see* Fats). If you have only a few pounds to lose, you may find that just switching to natural, unprocessed foods and eliminating meat will solve the problem.

Whether you are dieting or not, be sure to get some exercise everyday, preferably in the open air — the sun is still the best natural source of vitamin D. Besides burning up calories, exercise increases your oxygen intake, and oxygen is necessary for the complete digestion and use of foods in the system.

BOOK LIST

This chapter is by no means intended to be an exhaustive dissertation on all phases of nutrition. If you are interested in learning more the following books are good sources of information:

Let's Eat Right to Keep Fit by Adelle Davis
This is the modern "bible" of nutrition. The only problem with this book is the heavy emphasis on meats. Organ meats, which tend to be repositories for pesticides (from the animal's environment) and hormones (which are injected into the animals to fatten them more quickly) are stressed. In spite of this, the book provides a wealth of important information.

The California Way to Natural Beauty by Toni DeMarco
The author presents many ideas for health and beauty through natural means: balanced nutrition, cleansing diets, exercise, positive thinking. It contains fairly detailed explanations of what nutrition is all about and how the various nutrients function in the body.

Diet for a Small Planet by Frances Moore Lappé
Recipes for a Small Planet by Ellen Buchman Ewald
These two books give a detailed explanation of protein complementarity from a nutritional standpoint and from that of preserving the earth's resources while feeding its people.

Back to Eden by Jethro Kloss
Some of the ideas here are a bit "far out," as Mr. Kloss advocates a complete rejection of *all* animal products, including milk and eggs. However he includes lots of information about the health values of various foods and herbs and discusses natural healing methods.

The Save Your Life Diet by David M. Reuben
The importance of food fiber in the diet is discussed.

Prevention and *Organic Gardening and Farming*, Rodale Press
Published monthly, these magazines contain an abundance of information for growing healthful foods and living healthfully.

COMPLEMENTARY PROTEIN CHART

The following chart has been adapted from *Recipes for a Small Planet*; the amounts are reduced so that proportions can be easily adapted for cooking for one or two people. All the relationships have been tested to determine the exact complementary proportions for these particular ingredients.* Chances are good though, that you can substitute one whole grain or legume for another without drastically altering the protein content of the finished dish.

For greater exactness in computing your protein intake please use the dry measurements for the different ingredients. I have included some approximate cooked measurements only for convenience.

COMBINATION		GRAMS OF USABLE PROTEIN
⅓ c. rice (1 c. cooked)	+ 2 T. beans (⅓ c. cooked)	7.5
½ c. rice (1½ c. cooked)	+ 2½ t. soy beans or grits (5-6 t. cooked), or 5 t. soy flour	7.4
¼ c. rice (¾ c. cooked)	+ 1 T. brewer's yeast	6
⅓ c. rice (1 c. cooked)	+ 5⅓ t. sesame seeds or 1 T. tahini	5.33
⅜ c. rice (1⅛ c. cooked)	+ ½ c. milk	8.5
¼ c. rice (¾ c. cooked)	+ 2 T. wheat berries or 3 T. bulgar or 4 T. whole wheat flour *and* 2 T. soy beans or grits or 4 T. soy flour	10.25

*Lappé, Frances Moore, *Diet for a Small Planet*, Ballantine Books, Inc., N.Y., 1971, p. 123

COMBINATION		GRAMS OF USABLE PROTEIN
¼ c. rice (¾ c. cooked) *and* 2⅔ T. wheat berries or ¼ c. bulgar or ⅓ c. whole wheat flour	+ 1⅓ T. peanuts or 2 t. peanut butter *and* 1⅔ T. soy beans or grits, or 3⅓ T. soy flour	12
½ c. bulgar or ⅓ c. macaroni	+ ⅓ c. milk or 2 T. instant milk powder or 2 T. grated cheese	9.33
6 T. wheat berries or 10 T. bulgar or 12 T. whole wheat flour	+ 2 T. beans	11.5
¼ c. wheat berries or 6 T. bulgar or ½ c. whole wheat flour	+ 1 T. soy beans or grits, or 2 T. soy flour	8
¼ c. wheat berries or 6 T. bulgar or ½ c. whole wheat flour	+ 1 T. peanut butter or scant 2 T. peanuts *and* 2 T. milk (1 T. instant) *or* ¾ t. soybeans or grits, or 1½ t. soy flour	10.4
6 T. wheat berries or 10 T. bulgar or 13 T. whole wheat flour	+ 1 T. soy beans or grits, or 2 T. soy flour *and* 1 T. Tahini or 2 T. sesame seeds	14.25
½ c. cornmeal (3 tortillas)	+ 1⅓ T. soy beans or grits, or 2⅔ T. soy flour *and* ½ c. milk (2⅔ T. instant)	10
½ c. cornmeal	+ 2 T. beans	7
3 T. peanuts or 2 T. peanut butter	+ 1 T. soy beans or grits, or 2 T. soy flour *and* 3½ T. sesame seed or 1¾ T. Tahini	14.6
3½ T. peanuts or 2 T. peanut butter	+ 3 T. milk (1 T. instant)	10.5

COMBINATION		GRAMS OF USABLE PROTEIN
3 T. peanuts or scant 2 T. peanut butter	+ 4 T. sunflower seeds	13.75
2½ T. sesame seeds or 4 t. sesame butter or Tahini	+ 2 T. milk (2 t. instant)	4
2 T. sesame seeds or 1 T. Tahini	+ 4 t. beans	4.75
2 T. beans	+ ¼ c. milk (4 t. instant)	5.5
1 medium potato	+ 1 c. milk (⅓ c. instant)	9

Note: 1 c. milk = ¼ c. non-instant milk powder = ⅓ c. instant milk powder = ⅓ c. grated or ricotta cheese = ¼ c. cottage cheese.

COMPLETE PROTEIN FOODS

These foods contain high quality protein. You can eat them alone or use them to fill out amino acid deficiencies in lower quality protein foods. Watch for some surprises — corn and mushrooms both contain complete protein!

FOOD	APPROX. NPU	TOTAL GRAMS PROTEIN	GRAMS USABLE PROTEIN
Egg (1 medium)	94	6	6
Milk (1 c.)	82	9-10	7-8
Corn (1 medium ear)	72	4	3
Mushrooms (10 small or 4 large)	72	3	2
Hard cheeses (1 oz. 1 in. square cube)	70	7-10	5-7
Soft cheeses (1 oz.)	70	5-6	4-5
Brown rice (⅓ c. raw)	70	5	3
Wheat germ (2 T.)	67	3	2
Oatmeal (⅓ c. raw)	66	4	3
Soybeans (¼-⅓ c. raw)	61-65	17	10

For comparison, fish has an average NPU of 80, while meat and poultry have an average NPU of 67, lower than the NPU of most of these non-meat foods.

COOKING TALK

This chapter will, I hope, get you a little further down the road to speaking the language of cookery. I've included a dictionary of cooking terms to help you in cooking from written recipes. Comparatively few of the terms are used in the recipes in this book; I've included the extra terms in case you happen to come across them elsewhere.

At the end of the dictionary you will find thorough descriptions of cooking methods frequently used when cooking with natural foods. Familiarize yourself with several methods and adapt them to the dishes you will be cooking. In addition there are directions for making delicious homemade yogurt and tips on using herbs and spices to perk up your cooking.

Please don't let unfamiliar terms scare you. As you will see, most cooking terms are just fancy names for simple procedures.

COOKING TERMS

bake (roast) — to cook in an oven with dry heat.

baste — to spoon cooking liquid or fat over food while cooking to keep food moist and add flavor.

beat — to stir briskly to mix ingredients and incorporate air. Use a wire whisk, spoon, egg beater, or electric mixer.

bind — to blend ingredients with another so all ingredients will hold a shape. Used especially for bean and grain loaves and patties.

blend — to mix ingredients together until smooth.

boil — to heat liquid to the point that it bubbles readily (212⁰ for water) or to cook food in boiling liquid.

braise — to brown in a small amount of fat, then cover and cook slowly, often with the addition of liquid.

broil — to cook quickly a few inches under a broiler.

chop (cube, dice, mince) — to cut up into small pieces. Cube implies even pieces ½ inch or more in size. Dice is like cube but the pieces are ½ inch or less. Mince means to chop into very fine pieces.

coat (bread, dredge, dust) — to cover with a thin layer of another ingredient, often an egg and flour or batter mixture.

cream — to beat together a fat (oil or butter) with a sugar until they are smooth and light. Use a wooden spoon or an electric mixer.

crush — to extract juice and mince by pressing, especially garlic. Place garlic on cutting board and cover with the side of the blade of a French chopping knife. Rap the side of the blade sharply with the side of your fist. One or two blows should do it.

curdle — when ingredients separate and become lumpy instead of remaining smooth. This is something you want to avoid unless you are making cheese. Be careful when adding egg or milk to hot mixtures.

cut in (rub in) — to mix solid fat with flour until you have a crumbly textured mixture. This is done by cutting with a knife or pastry blender or rubbing with the fingers.

fry — to cook in fat.

fold — to add one ingredient to others already mixed together so that lightness is retained. Use a metal spoon, cut into the mixture with the side of the spoon, lift a spoonful of the mixture, and gently turn the spoon over. Repeat until the ingredients are thoroughly blended.

glaze — to brush surface with a liquid before baking, or to ice with a thin icing after baking.

grate — to break up into small pieces by rubbing against a grater.

grind — to break up into small pieces by putting food through a food mill, or blender, or by using a mortar and pestle.

knead — in bread baking. On a floured surface press the dough with the heel of the hand. Give the dough a quarter turn (so that the "north" side is now pointing "east"), lift one edge of the dough and fold it over. Press again. Repeat until the dough becomes elastic (it will spring back when pressed). Takes 5-15 minutes.

marinate — to soak in a liquid (often vinegar or a salad dressing) so that the food will absorb flavor from the liquid.

mash — to reduce to a finer texture by applying pressure.

parboil — to partially cook in boiling water. The cooking is then completed by another method.

pare (peel, scrape) — to remove the outer surface of a vegetable. Paring removes the thickest layer of vegetable. Scraping takes away the least. Peeling removes an intermediate amount. Since the greatest amount of vitamin and minerals in a vegetable are found just under its surface usually *none* of these methods should be used, except for removing dirt and imperfections that won't come off with a vegetable brush.

poach — to cook in liquid at a temperature just below boiling. Eggs may also be poached by cooking them in a special pan over water which is not quite boiling.

pre-heat — to heat oven or broiler to desired temperature before putting food in to cook. Some stoves have a special signal to tell you when the temperature you have selected has been reached. Otherwise allow 15-20 minutes for pre-heating.

proof — to dissolve yeast in warm water or stock and allow it to grow for about 5 minutes.

purée — to reduce food to a smooth, creamy texture by forcing it through a seive or food mill or by "buzzing" it in a blender.

rise — to expand and become higher and lighter. This occurs during baking with most baked goods, and also results from the growth of yeast in yeast breads and rolls.

roll out — to flatten a lump of pastry or cookie dough into a large, thin sheet, using a rolling motion of a rolling pin. You can also use a large, round jar if you don't have a rolling pin.

sauté — to fry in a small amount of fat. In French the word means "to jump," so the idea is to keep the food "jumping" by stirring frequently while cooking. Stirring will also distribute the fat over all the exposed surfaces of the food, thus locking in vitamins and minerals.

scald — to heat (especially milk) to a temperature between 160° and 190° F. Bubbles will form around the edges of the surface.

season — to flavor with salt, pepper, and other herbs and spices. It can also mean to prepare a new cast iron pan for cooking by rubbing oil over all cooking surfaces and then heating the pan in a 300° oven for several hours. After seasoning you should be able to wipe the pan clean with a damp cloth; soaping and scrubbing won't be necessary.

separate — to separate the whites from the yolks of eggs. Do this by gently pouring the yolk of the egg back and forth from one half of the cracked shell to the other until all the white has run off. If any speck of yolk ends up in the white remove it with a clean, dry spoon. If you need really stiffly beaten egg whites even a drop of yolk can foul up the works.

simmer — to cook in liquid at a temperature just below boiling, or to cook at a very low heat.

steam — to cook in steam rather than liquid. See the special section on ways to steam vegetables.

stew — to cook in liquid for a long period of time at a low heat.

stir — to combine ingredients using a circular motion. A calmer action than beating; try using a wooden spoon.

strain — to separate solids from liquids by pouring the whole mixture into a strainer. The liquid will pass through and should be caught underneath in a pan or bowl, while the solids will remain in the strainer. Strained food is food which has been puréed by forcing it through a food mill or strainer.

toss — to mix (salad and dressing) by scooping up, lifting, and dropping until all vegetables are glistening with a coating of salad dressing.

whip — to beat rapidly so that a great deal of air will be incorporated and the ingredient will eventually become fairly stiff. This process is used to make meringue or whipped cream.

STEAMING VEGETABLES

Steaming is the best method for cooking most fresh or frozen vegetables. Vegetables which soak or cook in large amounts of water lose many nutrients through leaching; vitamins and minerals are drawn out into the water, which is then usually thrown away. In steaming, less water comes in contact with the vegetables, therefore nutritional loss is minimized. You can steam vegetables in a number of ways.

Method I

Cook the vegetables in a steaming basket, either one made specifically for a certain pot or one of the little adjustable baskets which unfold to fit in a variety of pot sizes. With either type of basket first put some water in the pot. Use enough water so that it won't all boil away before your vegetables are cooked, but not enough to touch the bottom of the basket. Place the empty basket in the pot and bring the water to a boil. When a *lot* of steam is being produced place the vegetables in the basket, cover the pot, and reduce the heat to medium-low. The idea is to produce enough steam so that when the pot is covered it will be filled with steam and the air will be forced out. Exposure to air will cause a loss of nutrients. Keep the pot covered and continue to cook until the vegetables are crisp-tender.

Method II

If you don't have a basket you can use the sauté method for steaming your vegetables. Choose a pot with a tightly fitting lid. Over a medium flame, heat a tablespoon or two of oil or butter. When the fat is fairly hot add the vegetables and stir them until all the exposed surfaces are coated with a thin film of oil. This film will prevent nutrient loss. You may then add a tablespoonful or two or water to create steam (with very juicy vegetables like summer squash this is unnecessary). Cover, reduce heat to a simmer, and steam until vegetables are crisp-tender.

Method III

This method works well in "waterless" cookware, or any pan with a good, tightly fitting lid. Choose a pot which your food will nearly fill. Use about ⅛ inch of water, which is just enough to barely cover the bottom of the pan. Bring the water to a boil and as soon as it is steaming well, quickly pour in the vegetables. Cover the pan and reduce the heat to a simmer. Keep covered (don't peek!) and steam until vegetables are crisp-tender. Give the pot a good shake two or three times during the steaming process. Hold the lid on tightly and use the kind of movement the experts use for flipping pancakes. This will ensure that the vegetables cook evenly.

Timetable for Steaming Vegetables

The key to steaming vegetables is that "less is best" as far as cooking time is concerned. The only time you should increase any of the times is if you're using frozen vegetables that come out of the package in one big lump. Cooking may take a little longer because there are no spaces for the steam to get into until the vegetable has defrosted.

The only other time you'll have to increase cooking time (and this is not to be encouraged!) is if you're feeding someone like my mother who doesn't like her peas unless they're over-cooked. No wonder I never liked peas when I was a little kid!

COOKING TIME IN MINUTES

Artichokes, globe	18-20	Corn, fresh (on the cob)	5-6
Artichokes, Jerusalem	15-20	frozen	5-6
Asparagus, fresh	6-12	Eggplant	2-5
frozen	8-12	Greens, fresh	5-10
Beans, snap, fresh	7-10	frozen	8-10
frozen	10-12	Leeks	8-10
Limas	15-20	Mushrooms, whole	14-16
Beets, whole	30-45	Onions	6-8
sliced	6-8	Parsnips	6-8
Broccoli, fresh flowerets	6-8	Peas, fresh	6-8
whole head	12-15	frozen	10-12
frozen	10-12	Potatoes, whole	15-45
Brussels Sprouts, fresh	12-14	(depending on size)	
frozen	10-12	Sweet potatoes	15-45
Cabbage, fresh, quartered	10-15	Salsify	6-8
sliced or shredded	4-8	Summer squash	
Carrots, fresh, sliced	6-8	fresh	4-7
frozen	8-10	frozen	8-10
Cauliflower, fresh flowerets	6-10	Winter squash, halved	25-30
whole head	12-15	Turnips	15-20
frozen	10-12		

STIR-FRYING

Stir-frying is an excellent method for cooking vegetables. Because the cooking time is so short the vegetables retain their crunch, flavor, and nutrients. Some people I know who usually won't touch vegetables are crazy about them when they are stir-fried.

Before cooking, vegetables must be cut to a uniform thickness. Bean sprouts and snow peas are okay the way they are. Cut other vegetables into slices 1/8 inch thick. Break up broccoli or cauliflower flowerets and slice the stems.

When the vegetables are prepared, heat oil or butter in a frying pan or wok (with soy sauce or herbs if you like). When the oil is hot add the vegetables, stirring to coat all the vegetable surfaces with oil. Continue stirring over heat for 1-3 minutes (no more!) and serve.

PRESSURE COOKING

There are a lot of variations in pressure cookers and it's best to use yours in the way the manufacturer intended. If your pressure cooker comes with an instruction manual or you can prevail upon the previous owner for instructions, then use one of these two sources of information. If you can't get specific information on your cooker, use the general directions here.

Put the food in the cooker, lock on the cover, and place the cooker over high heat. When the contents are hot, steam will escape through a vent on the lid. Allow the steam to escape for a few minutes so that all the air will be expelled from the cooker. Put the weight on the cooker and continue cooking over high heat until the gauge reaches the desired pressure. *Immediately* lower the heat to the lowest flame that will sustain that pressure. The weight should rock gently. If there is no gauge on the cooker it will usually cook at 15 pounds pressure. Begin timing as soon as the desired pressure is reached. When the cooking time is over remove the cooker from the heat (place it in a pan of cold water for faster cooling) and allow the pressure to drop to zero before removing the lid or the weight.

Once the desired pressure is reached the weight on the cooker should always be gently rocking while a little steam escapes from beneath it. If the rocking and steam stop, cool the cooker immediately, remove the lid and clean out the vents which are probably clogged with food. Then begin the cooking process again, adjusting the cooking time. If the vents clog and you continue cooking the pressure inside the cooker will build up until finally the weight will blow off, followed by the food. This really doesn't happen that often; never if you're careful. Just be sure to put "dangerous" things like split peas or applesauce in small covered bowls in the cooker with about an inch of water in the cooker itself.

Many people are terrified of pressure cookers — sure that they'll explode. They do need to be used correctly, but if you use care there's no need for worry. After a couple of uses you'll wonder how you ever got along without one.

COOKING GRAINS

Whole grains will take longer to cook than devitalized white rice and wheat cereals. However, the nuttier, heartier taste and the additional vitamins, minerals, and proteins in the whole grains, makes it worth the little extra cooking time. Besides, it's not "working" cooking time, but rather "waiting" cooking time. Once you get the whole grains simmering you can pretty well forget them. Use the time to read a little, do your yoga exercises, whatever . . .

The length of time and amount of liquid needed for cooking grains is dependent on many factors: altitude, humidity, where and when the grain was grown, and other factors, some of which you probably won't know. Generally, use twice as much liquid by volume as grain. Simmer the grain, covered, for the amount of time given on the grain cooking table. The finished, cooked grains should be tender but not mushy; each kernel should be separate and the cooking liquid should be completely absorbed by the grain. Adjust your cooking methods until you get results which meet this standard. If the grains are too dry and hard try adding more water while cooking and/or lengthening the cooking time. If the finished grain is mushy or oozing extra water, next time use less water and cook for a shorter time. (For this time set the uncovered pan on a *very* low heat and let the steam escape or drain the grains in a colander or strainer.) Mushy grains won't hurt you, but they just don't look as appetizing as you'd like them to.

Method I
Bring twice as much salted water as grain to a boil. When the water is boiling rapidly stir in the dry grains very slowly so that the water never stops boiling. Cover the pot tightly and turn the heat down. Simmer the grains until they are tender.

Method II
Put the grain and twice as much cold, salted water in a pot. Bring to a boil, stirring as necessary to avoid sticking. Cover the pot, lower heat, and simmer until the grains are tender.

Method III
This is a variation on Method II and is useful for cooking two or more grains (or other foods) on one burner. Use small, stainless steel bowls, tin cans, etc. and fill them with the desired grain and a little less than twice as much water. Tightly cover each bowl or can with tinfoil. Place the covered bowls in

a large pot which has 1 to 2 inches of water in it (you can cook beans in this water while the grains are cooking). Cover the pot, bring the water in it to a boil, reduce the heat and simmer until the grains are tender.

Method IV
This method definitely enhances the nutty taste of whole grains with millet showing the most dramatic change in taste. Begin by heating oil or butter (with herbs if you like) in a saucepan. When the fat is hot add the grain and stir until every kernal is warmed through and coated with hot fat. Add twice as much water as grain, bring to a boil, cover, reduce the heat and simmer until the grains are tender.

Pressure Cooking
You can cook grains at 15 pounds pressure in a pressure cooker using any of the four regular cooking methods — just remember not to fill the cooker more than half full. To avoid clogging the vents in the cooker I prefer to use Method III. Put the covered bowls in the cooker, cover and bring to 15 pounds pressure (read your instruction manual to find how to do this with your cooker). Cook for the number of minutes given on the timetable. If you use one of the other methods watch the time carefully, or consider adding extra water and draining the cooked grains.

TIMETABLE FOR COOKING GRAINS

GRAIN	MINUTES OF REGULAR COOKING	MINUTES OF PRESSURE COOKING
Rolled oat, wheat, other rolled grains	5-7	not recommended
Bulgar, cracked wheat, other medium soft grains	15-20	5-10
Millet, buckwheat groats	25-30	10-15
Brown rice, barley, other medium hard grains	30-45	20
Whole wheat berries, rye berries, whole oats, other hard grains	60 (or longer)	30-35

COOKING DRY LEGUMES
(beans, peas, and lentils)

If you've never cooked dried legumes you may be in for a bit of a surprise. They do take quite a while to cook. The first time I made a baked bean dish "from scratch," I naively planned to serve it for lunch. It was finished in time for dinner that evening.

The trick to cooking beans without spending the whole day in the kitchen is to prepare the beans in large amounts and then freeze them for later use. I find it easiest to divide the cooked beans into small portions for freezing. Two tablespoons (⅛ cup) of dry beans will make about ⅓ cup of cooked beans, so I freeze the beans in ⅓ cup portions. If my recipe calls for ¼ cup (4 Tablespoons) of dry beans, I know to substitute 2 frozen portions, or ⅔ cup.

The ultimate solution to this problem is the pressure cooker which can reduce cooking time by more than 75 percent.

As with grains, the exact amount of cooking time and liquid will depend on any number of variables, some of which you may have no way of knowing. As a general rule I use about 4 or 5 times as much water as dry beans (more water for garbanzos). This proportion usually leaves a little extra stock, which is always welcome for making soups, stews, and breads. When cooking legumes in a regular pot you can add water as necessary to keep the beans from boiling dry. In a pressure cooker start with a little extra liquid since you won't be able to check the water level while the beans are cooking. Because of its tightly fitting lid and the shorter cooking time less water will be lost through evaporation than with a regular cooking pot.

REGULAR COOKING

Method I

This is the time honored way which all of our ancestors used to cook dry beans. Measure the dry beans into a large pot and cover the beans with water. Let the beans soak overnight. The following day, bring the beans and water to a boil (add more water if necessary), cover, and simmer until the beans are tender. (See timetable for approximate cooking times for different beans.) A trick with this method is to freeze the beans in the soaking water before cooking. This shortens the cooking time.

Method II

Instead of soaking the beans overnight put the dry beans in a pot with enough water to cover. Bring to a boil and cook for about five minutes, cover, and remove the pot from the heat. Let the beans soak in the hot water for 2 hours. Bring the beans and water to a boil and simmer until the beans are tender.

Method III

Bring water (about 5 times as much as the beans) to a rapid boil. *Slowly* add the beans to the boiling water; you must not allow the water to stop boiling while you are adding the beans. Cover the pot and simmer until the beans are tender. If you don't let the water stop boiling this method will cut the cooking time in half.

PRESSURE COOKING

Method I

Bring water to a boil in the uncovered cooker. Add beans, cover, and bring to 15 pounds pressure. Simmer until the beans are tender. (*See* timetable.)

Method II

Put beans and cold water in the pressure cooker. Cover, bring to 15 pounds pressure, and simmer until the beans are tender.

NOTE: Lentils and split peas cook more quickly than most other dried legumes. For regular cooking just bring them to a boil and simmer until tender. If you decide to cook lentils or split peas in the pressure cooker, put the legumes and water in a stainless steel bowl or tin can and cover tightly with foil. Place the bowl in the pressure cooker with an inch or two of water in the cooker itself and proceed as for pressure cooking Method II. This should prevent any clogging of the vents in the pressure cooker.

TIMETABLE FOR COOKING LEGUMES

LEGUME	REGULAR COOKING	PRESSURE COOKING
Lentils, split peas	1-1½ hours	15-20 minutes
Navy, soy, kidney, black, pinto cranberry, etc., beans	2 hours	25 minutes
Mung beans, small red beans	3 hours	30-35 minutes
Garbanzo beans	4 hours	45 minutes

YOGURT

If you've never gotten into yogurt before please do give it a try. While it's not the cure for all the world's problems that some claim it to be, it is a healthful, delicious food.

Yogurt is made by adding friendly bacteria to sweet milk and allowing the bactieria to grow, causing the milk to sour slightly and thicken. One cup of yogurt provides the same amount of usable protein as the milk from which it was made (about 1/5 of your daily protein requirement). The yogurt bacteria partially digests the sugar and protein in the milk, making the yogurt more easily digested than the uncultured milk. It's digestibility makes yogurt an excellent food for anyone recovering from stomach upset (caused by anything from a bout with the flu to too much pizza), and many people who are otherwise allergic to milk products find that they are able to eat yogurt without a problem.

In addition to being easily digested, yogurt seems to have a positive effect upon the digestion of other foods in the human system. If eaten regularly the yogurt bacteria continue to live and grow in the intestine, producing B vitamins and helping to keep a favorable balance of healthy bacteria in the human system — a balance which seems to make the host more resistant to diseases.

Such a wonder food must surely taste awful (like castor oil) you think? Well, if you've never tried it before yogurt can taste "funny," but with all those benefits it is worth acquiring a taste for it. At first, mix chopped fresh fruit and honey in with the yogurt when you eat it; gradually reduce the amount of fruit and honey as you learn to like the yogurt taste. Eventually you will like it with only a dab of honey, or perhaps even perfectly plain. Not only good as a food by itself, yogurt is a base for many salads, salad dressings, desserts, and can almost always be used as a substitute for mayonnaise, sour cream, or butter-milk.

Yogurt can be easily and inexpensively made at home. At current milk prices I can make a *half-gallon* of yogurt for about 75 cents, as compared to 35 cents -45 cents for a *cup* of commercial yogurt. The only prerequisites are clean, clean utensils and some way of keeping the yogurt warm (100^0-120^0 F) while it is incubating.

A commercial yogurt maker works well but has the disadvantages of making only a small amount of yogurt at a time, using electricity, and eventually wearing out. Instead, try using a deep soup pot or Dutch oven with a lid; the pot must be deep enough for quart or pint jars to fit inside when the lid is on. Set the pot on a folded towel, blanket, or several layers of newspaper. The covered jars, filled with yogurt ready to incubate, will go in the pot. Then pour warm water (115⁰-117⁰ F) into the pot until the water level is even with the necks of the jars or the pot is full. Put the lid on the pot and cover the whole thing with another blanket or towel. The blankets or towels are insulation to keep the water from cooling too quickly and provide an even heat for the incubating yogurt. *Don't* disturb the yogurt until it has thickened.

I have found the "soup pot method" to be the best for producing uniformly good yogurt in about three hours. If you wish, however, you may try:

1. Using your oven set at 100⁰ F.
2. Wrapping the yogurt jars in a sleeping bag.
3. Setting the yogurt over a pilot light.
4. Burying the jars in the ashes of a nearly spent campfire.
5. Putting the yogurt in a warm thermos bottle.
6. Setting the yogurt in a warm place in the house (on a T.V., radio, clothes dryer, etc.)

YOGURT TIPS

1. Check milk temperature carefully before adding the culture. If the milk is hotter than 120⁰ it will kill the culture; if the milk temperature drops below 100⁰ the culture will grow very slowly, if at all.

2. Make sure to stir the culture into the milk thoroughly as you want the culture distributed throughout the milk as much as possible.

3. Once you get the yogurt incubating, please *do not* move or stir it. Yogurt culture is very fussy and likes to stay still. Moving the incubating yogurt can delay culturing time considerably.

4. If you plan to add flavorings to your yogurt wait until it has been incubated, refrigerated, and thoroughly chilled.

5. Use *very* clean utensils when making yogurt.

6. Use fresh yogurt for the culture, i.e., homemade yogurt less than a week old or natural, commercial yogurt long before its expiration date.

Homemade Yogurt
1 quart

*2 c. whole milk or 2% milk	2 c. water
*1 generous c. instant milk powder (¾ c. non-instant)	2 t. yogurt (culture or starter)

1. Mix together the milk and milk powder. Use a wire whisk or blender to get out all the lumps. Heat the milk mixture to 180⁰ F.

2. Add the water. Pour the milk mixture into clean jars and allow it to cool to about 115⁰ F. The colder the water, the faster the mixture will cool. Don't let it cool below 110⁰ F.

3. Put the yogurt starter in a separate container. Remove about 1 T. warm milk from each jar and mix milk thoroughly with the starter. Then pour milk-starter mixture into the jars of warm milk and stir to distribute the starter throughout the milk. Cover the jars and place them into your incubating device. Please work quickly on this step so the milk won't have time to cool too much before incubating.

4. Allow the yogurt to incubate without disturbing it. It will take 3-10 hours to thicken depending on the weather and your incubation method. Check it in 3 hours to see if it is thick enough. If not, continue checking at intervals of ½-1 hour until it reaches the desired thickness. Refrigerate.

Time saver: If you don't have time to incubate your yogurt during the day mix it up just before you go to bed and let it incubate over night. In the morning it should be thick and ready to refrigerate.

Flavorings: Try stirring any of these into chilled yogurt:

honey	honey and vanilla
honey and fresh fruit	honey and cocoa or carob
homemade jams	honey and instant coffee
apple butter	honey and granola or familia

2 c. milk = 14 g.
1 c. milk powder = 21 g.
*Total = 35 g. usable protein

HERBS AND SPICES

Herbs and spices have been used for culinary and medicinal purposes for centuries. Evidence of their use is recorded in the Bible and the search for better spice routes resulted in Columbus "discovering" America. The earliest American settlers brought with them the seeds and plants of their favorite herbs and the native Americans taught them the use of others.

Simple foods become delicacies when prepared with the judicious use of herbs and spices. Do yourself the favor of becoming acquainted with a wide variety of them. Start with a collection of basic, staple seasonings and branch out from there. Every month or so treat yourself to a new seasoning — one you have never tried before — and start experimenting with it.

Store herbs and spices in a cool, dry, dark place; preferably in tightly closed glass containers. Seasonings should be within easy reach of the stove, but *do not* store them above the stove where steam from cooking will adversely affect them. In spite of the best care the flavors of herbs and seasonings will deteriorate with time. Check them, especially those you use infrequently, by sniffing them every now and then to see if they still retain their aroma (and flavor). Usually there won't be any noticeable deterioration in taste before six months to one year after you bought (or harvested) the herbs. If you find a jar which has lost its flavor, discard it, use it in compost, or make a "tea" for your houseplants.

Certain herbs cannot be bought in dried form simply because they do not dry very well. Borage (annual) and lemon balm (perennial) are two of these. Both are incredibly easy to grow, even in flower pots. You can dry them if you wish, just expect a certain loss of flavor. Others which you may enjoy growing are: thyme, rosemary, sage, chives (perennials), parsley (biennial), dill, sweet basil (annuals). All of these will do well in pots and if you have a little land you might want to expand your garden.

I haven't included a seasoning chart because I feel you'll learn more about seasonings by experimenting. See the recipes for seasoning suggestions. Remember, the taste of most seasonings is very similar to the smell. Your nose will be the best guide in finding experimental combinations which work well together. Since herbs shrink as they dry always use twice as much fresh as dried herb.

Staple seasonings:
  basil, sweet   onion
  chili powder   oregano
  cinnamon   parsley
  curry powder   pepper (white, black,
  garlic   or cayenne)
  marjoram   sage
  mustard (dry and/or   salt
    prepared)   thyme
  nutmeg

Test and experiment with:
  allspice   lovage
  anise   mace
  bay leaves   mints
  cardamom   rosemary
  chervil   saffron
  chives   savory
  cloves   shallots
  coriander   tarragon
  dill (weed and seed)   turmeric
  *ginger (dried and fresh)   vanilla
  leeks

---

*Dried and fresh ginger are not interchangeable in recipes as the flavors are almost entirely different. Preserve fresh ginger root by freezing it in a plastic bag. The amount needed can be cut or grated while frozen and the remainder returned to the freezer.

SETTING UP
YOUR KITCHEN

A kitchen reflects the kind of activity that goes on in it. If you hate every minute that you spend there, the kitchen and the food you cook will reflect that mood. But if love and happiness are two of the big ingredients in your cooking, you'll find that your kitchen will become a joyful place to be and the food you cook will be delicious. Arrange your kitchen to suit your personality — put pictures on the walls, display your natural foods, grow plants, use bright colors or natural wood textures.

For convenience, store foods and utensils so the ones used most often are easily accessible. Keep herbs close to, but not over, the stove so you can easily add a pinch of this or a dash of that while you cook.

Cooking with natural foods doesn't require all kinds of fancy cookware, so you can get along quite well with only a few utensils. A few suggestions though. Get cookware made of cast iron or stainless steel as these metals heat more evenly and last longer than cheaper cookware. Don't skimp on the quality of your knives. Get the best ones you can afford. With all small utensils try to make sure that they feel comfortable in your hand before you buy them — pantomime the jobs you'll use them for right there in the store.

Two "luxury" items which really are handy are a pressure cooker and a blender. Sometimes you can find good second-hand ones, or with a little comparative shopping you should be able to pick up new ones for less than $20 each.

The following list should help you to set up your kitchen for reasonable ease in cooking. You can get by with less — I once cooked for a friend, myself, and sometimes company for over a month using only a frying pan, baking pan, double boiler, paring knife, and a couple of spoons — but you'll have more flexibility with a few more utensils.

NECESSITIES

Frying pans with lids — 1 or 2
Saucepans with lids — 2 or 3
Soup pot or Dutch oven with lid
Wooden spoons — 3 or more
Slotted pancake turner
Grater
Knives for chopping — 2 small, 1 large
Cutting board
Measuring cups and spoons
Knife sharpener
Colander or strainer
Wire whisk
Mixing bowls — Pyrex, stainless steel, or stoneware bowls can double as casseroles
Small casseroles with lids — 2 or 3
Baking pan — 8"x8", 9"x9", or 7"x11", can double as extra casserole
Cookie sheets — 1 to 4
Can and bottle openers

NEARLY NECESSITIES

Ladle
Slotted spoon
Rubber scraper — Make sure it's rubber, not plastic
Bread pans
Muffin tins
Bread knife with serrated blade
Steaming basket
Double boiler — doubles as extra saucepans
Pie plates
Pastry blender
Cake pans
Candy thermometer
Pressure cooker
Blender

USEFUL LUXURIES

Tea kettle
Corkscrew
Pastry brushes
Tea strainer
Yogurt maker
Eggbeater or electric mixer

And anything else you're really into — an omelet pan if you make lots of omelets, a crêpe pan, pizza pan, coffee pot, etc.

MEASUREMENTS AND THEIR EQUIVALENTS

3 teaspoons (t. or tsp.) = 1 tablespoon (T. or tbsp.)
2 T. = ⅛ cup (c.)
4 T. = ¼ c.
5 T. + 1 t. = 5⅓ T. = ⅓ c.
8 T. = ½ c.
16 T. = 1 c.
2 c. = 1 pint (pt.)
2 pt. = 1 quart (qt.)
4 c. = 1 qt.
4 qt. = 1 gallon (gal.) liquid measure
8 qt. = 1 peck or chip, dry measure (like a peck of strawberries)
8 gal. or 4 pecks = 1 bushel

NATURAL FOODS TIPS

1. Store dry foods in glass jars. Use Mason jars if you have them. I've been saving 3 lb. honey jars for storing, but use whatever you can get. Empty coffee cans also make good canisters. Keep your foods where you can get at them easily, so you don't have to go through bag after bag or jar after jar to find the ingredient you are looking for. Label look-alikes, i.e., bulgar and steelcut oats.

2. Use measuring spoons or cups for scooping. That way you can measure and scoop all in the same movement — saves energy (your energy) and time.

3. Use a blender or a whisk to mix milk powder with water. When baking, stir the milk powder into the flour; then use the mixture as you normally would use plain flour.

4. Mix instant milk powder with *cold* water before adding the mixture to hot liquids.

5. To thicken sauces, mix cornstarch with cold water and slowly add this mixture to the hot sauce, stirring constantly.

6. To measure honey or molasses, oil the measuring cup first. The honey will slide right out.

7. Use measuring cups small enough to fit in your spice or herb jars; for instance, use two ¼ t. if the recipe calls for ½ t. of an ingredient. This way you'll avoid spilling.

8. Don't use Pyrex or crockery baking dishes for cooking on top of the stove unless they are labelled flameproof.

9. Put your freezer to work storing casseroles, cooked grains, or beans for quick dinners on nights when you haven't time to cook.

10. To save time learn to judge small measurements in your hand. Practice with salt. Measure a teaspoon, a tablespoon, etc., into your palm, observe carefully, and pour the salt back into the container. Then pour salt directly into your palm trying to approximate the measurement. Pour this amount into a measuring spoon and see how close you came to the right amount. It won't take long before you're accurate, and this is a very handy skill, especially when your seasonings come in shakers.

11. Use a pastry brush to oil casseroles and baking pans. If you're using a solid fat spread it over the pan surface with a paper towel. (White paper towels are more ecologically sound as the dyes in colored ones contain arsenic which retards their normal breakdown.) If a recipe calls for a pan to be greased and floured, grease the pan thoroughly, pour in a tablespoon or so of flour, then tilt the pan back and forth, tapping the pan until all the inner surfaces are coated with flour.

12. To skin fruits, like peaches or tomatoes, cover the whole fruits with boiling water and let them sit in the water for two or three minutes. Drain. Skin the fruit with a paring knife; the skin will slip right off.

13. If you have a sweet tooth you can increase sweetening in a dish without adding calories by adding a little ground coriander (up to ½ t.) to the honey called for in a recipe. This is probably psychological, but it does seem to work.

14. If you like onions and garlic, but don't like the taste they leave in your mouth, chew a little fresh parsley at the end of your meal. The parsley will neutralize the garlic or onion taste better than any commercial mouthwash.

THE RECIPES

To me, the best cook is one who uses simple, natural foods and prepares them in the most appetizing and nutritious ways possible. Good cooking is not a mysterious art shrouded in centuries of secrecy; some of the most delicious dishes are the simplest to prepare. For variety, and your own ego, it's nice to be able to make a few dishes that seem more complicated, although many fancy dishes are really much easier to make than you may have guessed. The recipes in this book are all pretty well foolproof, so long as you read and follow directions carefully. I haven't included sky-high soufflés that will collapse if a gnat walks across the ceiling. The recipes are good, healthful, tasty dishes which the average person should have no trouble learning to prepare.

For your convenience in planning a balanced diet any dish which provides significant amounts of protein has the protein content expressed in usable grams. Please check the chapter on nutrition so that you'll understand what "usable grams" of protein are. I've also included listings at the end of each recipe showing how the different protein sources complement each other. Avoid eliminating any of the protein sources (ingredients which are starred) from the recipes. If you absolutely cannot find a protein ingredient, for instance the wheat berries in the wheat-rice-soy combination, you may substitute a different combination, such as rice and soy or rice and beans. Check the complementarity chart first to be sure you're using the correct proportions for the most usable protein. In all probability you can also substitute one legume for another or one whole grain for another without radically changing the protein content of the dish.

CREATIVE COOKING

If you've never done much cooking I'd suggest following the recipes at first. Obviously, the recipes are designed to satisfy my taste buds, and your tastes may certainly vary from mine, so feel free to adjust the seasonings and non-protein ingredients to suit your own taste. Just remember though, if you want to add four cups of onions (or whatever) to a basic recipe, be sure that you're hungry enough to eat all the food that will result. Otherwise you'll not only have leftovers, but you will also not get as much protein in the portion which you do eat. The amount of protein in the total dish won't change; it will just be spread out through a larger quantity of food.

One of the most exciting things about natural foods is that there are so many things you can do with them. Once you begin to develop a positive attitude about your cooking ability start trying variations on the recipes — vary seasonings, vegetable ingredients, etc. Some of the most delicious dishes are discovered by just tossing different foods together, and adding a little of this and a pinch of that, until *voilà*, you have an entirely new, different, and exciting taste experience. If you are entirely new to cooking I wouldn't start just tossing things together right away. Give yourself a chance to get to know a variety of flavors and cooking methods and then go ahead and experiment. *Bon appetit!*

You will notice as you read the recipes that I haven't included any recipes for "vegetarian meat" or other meat substitutes. There are two reasons for this. First of all, I just can't get into the amount of preparation necessary for preparing these products at home. Second, I would rather eat real soybeans, wheat, or whatever, than imitation anything. If you feel that you *have* to have imitation bacon or hamburgers check your market for soy-based products or with the Seventh Day Adventists in your area — they've been successfully using meat substitutes for years.

In much the same way, if you can't or won't use eggs, there are egg replacers or substitutes on the market. The decision to use one of these, and if so which one to use, really must depend on the individual and his or her needs. The frozen liquid type is low in saturated fat and cholesterol, contains a fair amount of protein, and can be used almost like a regular egg. Unfortunately it does contain real egg whites (so it's no good for those allergic to eggs) and chemical preservatives. The powder type replacer contains no egg or other animal products and no preservatives; it is intended to act mainly as a binding agent in baking and cooking and won't make imitation scrambled eggs. The powder cannot be considered a nutritional substitute for real eggs as it contains no protein. If you decide to go the replacer route check your market or natural food store for the product that best fits your needs.

MENTAL ATTITUDE

Mental attitude has a great deal to do with enjoyment of foods. I think that one of the surest ways to be disappointed with any vegetarian dish is to spend all your eating time searching for the "meat flavor." Those who do this cheat themselves, as they miss all the other flavors while they search for that particular one. After all, you wouldn't expect egg to taste like hamburger, so you shouldn't expect pilaf to taste like steak. If you expect a vegetable dish to taste like a vegetable dish you'll find that it will satisfy the mind, the palate, and the tummy. If you expect it to taste like something it's not, then it won't satisfy.

Your mental attitude will, and should, influence your choice of foods. Learn to listen for your body's signals. As you become attuned to your body's needs you'll find that it will tell you what it needs to eat. For instance, if you crave a green salad with chunks of cheese, chances are that a salad is what you need to fill your nutritional needs right then. If you aren't in the mood for rich food you should plan a menu of simply prepared foods like salads, simple grain dishes, or yogurt with fruit. When you want simple food, rich food won't taste right, and when you want rich food, simple food won't satisfy you. If you learn to listen to the little voice inside you, you will probably be eating the foods your body needs most. Of course, if the little voice you hear consistently says "chocolate" it's probably your sweet tooth rather than your real needs that you are hearing. You'll have to learn to recognize the differences.

Although I can't prove it scientifically, I also believe that mental attitude has a lot to do with how well your body uses the food which you eat. If you really believe that a food is good for you it will be, and your body will use the food in the best way possible. My grandfather eats the most nutritionally worthless diet I have ever seen, but he really believes that the foods he likes are good for him. He's still happily plugging along at the age of 86. For myself, I find that it's easier to believe in my food if I know it has some nutritional worth. I try to eat natural foods and avoid junk. If you have to eat junk food, get good quality junk and try to concentrate on any positive qualities it may have while you eat it. If you dwell on the positive it may actually make the food more nutritious or at least, hopefully cancel out some of the negative qualities.

COOKING WISDOM

A few words of wisdom before you begin. If you've never eaten natural foods before don't try to make the switch in one giant step by tossing out all your instant food packages and stocking your pantry with all kinds of natural foods you don't know how to use. Instead, go gradually. Start buying seasonal fresh fruits and vegetables and learn to prepare them well. If you've been living on canned goods you may never have tasted "real" vegetables before. For main dishes start with familiar things like spaghetti and macaroni and cheese, but substitute whole grain noodles for the white flour noodles you've used before. Substitute brown rice for white rice, then gradually add other whole grains to your diet. If you're just beginning to reduce your meat consumption try some of the more highly seasoned dishes first — curries, creole, and stir-fry dishes. As you eat less meat and refined food your sense of taste will become more acute. You will begin to appreciate and enjoy many delicate flavors which may have been masked by your old eating habits.

The first time you make a shopping expedition to a natural foods store it's a good idea to make a shopping list. Otherwise it's very easy to go wild and buy a little (or a lot) of everything you see. Choose a few recipes you want to try and buy the foods you need for those recipes, plus a little extra to store away. Then start trying the recipes, one or two a week at first. Gradually you'll find that you're eating more and more natural food and less instant food from the supermarket. Don't be in a rush — dry, natural foods will keep for a long time. You don't have to be in any hurry to eat them up. I'm a firm believer in shopping lists even after you've been cooking for a long time. They save shopping time, and you're more likely to come home with everything you need. It's ever so easy to have an important ingredient slip your mind while shopping, only to realize you don't have it when you start to prepare a dish you've really been looking forward to eating. To avoid disappointment, write it down!

For more enjoyable cooking try to elicit some help in the kitchen. When you and your roommate or guests work together nobody needs to be alone in the kitchen. Many hands *do* make light work. You'll all be able to add your own personal touches, and when you eat the food that you've prepared together you'll begin to understand the significance of "breaking bread" together. Cooking and eating together can be almost a model of the world as it should be; people working together, giving of themselves, so that all of them can enjoy and find fulfillment in the result.

BREAKFAST & BRUNCH

Nutritionists are of two minds concerning breakfast. Some believe that a big breakfast with lots of protein is essential for getting off to a good start for the day. Others think that since breakfast is a meal which breaks the fast since dinner the night before, it's easier on the system to have a small, simple meal of fruit and perhaps a little yogurt or a slice of toast. You will have to experiment to discover which method works best for you.

Even if you don't get into eating big breakfasts, you'll find that egg and pancake recipes will make delicious quick meals. Use them for simple luncheons or suppers. You can even use the cereals for other meals if you haven't been too strongly conditioned to believe that cereals are breakfast food and nothing else.

For a different and delightful get-together invite a few friends over for brunch. Serve plenty of fresh fruit, yogurt, toast or coffeecake, teas or coffee, and eggs or pancakes. It's a great way to kick off an active afternoon of swimming, boating, hiking, or watching a football game.

CEREALS

Granola

4 cups

If you're used to eating super-sweet commercial cereals you may want to add more honey to this recipe, especially the first few times you make it.

*1½ c. rolled oats
*½ c. rolled wheat
*¼ c. soy grits
*⅓ c. sunflower seeds
*2 T. instant milk powder
   (1½ T. non-instant)

*2 T. wheat germ
¼ t. salt
¼ c. oil or melted butter
¼ c. honey
1 t. vanilla
¼ c. or more raisins

1. In a large bowl stir together all the dry ingredients except the raisins.
2. Heat the oil, honey, and vanilla in a small saucepan until the mixture becomes very runny.
3. Pour the hot liquid over the dry ingredients and stir thoroughly. Coat all the dry ingredients with liquid.
4. Empty the mixture into a flat bottomed pan and toast the cereal in a 350° oven. Stir every five minutes to assure even toasting. Toast for 15-25 minutes depending on how dark you like your cereal.
5. Allow the toasted cereal to cool before mixing in the raisins. Store in airtight containers.
6. Serve with milk and honey.

VARIATIONS

1. Substitute sesame seeds for all or part of the sunflower seeds.
2. Add ½ c. shredded coconut to the dry ingredients before toasting.
3. Substitute ¼ c. sunflower seeds and 3 T. peanuts for the ⅓ c. sunflower seeds.
4. Add other chopped dried fruit.

5. Substitute real maple syrup for all or part of the honey.

6. Substitute ½ c. flaked triticale for the rolled wheat or for ½ c. of the rolled oats.

2 c. rolled cereal + ¼ c. soy grits = 32 g.
⅓ c. sunflower seeds + 2 T. milk powder = 8 g.
2 T. wheat germ = 2 g.
***Total = 42 g. usable protein**

Familia

4 cups

This is a variation on a Swiss recipe.

*1½ c. rolled oats	¼ c. diced, dried apples
*½ c. rolled wheat	¼ c. diced, dried apricots
*⅓ c. sunflower seeds	¼ c. raisins
*½ c. instant milk powder	¼ t. salt
(6 T. non-instant)	
*¼ c. toasted wheat germ	

Stir all the ingredients together and serve with honey and milk or yogurt.

VARIATIONS

1. Experiment with different dried fruits, either for a taste change or if you can't get one of those listed. Traditionally, familia is made with apples, but yours doesn't have to be.

2. Traditional familia also contains almonds and hazelnuts. Substitute these for the sunflower seeds if you wish.

3. Add chopped, seasonal fresh fruit when you serve the cereal.

4. Substitute ½ c. flaked triticale for the rolled wheat or for ½ c. of the rolled oats.

2 c. rolled cereal + ⅓ c. instant milk powder = 28 g.
⅓ c. sunflower seeds + 2 T. milk powder = 8 g.
¼ c. wheat germ = 4 g.
***Total = 40 g. usable protein**

Millet Cereal

1 serving

*¼ c. whole, hulled millet   dash cinnamon
*¼ c. milk   1 T. raisins
¼ c. water   milk and honey to taste
dash salt

1. Let the millet soak in the milk overnight in the refrigerator.

2. Bring the water, salt, and cinnamon to a boil. Slowly trickle in the milk and millet mixture, pouring slowly enough so that the water never stops boiling. Cover and reduce heat. Simmer 20-25 minutes.

3. Serve with milk and honey.

¼ c. millet = 2 g.
¼ c. milk = 2 g.
Probable complementarity = 1 g.
*Total = 5 g. usable protein

Cinnamon Oatmeal

1 serving

This is a delicious change from plain oatmeal. It's hot and filling on a cold winter morning.

¾ c. water   *1 T. soy grits
⅛ t. salt   cinnamon to taste
1 T. raisins   (¼ t. or more)
*⅓ c. rolled oats   milk and honey to taste

1. In a small saucepan bring the water, salt, and raisins to a boil.

2. Stir in the oats, soy grits, and cinnamon. Cook, uncovered, about 1 minute. Lower heat, cover, and simmer for about 5 minutes or until the oats are tender and have absorbed all the water.

3. Serve with honey and milk.

VARIATIONS

1. Substitute ⅓ c. rolled wheat or flaked triticale for the rolled oats.

2. Substitute ⅓ c. bulgar or cracked wheat for the rolled oats and increase simmering time to 20 minutes. This can also be a filling supper when camping or when you're pressed for preparation time.

*⅓ c. oats + 1 T. soy grits = 8 g. usable protein

Cornmeal Mush

2 servings

2 c. boiling water	***2⅔ T. instant milk powder**
***½ c. cornmeal**	**(2 T. non-instant)**
***4 t. soy grits**	**½ c. cold water**
	¼ t. salt

1. In the top of a double boiler bring the two cups of water to a boil over direct heat.

2. In a bowl, combine all the other ingredients. Slowly stir these ingredients into the boiling water. Continue to cook over direct heat for about 3 minutes, stirring constantly.

3. Set the top of the double boiler over boiling water, cover, and continue to cook for about 15 minutes. Serve with milk and honey.

VARIATION

Fried Mush: Turn the finished mush into a well-oiled loaf pan and refrigerate until the mixture is solid; overnight is best. Cut the solid mush into slices and fry the slices in a good quantity of hot fat over a medium-high flame. Allow the mush to fry until it is well-browned on the bottom before turning it once to fry it on the other side. Serve with honey or maple syrup.

*½ c. cornmeal + 4 t. soy grits + 2⅔ T. milk powder = 10 g. usable protein

Sesame Rice Cereal

2 servings

*½ c. raw brown rice
*2⅔ T. sesame seeds
1 c. water

⅛-¼ t. salt
honey and milk to taste

1. Buzz the raw rice and sesame seeds in the blender for a full minute or a little longer. The rice should be well cracked. Stop buzzing before it gets to the powdery flour stage.
2. Bring the water and salt to a boil and add the ground rice and sesame mixture. Cover, reduce heat, and simmer until the rice is tender, 20-25 minutes.
3. Serve with honey and milk.

*½ c. brown rice + 2⅔ T. sesame seeds = 8 g. usable protein

Peanut Cereal

1 serving

A rich and creamy cereal — a good start for a hard day of work or play.

⅛ t. or more salt
  (depending on whether
  your peanut butter
  is salted)
¾ c. water

*3 T. bulgar or steel-cut oats
*2 T. peanut butter
*¼ c. milk
  raisins (optional)

1. Bring the water and salt to a boil. If your peanut butter is unsalted you may want to use more salt.
2. Add the grain, peanut butter, and as many raisins as you like (for sweetness). Reduce heat, cover, and simmer until the cereal is smooth and creamy, 15-20 minutes.
3. Serve with *at least* ¼ c. milk, and honey if you wish.

3 T. bulgar + 1½ t. peanut butter + 1 T. milk = 5.0 g.
4½ t. peanut butter + 2¼ T. milk = 7.5 g.
¾ T. milk = .5 g.
*Total = 13.0 g. usable protein

EGGS

Boiled Eggs

"Boiled" eggs are cooked by simmering. Cooking eggs in rapidly boiling water will cause the protein to toughen.

In a saucepan, cover the eggs with cold water. You can add a little salt to help keep the shells from cracking. Bring the water to a boil. As soon as it boils reduce the heat so the water boils very slowly but constantly. Continue cooking until the eggs are done. The exact amount of cooking time will vary with your eggs, your stove, and your cookware.

Soft cooked eggs - 2 to 5 minutes

Hard cooked eggs - 15 to 20 minutes

As soon as hard cooked eggs have finished cooking plunge them into cold water. This stops the cooking and keeps the yolks from discoloring. For easier peeling use eggs that are 2 or 3 days old. If the raw egg is very fresh the cooked egg will be really hard to peel.

Poached Eggs

Bring lightly salted water to a boil; reduce the heat so the water temperature is just slightly below boiling. Break the eggs, one at a time, into a dish and gently slide each egg into the hot water. Allow the egg to cook in the hot water over low heat for 3-5 minutes, or remove the pan from the burner and allow the eggs to sit in the hot water for about 8 minutes, or until the egg is set. Remove cooked eggs from the water with a slotted spoon to allow the water to drain from the egg.

If you have an egg poacher, oil or butter the individual molds and break an egg into each one. Cook over, not in, boiling water for 4-5 minutes.

Fried Eggs

Heat oil or melt butter over a medium-low flame. Carefully break the eggs into the hot fat and cook until the eggs are set. To speed up the process pour a tablespoon of water into the pan and cover. The steam produced by the water will cook the top of the egg more quickly. Don't try to rush the process by turning up the heat — the bottom of the egg will burn, the top stay raw, and the protein will toughen.

If you must have your eggs "over lightly" use a well-seasoned cast iron frying pan. Slide a pancake turner under the nearly cooked egg, supporting the yolk, and *gently* turn the egg over and cook for a few more seconds. And practice, practice, practice!

Scrambled Eggs

Beat the eggs with a little water, salt, and pepper if you like, in a bowl. In a frying pan heat oil or melt butter over a medium heat. When the fat is hot pour in the eggs and stir gently with a wooden spoon or pancake turner until the eggs are set.

For quick scrambled eggs omit beating the eggs in a bowl. Break them into the hot fat and stir them rapidly while they cook.

French Toast

2 medium servings

A quick and easy meal.

*4 slices whole grain bread	salt and pepper to taste
*1 egg	butter or oil
1-2 T. milk	

1. Beat the egg with a little milk and seasonings. Dip the bread in the egg mixture, coating both sides of each slice.

2. Fry the dipped bread in hot melted butter or oil, turning each slice when it is golden brown on the bottom. When both sides are golden brown serve with honey, maple syrup, yogurt, or preserves.

4 slices whole grain bread = 4-12 g.
1 egg = 6 g.
*Total = 10-18 g. usable protein

Eggs and Potatoes

1-2 servings

This is a yummy breakfast and a good way to use up leftover potatoes. You can vary it by adding different herbs.

1½ T. oil or butter
*1 medium potato (prefer-
 ably cooked), sliced
 or diced

*2 medium eggs
 salt, pepper, and other
 seasonings to taste

1. Heat the oil or butter in a frying pan. Add the potato pieces and sauté until they are warmed through.

2. Beat the eggs in a bowl. Pour the beaten eggs over the potatoes, add seasonings, and continue to sauté until the eggs are set.

2 eggs = 12 g.
1 medium potato = 1.2-2 g.
*Total = 13.2 -14 g. usable protein

Eggs and Mushrooms

1-2 servings

2 T. butter
*¾-1 c. sliced mushrooms

*2 medium eggs
 salt and pepper to taste

1. Melt the butter in a frying pan and sauté the mushrooms in the butter until they soften.

2. Beat the eggs in a bowl and pour the beaten eggs over the mushrooms. Continue stirring over medium heat until the eggs are set.

2 eggs = 12 g.
¾-1 c. mushrooms = 1-3 g.
*Total = 13-15 g. usable protein

Western Eggs
1-2 servings

Try making western sandwiches by serving these eggs between two slices of whole grain toast.

1-2 T. oil or butter	*2 eggs, beaten
1-2 T. chopped onion	salt and pepper to taste
2-4 T. chopped green pepper	

1. Heat oil or butter in a frying pan. Sauté the onion in the hot
   fat until soft. Add the green pepper and sauté for a minute
   or two longer.
2. Add the beaten egg to the vegetables and stir over medium
   heat until the eggs are set.

*2 eggs = 12 g. usable protein

OMELETS

An omelet can be a beautiful meal. It takes a little practice to
learn to make one perfectly, but once you get the hang of it
you'll find that they really aren't difficult to make at all.

For best results use an omelet pan or a frying pan with
sloping sides. An omelet cooked in a pan with straight sides is
difficult to remove from the pan in one piece. Make your
omelets to suit the size of your pan. You'll usually get better
results using a small pan and making several two egg omelets
rather than using more eggs and a larger pan.

If you're going to fill the omelet with vegetables sauté the
vegetables first and set them aside. Scatter the cooked vegetables over the surface of the omelet just before you fold it over.

Basic Omelet
1-2 servings

1-2 T. butter	1-2 T. water
*2 eggs	salt and pepper to taste

1. In a bowl, beat the eggs with the water and seasonings.

2. Heat the omelet pan. Melt the butter in the hot pan, swirl- ing the butter around until it coats all of the pan's cooking surfaces.

3. As soon as the butter stops bubbling add the beaten egg. Tilt the pan back and forth so the egg covers the entire bottom of the pan.

4. Using a fork, lift one edge of the omelet and tilt the pan so the liquid egg on top runs to the bottom of the omelet. Repeat with another edge until the omelet is no longer runny on top. Then let the omelet cook over a medium flame until the surface is softly set, 30-60 seconds.

5. Add fillings if desired.

6. Using a fork or pancake turner fold the omelet in half. Slide out onto a plate and serve.

*2 eggs = 12 g. usable protein

Cheese Omelet

1 serving

*1 T.-⅓ c. grated cheese
*1 Basic Omelet

Make a basic omelet. When the omelet is nearly cooked sprinkle the surface with grated cheese. Let the cheese melt slightly, fold the omelet over, and serve.

VARIATION

Cheese-Mushroom Omelet: After the cheese begins to melt scatter sautéed mushrooms over the surface. Then fold the omelet over and serve.

2 eggs = 12 g.
⅓ c. cheese = 7 g.
*Total = 19 g. usable protein

The amount of protein in this omelet depends upon the amount of cheese you use.

Mushroom Omelet

1 serving

*½-1 c. sliced mushrooms   *1 Basic Omelet
1-2 T. butter

1. Sauté the mushrooms in butter until they soften. Set aside.
2. Make a basic omelet. Scatter the sautéed mushrooms over the surface of the softly set omelet just before folding it over.

2 eggs = 12 g.
½-1 c. mushrooms = 1-2 g.
*Total = 13-14 g. usable protein

Western Omelet

1 serving

1-2 T. butter   2-6 T. chopped green pepper
1-3 T. chopped onion   *1 Basic Omelet

1. Sauté the onion and then the green pepper in the butter until soft. Set aside.
2. Make a basic omelet. Scatter the sautéed vegetables over the surface of the omelet just before folding it over.

*2 eggs = 12 g. usable protein

Squash and Sesame Omelet

1 serving

½ c. diced summer squash   1-2 T. butter
*1 T. sesame seeds   *1 Basic Omelet
*1 T. chopped onion
   (optional)

1. Sauté the squash, sesame seeds, and onion in the butter until soft. Set aside.

2. Make a basic omelet. Scatter the vegetable and seed mixture over the surface of the omelet just before folding it over.

2 eggs = 12 g.
1 T. sesame seeds = trace
*Total = 12 g. usable protein

Baked Noodle Omelet

1 large or 2 small servings

This can be a one dish meal for breakfast, lunch, or a quick supper.

*¼ c. whole wheat
  macaroni, cooked
1-2 T. chopped onion
1-2 T. chopped green pepper
*3 medium mushrooms,
  sliced
1-2 T. oil or butter

*2 eggs
*¼ c. milk
*⅓ c. grated cheese
dash thyme
dash cayenne
salt to taste

1. Sauté the vegetables in a little oil or butter until they soften.

2. In a bowl beat together the eggs, milk, cheese, and seasonings. Stir in the cooked macaroni and sautéed vegetables.

3. Pour the mixture into a well-oiled casserole and bake at 325⁰ until set, 15-20 minutes. Or, pour the mixture into an oiled frying pan and cook covered over very low heat until set, 10-15 minutes.

¼ c. macaroni + ¼ c. milk = 7 g.
2 eggs = 12 g.
⅓ c. cheese = 7 g.
3 mushrooms = 1-2 g.
*Total = 27-28 g. usable protein

Egg Foo Young

1 or 2 servings

Egg Foo Young is basically a bean sprout omelet. I've included sliced carrot for crunch. Feel free to add or substitute water chestnuts or bamboo shoots if you have them. Serve with brown rice for a filling meal.

1-2 T. oil
a few gratings fresh ginger
2 scallions or 1 leek, sliced
½ carrot, sliced
½ stalk celery, sliced

¼-½ c. bean sprouts
***2-3 mushrooms, sliced**
***2 eggs**
¼ t. salt
1 t. tamari soy sauce

1. Heat the oil in a flat bottomed frying pan (not a wok). Stir-fry all the vegetables in the order in which they are listed, adding each vegetable as soon as the previous one is coated with oil. It should take only a few minutes.

2. In a bowl, beat together the eggs, salt, and tamari. Pour the egg mixture over the vegetables in the frying pan. Reduce heat to medium-low and stir the eggs and vegetables for a minute or so until the eggs are beginning to cook but are still wet. Spread the mixture out over the bottom of the pan and continue to cook until the omelet is set. Cut into wedges for easier serving.

2 eggs = 12 g.
2-3 mushrooms = 1-2 g.
***Total = 13-14 g. usable protein**

"BAKING" PANCAKES

Pancakes are traditionally considered to be a type of bread, so they are "baked" on a griddle or frying pan. Most of us think of the process as frying, but to be correct we'll go along with the experts and bake our pancakes.

Heat your griddle or frying pan until it is fairly hot; with a well-seasoned pan you may not even have to use any fat other than that in the recipe itself. The griddle is hot enough when a drop of cold water dances and sputters across the griddle surface. If the griddle is too cool the water will boil; if it's too hot the water will disappear when it touches the griddle surface.

When the griddle is heated make a pancake by gently pouring about ¼ cup of batter onto the griddle. When *many* bubbles have formed on the surface of the cake lift it with a pancake turner. If the bottom of the pancake is brown enough to suit your fancy flip the cake over and cook it for a minute or two on the other side. If the bottom of the cake isn't dark enough for you, return it to the griddle for another minute or two before flipping the cake over. In any case, never flip the pancake more than once.

If pancakes must be kept warm until you're ready to serve them keep them in a 200° oven. Stack them with towels between the cakes. Unless you're making some kind of elegant crêpe dish I think you'll enjoy your pancakes more if you eat them as they cook, rather than trying to hold them and serve them all at once.

WAFFLES

The pancake recipes can be used for making waffles, although you may wish to add 2 to 3 tablespoons more oil or butter to the batter. Fill a heated waffle iron ⅔ full, close it, and bake about 4 minutes or until it stops steaming. Open the iron and remove the waffle. If done, it will come away from the iron easily.

A well-seasoned waffle iron should never need extra greasing before baking waffles. Follow the manufacturer's instructions for seasoning.

For both pancakes and waffles mix wet and dry ingredients until moist. The batter may be slightly lumpy. The less you mix, the lighter your cakes will be.

Serve pancakes and waffles with a topping of butter and honey, syrup, or fruit jelly or preserves. Or top them with ice cream for a filling dessert.

Whole Wheat Pancakes

10 cakes

*1 egg, beaten
*¾ c. milk
1 t. baking powder
*¾ c. whole wheat flour

1 T. oil or butter
1-2 t. honey
¼ t. salt

1. Beat the milk, oil, honey, salt, and baking powder into the beaten egg.
2. Stir the flour into the liquid mixture.
3. Bake on a hot, greased griddle or frying pan.

VARIATION

Triticale Pancakes: Substitute ¾ c. triticale flour for the whole wheat flour.

⅜ c. milk + ¾ c. whole wheat flour = 10.5 g.
⅜ c. milk = 3 g.
1 egg = 6 g.
*Total = 19.5 g. usable protein

Cornmeal Pancakes

12 cakes

*1 egg, beaten
*1 c. milk
1 t. baking powder
¼ t. salt
*½ c. cornmeal

*4 t. soy grits
*½ c. whole wheat flour
1-2 t. honey
1 T. oil

1. Beat the milk, honey, oil, salt, and baking powder into the beaten egg.
2. Stir all the other ingredients into the liquid mixture. Let the mixture set for a few minutes to allow the liquid to soften the soy grits.
3. Bake on a well-greased griddle or frying pan.

½ c. cornmeal + 4 t. soy grits + ½ c. milk = 10 g.
½ c. whole wheat flour + ¼ c. milk = 7 g.
¼ c. milk = 2 g.
1 egg = 6 g.
*Total = 25 g. usable protein

Sesame Pancakes

10 cakes

These are my favorites. Yummy, with the subtle taste of sesame.

*1 egg, beaten
*¾ c. milk
1 T. oil
1-2 T. honey

*⅓ c. sesame seeds
*¾ c. whole wheat flour
¼ t. salt
1 t. baking powder

1. Beat the milk, oil, and honey into the egg. Stir in the dry ingredients in the order listed.
2. Bake on a well-greased griddle or frying pan.

⅜ c. milk + ¾ c. whole wheat flour = 10.5 g.
⅓ c. sesame seeds + about ¼ c. milk = 8 g.
⅛ c. milk = 1 g.
1 egg = 6 g.
*Total = 25.5 g. usable protein

Oatmeal Pancakes

12-14 cakes

*1 egg, beaten
*½ c. yogurt or buttermilk
*½ c. milk
¼ t. salt
½ t. baking soda

½ t. baking powder
1 T. oil
2 T. honey
*½ c. rolled oats
*½ c. whole wheat flour

1. Beat the yogurt, milk, salt, soda, and baking powder into the beaten egg.

2. Beat in the oil and honey, and finally the oats and flour.

3. Bake the pancakes on a hot, well-greased griddle or frying pan.

½ c. milk + ½ c. oats + ½ c. whole wheat flour = 14 g.
½ c. yogurt = 4 g.
1 egg = 6 g.
*Total = 24 g. usable protein

Buckwheat Pancakes

10 cakes

*1 egg, beaten
*¾ c. milk
1 t. baking powder
*¼ c. buckwheat flour
*½ c. whole wheat flour

1 T. oil or butter
1 T. honey
1 T. molasses
¼ t. salt

1. Beat the milk, honey, molasses, oil, salt, and baking powder into the beaten egg.

2. Stir in the flours.

3. Bake on a hot, greased griddle or frying pan.

⅜ c. milk + ¼ c. buckwheat flour + ½ c. whole wheat flour = 10.5 g.
⅜ c. milk = 3 g.
1 egg = 6 g.
*Total = 19.5 g. usable protein

SOUPS, SALADS & SANDWICHES

These three have more in common than their initial letter. Try them singly for a light meal or in combination for a more substantial repast.

SOUPS

If you've ever been snowed in on a cold winter's night you know there's nothing better for warming up your insides than a big bowl of steaming hot soup eaten with thick slices of freshly baked homemade bread. Make a big pot of soup and reheat the leftovers for lunch the next day. Try soup cold straight from the refrigerator. (For cream soups reheat without boiling, preferably in the top of a double boiler.)

Save the water from steaming vegetables to make stock for soup. Add onion skins, midribs from greens, potato peels, celery leaves, or almost any vegetable matter which you might normally discard. Simmer for about 30 minutes. Strain the stock and use the liquid in your soup.

Use the recipes as a starting point. With a little imagination you can concoct all kinds of delicious soups by adding a little of this and a little of that.

Cheese and Potato Soup

3 cups

1-2 t. butter	dash thyme
½ medium onion, chopped	1 c. water or stock
*1 medium potato, diced	¼ t. salt, or to taste
1 carrot, chopped	*⅓ c. grated cheese
1 t. sage	(mild cheddar)
dash cayenne	*1 c. milk

1. Melt the butter in a saucepan. Sauté the vegetables until the onions become transparent.

2. Add herbs and stock. Bring to a boil, cover, reduce heat, and simmer for about 20 minutes or until the vegetables are tender.

3. Over low heat stir in the salt and grated cheese. Continue stirring until all the cheese is melted.

4. Add milk and continue to simmer over low heat until the soup is hot again. Do not boil.

1 potato + ⅓ c. grated cheese = 9 g.
1 c. milk = 7 g.
*Total = 16 g. usable protein

Spicy Bean-Wheat Soup

3 cups

*2 T. dry beans (pinto, navy, garbanzo), cooked	2 c. stock or water
*6 T. wheat berries, cooked	1 t. cardamom
1 T. oil	dash thyme
1 medium onion, chopped	dash cayenne
1 carrot, sliced	*2 large or 5 small
2 stalks celery, sliced	mushrooms, sliced
	salt to taste

1. In a saucepan heat the oil and sauté the onion, carrot, and celery for a few minutes. Add the herbs and sauté for a few more minutes.

2. Add the stock, bring to a boil, cover, reduce heat, and simmer until the vegetables are tender, about 30 minutes.

3. Add the drained, cooked beans and cooked wheat berries. Continue to simmer until the beans and wheat berries are heated through.

4. Add the sliced mushrooms for the last 5 minutes of cooking.

5. Salt to taste and serve.

VARIATION

Substitute triticale berries for the wheat berries.

2 T. beans + 6 T. wheat berries = 11.5 g
mushrooms = 1 g.
*Total = 12.5 g. usable protein

Lentil Soup

2 cups

*2 T. dry lentils	**⅛-¼ t. thyme**
(preferably red), cooked	***⅓ c. raw brown rice**
1 small onion, chopped	**dash cayenne**
½ clove garlic, minced or	**2 c. water or stock**
dash of garlic powder	**1 bay leaf**
1 carrot, chopped or sliced	**½ t. salt**
2 stalks celery, sliced	
⅛ t. marjoram	

1. In a saucepan heat the oil and sauté the vegetables for a few minutes.

2. Add the herbs and rice and sauté for a few minutes more. Add the water or stock, bring to a boil, cover, reduce heat, and simmer until the rice is tender, 30-45 minutes.

3. If you can't get red lentils you may wish to rinse the drained lentils. I'm sure you lose some minerals, but I find the stock from the green lentils to be a very unappetizing color. Add the drained lentils to the soup and continue cooking long enough to heat the lentils through. Add salt and serve.

Note: If you have decided not to use the lentil stock in the soup save it for baking bread, especially rye bread, as it gives it a nice, dark color.

*2 T. lentils + ⅓ c. rice = 7.5 g. usable protein

Thick and Creamy Mushroom Soup

3 cups

Spoon leftovers over steamed snap beans for a delicious, fancy vegetable dish.

1 c. stock or water
1 stalk celery, sliced
1-2 T. butter
*1½-2 c. sliced mushrooms
½ t. salt

*1 potato, cut in large
   chunks
¼ t. nutmeg
dash cayenne
1-2 T. red wine (optional)

CREAM SAUCE
½ T. butter
1 T. whole wheat flour
*⅔ c. instant milk powder
   (½ c. non-instant)

*1 c. milk
bay leaf

1. Simmer the celery and potato in the stock until they are tender. For more flavor leave the peel on the potato while cooking — slip it off when done. Purée this mixture in a blender or food mill.

2. While the stock is simmering make a cream sauce. In a bowl beat the milk powder into the milk. Melt the butter in a frying pan. Stirring constantly add the flour, then the milk mixture. Finally add the bay leaf. Cook over low heat, stirring constantly, until thickened or put the sauce into a 350° oven to thicken, about 15 minutes.

3. Cool the purée and cream sauce slightly and mix them together, preferably in a blender. Set aside.

4. Sauté the mushrooms and seasonings in butter or a combination of butter and oil until tender. Add the wine and lower the heat. Slowly stir in the purée and cream sauce mixture. Heat gently over low heat. Do not boil.

1 potato + 1 c. milk = 9 g.
⅔ c. milk powder = 14 g.
mushrooms = 2-5 g.
*Total = 25-28 g. usable protein

Black Bean Soup

1 quart

*¼ c. dry black beans,
   cooked with a bay leaf
*¼ c. rice or barley
1 T. butter
½ medium onion, chopped
2 stalks celery, chopped
   (optional)
2 c. stock or water
½ t. oregano
¼ t. thyme

⅛ t. dry mustard
dash cayenne
¼ t. salt
*1 c. milk or ⅓ c. instant
   milk powder (¼ c.
   non-instant) dissolved in
   1 c. stock
¼ c. or more tomato juice
   (optional)

1. The black beans should be drained after cooking. For a prettier soup rinse the cooked beans with clear water. If you don't mind the color of the bean stock use it in the soup. Otherwise substitute a milder stock or plain water.

2. In a sauce pan melt the butter and sauté the vegetables for a few minutes.

3. Add 2 c. stock and seasonings. Bring to a boil and add rice or barley. Cover and simmer about 30 minutes.

4. Add the drained black beans and bay leaf to the soup and continue simmering for about 15 minutes.

5. Reduce the heat and add the milk and tomato juice. Keep over low heat until the soup is warmed through. Do not boil. Serve with whole grain bread.

¼ c. rice or barley + ⅓ c. milk = 6 g.
¼ c. beans + ½ c. milk = 11 g.
2⅔ T. milk = 1 g.
*Total = 18 g. usable protein

Tomato Rice Sesame Soup

3 cups

This soup has a strong garlic flavor. For a milder soup substitute a dash of garlic powder for the minced garlic.

1-2 T. oil
1 clove garlic, minced
*¼ c. sesame seeds
*¼ c. rice or barley
½ c. water or stock
1 small carrot
1 small stalk celery

1½ c. tomato juice
1 t. oregano
*½ c. milk
*⅓ c. instant milk powder
  (¼ c. non-instant)
salt to taste

1. Sauté the garlic in the oil until the garlic is soft. Add seeds and grain and sauté for a minute or two more. Add water, bring to a boil, cover, reduce heat, and simmer for 15 minutes.

2. Put the tomato juice, carrot, celery, and oregano in your blender and "buzz" until smooth. Add the vegetable juice mixture to the simmering ingredients. Continue to simmer, covered, until the grain is tender.

3. Beat the milk powder into the liquid milk (in the blender since you've already used it). Slowly stir the milk into the soup. Simmer just until the soup is heated through, but do not boil. Add salt and serve.

¼ c. sesame seeds + 1 T. milk powder = 6⅓ g.
¼ c. rice + 2 T. milk powder = 5⅔ g.
2⅓ T. milk powder = 3 g.
½ c. milk = 3.5 g.
*Total = 18.5 g. usable protein

Vichyssoise (Leek and Potato Soup)

If you eat this hot it's leek and potato soup. If you chill it first it's vichyssoise, an American dish with a French name. I'm told the French have never heard of it. Still and all, it's good on a hot summer day!

*3 potatoes
1 T. butter
3-4 leeks
*⅔ c. instant milk powder
   (½ c. non-instant)
1 c. water

*1 c. milk
2 T. dried parsley (4 T. fresh)
¼ t. thyme
¼ t. summer savory
1 t. tamari soy sauce
1 t. dill seed

1. Steam the potatoes about 30 minutes and slip off the skins. In the blender process one potato, the water, and the milk powder until smooth. Set aside.

2. In a saucepan or soup pot sauté the leeks in the butter until soft. Add the puréed mixture, milk, and seasonings. Cut the other two potatoes into chunks and add. Cover and turn the heat low. Simmer for an hour or longer. For best results don't let the soup boil. Refrigerate.

*3 potatoes + 1 c. milk + ⅔ c. milk powder = 27 g. usable protein

Vegetable Soup

4 cups

My vegetable soup recipe is constantly changing. This is it right now. Feel free to add any special touches of your own.

*2 T. dry soybeans, cooked
*2 T. wheat berries, cooked
*¼ c. brown rice
1-3 T. oil
1 onion, chopped
1 c. chopped carrots
1 c. chopped celery
1 c. shredded cabbage
1 c. mixed vegetables (corn, beans, peas, limas, anything you might find in your refrigerator)

2 c. water or stock
1 c. fresh tomatoes, skinned and chopped or canned
1 bay leaf
celery leaves
¼ t. thyme
1 T. dried parsley
few drops tamari soy sauce
dash garlic powder and cayenne
1 t. salt to taste

1. In a soup pot heat the oil; sauté the vegetables in the order listed. As each one softens, add the next.

2. Add water or stock, seasonings, rice, and cooked soybeans and wheat berries. Bring to a boil, cover, reduce heat, and simmer for at least 1 hour.

3. About ½ hour before you're ready to serve the soup, stir in the tomatoes. Continue simmering until the soup is heated through and the flavors mingle.

4. Adjust seasoning to taste.

VARIATION

Substitute triticale berries for the wheat berries.

*2 T. soybeans + 2 T. wheat berries + ¼ c. rice = 10.25 g. usable protein

Garden Soup

4-6 cups

This could also be called "clean out the refrigerator soup." The flavor is different from other vegetable soups because of the seasonings and pot herbs.

*¼ c. dry beans
*¾ c. wheat berries
about 2 c. stock
2 carrots, chopped
1-2 scallions, chopped
1 small zucchini, sliced
2. c. tomato juice
⅛ t. garlic powder
¼ t. summer savory
¼ t. rosemary
¼ t. tamari soy sauce

1 small turnip, diced
1 c. shredded greens (chard,
    sorrel, lamb's quarters,
    borage, spinach, etc.)
¼-½ c. sliced mushrooms
1 sage leaf
½ t. salt
handful of snow peas
    or snap beans
yellow squash slices

1. Bring the stock to a rapid boil. Slowly add the dry beans, but never let the water stop boiling. Simmer for 1 hour. Add wheat berries and simmer for another hour.

2. Add the carrots and scallions and continue to simmer for another 30 minutes.

3. Add all the other ingredients in the order listed, plus any other leftover vegetables you may have in the fridge. Simmer 10-15 minutes or until you are ready to eat. (For best flavor don't let the snow peas cook too long. Their crunch is their best feature!)

*¼ c. dry beans + ¾ c. wheat berries = 23 g. usable protein

Oatmeal Soup

4 cups

This is a hearty, flavorful soup, especially good on a cold day when you want something hot in a hurry. It takes only about 15 minutes to make from start to finish.

*½ c. rolled oats
1 T. oil
1 medium onion, chopped
1 clove garlic, minced
1½ c. stock
*1 T. soy grits

*⅓ c. instant milk powder
  (¼ c. non-instant)
1½ c. peeled and chopped
  tomatoes or tomato juice
1 T. miso or tamari soy sauce
⅛-¼ t. salt

1. In a heavy dry saucepan, toast the rolled oats over a medium heat, stirring almost constantly, until they are golden brown. Watch carefully. Once the oats get warm they can burn very easily. Remove the oats from the heat and set them aside.

2. In a saucepan heat the oil and sauté the onion and garlic until soft. Add the stock, soy grits, toasted oatmeal, and 1 cup of the tomatoes; bring the soup to a boil over medium heat. Cover and reduce heat to a simmer. Simmer for about 5 minutes.

3. Dissolve the milk powder in the remaining ½ cup of tomatoes and stir this mixture into the soup.

4. Remove about ½ cup of the soup from the pot and allow it to cool slightly. Dissolve the miso or tamari in this warm soup and add the mixture back to the soup pot.

5. Add salt to taste.

½ c. rolled oats + 1 T. soy grits = 8 g.
⅓ c. milk powder = 7 g.
*Total = 15 g. usable protein

Cream of Celery Soup

3 cups

This is a delicious first course. If you add milk powder it can make a full meal.

1 T. butter	¼ t. thyme
1 medium onion, chopped	¼ t. summer savory
1½ c. chopped celery,	1 T. miso or tamari
including leaves	*1 c. milk
1 c. water or stock	½ t. salt, or to taste

1. In a soup pot melt the butter and sauté the onions and celery for a few minutes until they soften and the onion becomes transparent. If your celery has few leaves add ½ t. celery seed to compensate. Add the water or stock, bring to a boil, cover, reduce heat, and simmer for about 30 minutes.

2. Stir in the thyme and summer savory. Remove a small amount of stock from the pot and allow it to cool slightly; dissolve the miso in the stock and add the solution back to the soup. Add the milk and cover the pot. Simmer the soup for another 30 minutes or until the celery is tender and you are ready to serve it. Do not boil. Add salt to taste just before serving. Be careful with the salt as both miso and celery are very salty. Even ½ t. may be more than you like.

VARIATIONS

1. Potato Celery Soup: Add 1 or 2 diced potatoes when you sauté the vegetables.

2. Protein-rich Celery Soup: Dissolve ⅓-⅔ c. milk powder in the milk before adding to the soup. This will add 7-14 g. usable protein.

*1 c. milk = 7 g. usable protein

Cream of Chard Soup

3 cups

This soup makes a quick and easy first course. White milk, yellow butter, and bright green chard make it pretty too. You can substitute other greens for the chard.

1 T. butter	1 T. whole wheat flour
1 medium onion,	*2 c. milk
finely chopped	dash cayenne
3 leaves Swiss chard, stems	dash nutmeg
and leaves chopped sep-	salt and pepper to taste
arately or 3 c. other greens	

1. In a saucepan melt the butter over a medium-low flame. Sauté the onion and chard stems until soft. Sprinkle the whole wheat flour over vegetables and stir. Sauté until the flour is moistened with melted butter.

2. Stir in the milk and continue to cook until the soup is warmed through. Add the chopped chard leaves (make sure they are finely chopped) and stir into the soup. Add nutmeg and cayenne. Continue to heat until the chard wilts. Add salt and pepper to taste.

VARIATIONS

Substitute any other greens for the Swiss chard. The flavor will vary but this is a good, basic recipe. Use whatever you have, spinach, leaf lettuce, endive, etc.

*2 c. milk = 14 g. usable protein

Cream of Asparagus Soup
2-3 cups

A great way to use up the tough ends you've snapped off fresh asparagus.

2-3 c. raw, chopped asparagus	1 stalk celery, chopped
1 c. vegetable stock or water	1 T. whole wheat flour
1 T. butter	*1 c. milk
1 medium onion, chopped	salt, cayenne, and paprika to taste

1. Cook the asparagus in the vegetable stock until the asparagus is very tender, 30 minutes or more.

2. In a saucepan or soup pot melt the butter and sauté the onion and celery until soft. Stir in the whole wheat flour and stir until the flour is very moist. Stir in the asparagus and stock and slowly bring the mixture to a boil, stirring frequently. Add the milk, reduce heat, and simmer until the soup is heated through.

3. Purée the soup. If you purée it in a blender you will have more soup, but it will be smoother if you put it through a sieve or food mill. Return the soup to the pot and reheat for a few minutes. Add salt and cayenne to taste and as much paprika as you like for color.

*1 c. milk = 7 g. usable protein

Creamed Winter Squash or Pumpkin Soup

4-5 cups

Hot and filling on a cold November evening.

2 c. cooked, peeled, mashed
  or puréed winter squash
  or pumpkin
2 T. butter or oil
¼ c. whole wheat flour
*2 c. milk

1 c. stock or water
½-3 t. grated fresh ginger
½ t. salt
dash cayenne
1-2 T. honey

1. Prepare the squash by halving it, scooping out the seeds, and steaming it until tender. Peel and mash the cooked squash. Save any extra to serve as a vegetable.

2. In at least a 2 qt. saucepan melt the butter or heat the oil. Add the whole wheat flour, stirring until the flour absorbs all the fat. Add 1 cup of milk and continue to heat the mixture over a medium flame, stirring often, until it thickens and then boils.

3. Add the second cup of milk, stock, cooked squash, seasonings, and honey. Pour the soup into a blender and process until everything is smooth. Return the soup to saucepan and keep it over a low flame until you are ready to serve it.

*2 cups milk = 14 g. usable protein

CLEAR SOUPS

These don't provide significant amounts of protein, but they are nice and easy for a first course or a late night snack.

Minestrone

4 cups

This is good with lasagna or other Italian food.

¼ c. dry beans, cooked
   (a combination of black,
   kidney, and pinto beans)
1 T. olive oil
1 small carrot, chopped
1 stalk celery, chopped
1 turnip, peeled and diced
¾-1 c. fresh snap beans,
   broken in inch long pieces
1 medium zucchini, sliced
1 c. water or stock

leftover juice from Summer
   Squash Bake and tomato
   juice to make 1 c. juice
tomato juice and/or water
   to make 1 c.
1 t. oregano
¼ t. sweet basil
¼ t. tamari
¼-½ t. salt
whole wheat macaroni
   (optional)
grated cheese

1. Heat the oil and sauté all the vegetables in the order listed. Add the cooked beans and 1 c. water or stock. Bring to a boil, cover, reduce heat, and simmer for 30 minutes.

2. If you don't have leftover juice from the squash dish make the juice by combining:
   1 c. tomato juice   ¼ t. sweet basil
   1 T. olive oil   ¼ t. salt
   1 t. oregano   ¼ t. honey
   Add this juice, or the leftover juice, to the soup.

3. Add the rest of the tomato juice, seasonings, tamari, and macaroni. Simmer 15-30 minutes.

4. Serve with a grating of cheese on top.

Note: Please don't substitute other oil for the olive oil or you won't end up with the same flavor. The dry beans are used mostly for color, but they also provide protein which can be complemented in the rest of your meal.

Green Soup

2 cups

This is almost like a hot salad for a cold day. Toss in any green vegetable leftovers you may have in your refrigerator.

1-2 t. oil
1 scallion, including top, chopped
1 medium mushroom, sliced
1 T. diced green pepper
1 small zucchini, sliced
1 c. stock or water

¼ t. summer savory
¼ t. salt or to taste
few drops tamari soy sauce
handful green snap beans
handful fresh greens
   (spinach, lettuce, escarole, endive, etc.)

1. Heat the oil in a small saucepan and sauté the scallion, mushroom, green pepper, and zucchini for a few minutes. Add the stock and bring to a boil.

2. Add the seasonings and green beans. Simmer until the vegetables are tender.

3. Add the fresh greens and simmer for about 1 minute.

Tri-color Soup

2½ cups

I once heard that a balanced meal should include foods of several different colors. If that's true, this soup must be loaded with food value. At any rate it's a beautiful appetizer or first course.

1 T. oil
2 or 3 fresh beets, peeled and thinly sliced
1 carrot, thinly sliced
½ c. fresh snap bean pieces
dash curry powder

2 c. stock or water (for best color use at least part beet stock)
¼ t. salt or to taste
¼-½ t. miso or tamari soy sauce

1. Heat the oil. Sauté the beets, then the carrots, and then the beans. Be sure each vegetable is well coated with oil before

adding the next. The oil will seal the color in the vegetables, especially the beets. Add the curry powder and sauté for a few more seconds.

2. Add the stock or water, bring to a boil, cover, reduce heat, and simmer for about 10 minutes.

3. Add salt and miso or tamari to taste. If using miso be sure to dissolve it in a little warm water before adding it to the soup.

Sorrel Soup

3 cups

A good, appetite stimulating first course. Use sorrel if you possibly can. Otherwise you can substitute other fresh greens, but the taste will change.

1 T. oil	3 c. chopped sorrel
1 medium onion, chopped	2 T. chopped fresh sweet basil
1 carrot, sliced	(1 T. dried)
1 medium mushroom, sliced	1 T. miso or tamari
2 c. water or stock	dissolved in 1 c. water
	¼ t. salt

1. Sauté the onion, carrot, and mushroom in the oil. Add water or stock, bring to a boil, reduce heat, cover, and simmer for about 20 minutes or until the carrot is tender.

2. Add the chopped sorrel and sweet basil. Cover again and simmer for about 3 minutes.

3. Dissolve the miso in a cup of warm water; add the miso and water mixture to the soup. Heat just enough to warm the soup. Add salt to taste.

Curried Summer Squash Soup

4 cups

As you eat more and more of this soup it tastes better and better.

1 T. oil	dash cayenne
1 small onion, chopped	1½ c. water or stock
2 summer squash, cut in	1 T. miso or tamari
chunks	salt to taste
½ t. curry powder	

1. Sauté the onion and summer squash in the oil. Add the curry powder and cayenne and sauté for a minute. Add water or stock, bring to a boil, cover, and simmer for about 30 minutes.

2. Remove about ½ c. liquid from the soup and let it cool slightly. Dissolve the miso in the cooled liquid and add the mixture to the soup. Add salt if you wish. (I think the soup doesn't need salt but you may like a little.)

Use Up The Stock Soup

This is just what its name suggests. It is easy to make and uses only basic, staple foods. Adjust the amount of vegetables according to the amount of stock you need to use up.

1 T. olive oil	3-4 c. stock
1 clove garlic, minced	about ¼ t. summer savory
1 onion, chopped	about 1 t. sweet basil
1-2 carrots, chopped	1 T. or more tamari or miso
1-2 stalks celery,	salt to taste if needed
chopped	

1. Sauté all the vegetables in the olive oil. Add the stock and herbs and bring to a boil. Reduce heat and simmer until the vegetables are tender.

2. Add tamari or miso (dissolved in warm stock) and salt if necessary.

VARIATION

If you have any bits of leftover vegetables sitting around in the refrigerator add them to the simmering soup.

Gaspacho

4 cups

Chilly and refreshing on a steamy summer day.

1 c. tomatoes, peeled
  and chopped
1 c. tomato juice
½ sweet green pepper,
  chopped
1 small summer squash or
  cucumber, chopped

1½ t. sweet basil
¼ t. salt
1 small scallion or a
  few fresh chives, chopped
2 T. olive oil
1 T. lemon juice

Purée everything in the blender and chill until ready to serve, at least 2 hours.

VARIATION

Dice all the vegetables and combine all the ingredients; chill for at least 2 hours.

SALADS

One of my favorite meals is a big tossed salad, full of colorful vegetables and chunks of cheese. A simple meal, but oh, so delicious! Many nutritionists recommend eating at least one salad of raw greens each day — especially for its vitamin and enzyme content. Keep salad greens refrigerated until you are ready to use them, and wash them quickly without soaking. Salad foods with intact peels, such as apples and potatoes, need not be refrigerated as the peel will prevent vitamin loss. However, once the food is cut or peeled vitamin loss will occur if the food is left unrefrigerated. After washing, dry all salad foods thoroughly so the oil from the dressing will cling to them and prevent any further vitamin loss.

In addition to green salads experiment with others. A cool Creamy Cucumber Salad will go well with a hot curried dish, while a spicy salad would go well with a mildly flavored quiche. Experiment to find your favorite combinations.

VEGETABLE SALADS

Green Salad

If you're accustomed to eating only iceberg lettuce you'll probably want to include some of it in your salads for crunch. However, for vitamin content it's better to use darker greens for the main part of the salad. In general the darker the green is, the more vitamins and minerals it has. I've found that the more I eat of other greens, the more appealing they become; iceberg lettuce has gradually lost its place of importance. Somehow its bland taste just can't compete any longer with sweet leaf lettuce, buttery Boston lettuce, or sturdy Romaine.

Salad greens should be washed quickly in cold water and then dried by shaking them *hard*, patting them dry between terrycloth towels, or using a lettuce spinner. Greens must be dry for the oil in the salad dressing to stick to them. Greens will keep longer if they aren't washed before being stored in the refrigerator. However, salads are quicker to make if the greens are pre-washed so all you have to do is tear and toss when you are ready to eat. Choose the system which goes best with your lifestyle. Once they're picked, store all greens in the refrigerator to avoid vitamin loss.

To "officially" be a green salad the salad should contain nothing but raw salad greens.

1. Wash and dry the leaves of various greens, such as:

borage	lamb's quarters
cabbage	lettuce (iceberg, Romaine,
chard	leaf, red, Boston, butter)
corn salad	sorrel
dandelion greens	spinach
endive	watercress
escarole	wild greens (in small
kale	amounts)

2. Tear the greens into small pieces and place them in a large bowl. Pour a tablespoonful of oil on top and toss gently until the greens are coated with a thin film of oil. The film locks in vitamins and minerals which may be lost if the greens are left exposed to room temperature air.

3. Refrigerate until ready to serve. Serve with your favorite dressing.

Tossed or Chef's Salad

This is one of my favorite meals. You have the choice of tossing the finished salad or arranging the extras on top of the greens. Salads are a great place to try out your creativity; they can be different every time you make them.

1. Prepare a green salad.

2. Add any or all of the following:

broccoli, raw florets	mushroom, raw slices
carrot, raw slices	radishes
cauliflower, raw florets	scallion or onion slices
celery, raw slices	sprouts
*cheese chunks	summer squash, raw chunks
cucumber slices	*sunflower seeds and
*egg, hard-cooked chunks	peanuts (4 to 3 ratio)
*garbanzo beans, cooked	toasted croutons
and drained	tomato chunks
green pepper, chunks	turnip, grated raw
or slices	vegetables, cold cooked
Jerusalem artichoke	
grated	

3. Toss gently or arrange in salad bowls. Serve with your favorite dressing. The amount of protein will vary.

TOSSED SALAD COMBINATIONS

1. Leaf lettuce, tomatoes, mung bean or alfalfa sprouts.

2. Spinach and raw mushroom slices.

3. Leaf lettuce, Swiss chard, kale, tomatoes and Swiss cheese chunks.

4. Spinach, raw mushroom slices and alfalfa sprouts.

5. Romaine lettuce, shredded cabbage, carrot slices, raw mushroom slices, tomatoes and sunflower seeds.

6. Romaine lettuce, leaf lettuce, tomatoes, chunks of cheese and hard-cooked egg.

7. Leaf lettuce, Swiss chard, tomatoes, carrot slices, celery, summer squash slices and chunks of cheese.

8. Leaf or Boston lettuce, cauliflower florets, raw mushroom slices, chunks of cheese and sunflower seeds.

The more I think about it the harder it is to imagine how any tossed salad could be a flop, as long as you use fresh ingredients. So put together whatever you have on hand and enjoy!

Tomatoes and Cucumbers
2 servings

1 tomato, cut in chunks	**2 T. vinegar**
1 cucumber, sliced	**honey, salt, and pepper**
2 T. water	**to taste**

1. Prepare the vegetables and place them in a large bowl.

2. In a separate bowl combine the water and vinegar. Add enough honey to neutralize the acid taste. (Test by tasting — all good cooks taste while they cook.) Add a dash or two of salt and pepper.

3. Pour the vinegar dressing over the vegetables and allow them to marinate for 15-20 minutes before eating, if you can wait that long!

VARIATION

Serve the dressing over sliced cucumbers.

Curried Carrot Slaw

2 servings

Sweet and spicy!

2 carrots, grated　　　　　　**2-4 T. raisins**

DRESSING
¼ t. curry powder　　　　　**1 t. honey**
** (or to taste)**　　　　　　　**2 T. oil**
2 t. cider or wine vinegar

1. Stir together the curry powder, vinegar, and honey. Add the oil and stir or shake well.

2. Pour the dressing over the carrots and raisins and toss the salad.

Pickled Beets

2-4 servings

1 c. cooked, peeled, and　　**½ c. vinegar**
** cut beets (canned are fine)**　**⅓ c. honey**
1 c. beet stock　　　　　　　**salt and pepper to taste**

1. Combine the stock, vinegar, and honey. Heat them slightly to dissolve the honey more quickly. Add salt and pepper to taste.

2. Pour the liquid over the beets and refrigerate 4 hours or longer.

VARIATION

Pickled Beets with "Beet Eggs": Add peeled, hard-cooked eggs to the beets and liquid. Refrigerate. Yes, the eggs will be purple, and so good!

Broccoli, Mushroom, and Bean Sprout Salad

This is more filling than a lettuce salad, so don't go overboard when you start chopping vegetables.

**raw broccoli, florets
broken up and stems
thinly sliced**

**sliced raw mushrooms
mung bean sprouts**

1. Combine the vegetables in any proportion.
2. Toss the vegetables with the blue cheese dressing and serve the salad either alone or on a bed of greens.

All of the ingredients supply small amounts of protein. The final amount will depend on the final amounts of food.

Creamy Cucumber Salad

2-4 servings

**1 cucumber, quartered
lengthwise, and sliced
*½ c. yogurt
dash of salt and pepper**

**1 t. dried dill weed
(2 t. fresh)
1 t. dried sweet basil
(2 t. fresh)**

1. Prepare the dressing by stirring crumbled herbs, salt, and pepper into the yogurt.
2. Add cucumber slices and stir gently.
3. This salad tastes best (especially if dried herbs are used) if allowed to marinate in the refrigerator overnight.

*½ c. yogurt = 4 g. usable protein

Cole Slaw

2-4 servings

1-2 c. grated or thinly
  sliced cabbage (combine
  red and green cabbage
  for a prettier slaw)

1 small carrot, grated
2 T. grated or finely
  diced green pepper

DRESSING

2 T. apple cider vinegar
1 t. honey

*½ c. yogurt
dash salt and pepper

1. Stir the dressing ingredients together. Adjust the amounts of honey, salt, and pepper to suit your taste.

2. Pour the dressing over the grated vegetables and toss lightly to coat the vegetables.

3. Refrigerate until ready to serve.

*½ c. yogurt = 4 g. usable protein

FRUIT SALADS

Simple Fruit Salad

2-4 servings

1 apple, cut in chunks
1 orange, sectioned and
  cut in chunks
1 banana, sliced

¼ c. pineapple chunks
2 T. lemon juice
1 t. honey
a few sprigs fresh mint
  (optional)

1. Combine the honey and lemon juice to make a dressing for the salad. Pour over the fruits and toss gently.

2. Garnish with mint sprigs and chill until ready to serve.

VARIATION

Substitute mint vinegar for the lemon juice and increase the amount of honey.

Creamy Fruit Salad

2 large or 4-5 small servings

*1 c. yogurt
1-2 T. honey
1 c. pineapple chunks

1 apple, cut in chunks
¼ c. sliced strawberries
*raw sunflower seeds

1. Beat the honey into the yogurt. Gently stir in all the fruits. Refrigerate for at least 2 hours to allow the flavors to mingle.

2. Serve well chilled with a sprinkling of sunflower seeds topping each serving.

1 c. yogurt = 8 g.
sunflower seeds = small amount protein
*Total = 8 g. usable protein

Ambrosia Salad

2 large or 4-5 small servings

*1 c. yogurt
1 t. lemon juice
1 T. honey
1 apple, chopped

1 orange, sectoned and chopped
¼-⅓ c. pineapple chunks
⅓ c. (or more) shredded coconut

1. Beat the yogurt, lemon juice, and honey together until smooth. Gently stir in all the rest of the ingredients.

2. Chill for at least 2 hours before serving.

*1 c. yogurt = 8 g. usable protein

Creamy Grape Salad
2 servings

1 c. white grapes	*1 c. yogurt
¼ c. raisins	2 t. honey

1. Combine all the ingredients, stirring thoroughly but gently. Adjust the amount of honey to suit your taste.
2. Chill until ready to serve.

*1 c. yogurt = 8-9 g. usable protein

MAIN DISH OR FULL MEAL SALADS
These all provide fairly large amounts of usable protein.

Three Bean Salad
2-4 servings

I think this is the best three bean salad I've ever tasted. It will serve two as a main dish or several as a side dish.

*¼ c. black beans, cooked	dash cayenne and garlic
*¼ c. garbanzo beans,	powder
cooked	½ t. salt
1 scallion, chopped	⅛ t. dry mustard
1 stalk celery, chopped	2 T. vinegar
1 t. oregano	3 T. oil
⅛ t. cumin	1 c. steamed snap beans
¼ t. summer savory	*⅓ c. grated cheese

1. If possible cook the dry beans separately to preserve their colors. Plunge them into ice water to cool them quickly. Drain.
2. Combine all the ingredients and toss gently.
3. Refrigerate the salad for at least 2 hours to allow the vegetables time to marinate. Serve on a bed of raw greens.

*½ c. beans + ⅓ c. grated cheese = 22 g. usable protein

Spring Delight Salad
2-4 servings

This makes a meal for two or a side dish for several.

DRESSING

½ avocado, mashed
*1 c. yogurt
*⅓-⅔ c. instant milk
  powder (¼-½ c.
  non-instant)

1-2 T. honey
dash coriander
½ t. salt

SALAD

assorted diced fruit: pear,
  apple, orange, banana,
  pineapple, melon,
  avocado, peach, kiwi,
  papaya, mango, etc.

*½ c. bulgar, cooked
  with ½ t. salt
1 T. orange or lemon juice

1. After the bulgar is cooked press it into a mold (a small, round-bottomed bowl is good) and refrigerate until set.

2. Prepare the fruit, toss it gently with the orange or lemon juice to prevent discoloring, and chill.

3. Prepare the dressing. Stir the yogurt into the mashed avocado. Beat in the milk powder — the more milk powder you can beat in, the higher the protein. Beat in the honey, coriander, and salt. Chill.

4. To assemble the salad invert the bulgar mold on the center of a serving plate. Arrange the fruit around the bulgar, and pour dressing over all. Extra dressing can be spooned over individual servings.

VARIATION

Crumble the chilled bulgar into the fruit and toss with the dressing.

½ c. bulgar + ⅓ c. yogurt = 9 g.
⅔ c. yogurt = 4-6 g.
⅓ + ⅔ c. milk powder = 7-14 g.
*Total = 20-29 g. usable protein

Potato Salad

2-4 servings

This serves 2 or 4 people, unless one of them is my brother. In that case it serves one.

*3-4 medium potatoes,
  steamed, skinned,
  and chopped
*1-2 hard-cooked eggs
5 chives or 2 scallions
½ medium cucumber
1 stalk celery
*½ c. yogurt

*⅔ c. instant milk powder
  (½ c. non-instant)
1 t. lemon juice or vinegar
½ t. summer savory
dash tarragon
dash cayenne
¼ t. salt, or to taste

1. Chop all the vegetables and the eggs into a large bowl. Add any extra touches of your own — chopped green pepper, chopped olives or pickles, etc.

2. In a separate bowl beat the milk powder into the yogurt. Stir in the lemon juice and the seasonings. Pour this dressing over the vegetables and stir gently. Refrigerate until ready to serve.

1-2 eggs = 6-12 g.
2 potatoes + ⅔ . milk powder = 18 g.
1-2 potatoes = 1.2-4 g.
½ c. yogurt = 4 g.
*Total = 29.2-38 g. usable protein

Herbed Macaroni Salad

2-4 servings

This makes a good, cool main dish for a summer meal.

DRESSING

*¼ c. yogurt
*⅔ c. instant milk powder
   (½ c. non-instant)
1 t. vinegar
¼ t. tamari soy sauce

⅛ t. ground cumin
¼ t. summer savory
¼ c. thyme
½ t. salt

SALAD

*½ c. whole wheat macaroni,
   cooked
¼ c. chopped celery

⅓ c. grated carrot
2 scallions, chopped
¼ c. diced green pepper

1. Beat the milk powder into the yogurt. Beat in the vinegar, tamari, and seasonings.

2. Add all the other ingredients to the dressing and toss lightly. Chill until ready to serve (at least 2 hours).

½ c. macaroni + 2⅔ T. milk powder = 14 g.
2⅔ T. milk powder = 4 g.
⅓ c. milk powder = 7 g.
¼ c. yogurt = 2 g.
*Total = 27 g. usable protein

Tabooley

2-3 servings

This is a variation on a traditional Middle Eastern salad. Feel free to adjust the amounts of vegetables to suit your own taste.

*10 T. cracked wheat, raw
2 T. dried parsley (4 T.
   fresh), minced
1 T. dried mint (2 T.
*2 T. dry garbanzo beans,
   cooked tender
3 scallions, chopped

1 stalk celery, chopped (⅔ c.)
½ small cucumber, sliced
½-2 medium tomatoes,
   chopped
½ t. salt
1 T. oil (preferably olive)
3 T. lemon juice

1. Put the cracked wheat, parsley, and mint in a bowl. Cover with 2 cups boiling water and let soak for 2 hours. Drain, pressing out as much water as possible.

2. Combine all the ingredients in the order listed, pouring the oil and lemon juice over all. Toss lightly and mix the ingredients.

3. Refrigerate until thoroughly chilled, at least 2 hours.

*10 T. cracked wheat + 2 T. beans = 11.5 g. usable protein

SALAD DRESSINGS

The BEST French Vinaigrette Dressing

My sister brought this recipe back from Paris. It's easy as anything and really brings out the taste of the vegetables in your raw salads. Make as much or as little as you need. Remember, the trick with all oil and vinegar dressings is to always use three times as much oil as vinegar.

½ part Dijon mustard
   (⅛ part dry mustard)

1 part cider, wine, or
   herb vinegar
3 parts salad oil

1. Mix the mustard and vinegar together until smooth. Add the oil and stir or shake briskly to mix.

2. Serve as is or add herbs to taste: sweet basil, oregano, summer savory, dillweed, sweet basil. Invent your own!

Sesame Dressing

Put some cheese in your salad to complement the tahini.

1 T. tahini or sesame butter   **½ t. tamari**
4-5 t. lemon juice   **water**

1. Blend the tahini, lemon juice, and tamari together until smooth.
2. Blend in water, a teaspoonful at a time, until the consistency is the way you like it for salad dressing.

American French Dressing

The red kind — another recipe which the French have never heard of.

1 part vinegar   **3 parts oil**
2 parts tomato juice

1. Thoroughly stir or shake all the ingredients together.
2. Add a dash of garlic powder and herbs to taste (sweet basil and oregano are good).

Herbed Buttermilk Dressing

Feel free to alter the herbs as you wish to create your own favorite dressing.

*½ c. buttermilk   **½ t. oregano**
1 t. lemon juice   **dash ground cumin**
¼ t. tamari soy sauce   **dash cayenne**
¼ t. marjoram   **¼ t. salt**

Stir everything together and serve on raw vegetable salads.

*½ c. buttermilk = 3.5-4 g. usable protein

Olive Oil and Buttermilk Dressing

Easy and delicious. Enough for one salad, but make more if you wish.

1 t. olive oil
1 T. buttermilk
⅛-¼ t. summer savory

⅛-¼ t. sweet basil
dash garlic powder

Stir all the ingredients together and pour over your salad. Or sprinkle the herbs over your salad. Drizzle the olive oil over the herbs; finally pour buttermilk over all.

Blue Cheese Dressing

⅔ cup

The first time I made this I was amazed at how easy it was. I thought that I would surely have to play with seasonings, etc. for a while before the dressing came out the way I wanted it. I was wrong!

*½ c. yogurt
*2-4 T. crumbled blue cheese

¼ t. lemon juice

Stir all the ingredients together and chill. Serve on raw vegetable salads.

½ c. yogurt = 4 g.
2-4 T. blue cheese = 2-6 g.
*Total = 6-10 g. usable protein

Green Goddess Dressing

1 cup

The chives and parsley give this dressing lots of flavor and the parsley keeps you from getting onion breath.

*¾ c. buttermilk   1 t. lemon juice
5 chives or 2 scallions,   dash tarragon
  chopped
about ⅓ c. chopped
  fresh parsley

1. Thoroughly mix all the ingredients together or buzz them in the blender for a minute or two.
2. Refrigerate for several hours to allow flavors to mingle.

*¾ c. buttermilk = 6 g. usable protein

Easy Thousand Island Dressing

¾ cup

Use this on green salads or in Reuben sandwiches

*½ c. yogurt   dash dry mustard
2 T. catsup   dash tarragon
1 T. pickle relish or   ¼ t. tamari soy sauce
  chopped sweet pickle

Stir all the ingredients together and refrigerate to allow flavors to mingle.

*½ c. yogurt = 4 g. usable protein

The Easiest Salad Dressing of All

If you like plain buttermilk or yogurt just top your vegetable salad with one of them. You can add herbs if you wish (summer savory is nice) but it isn't really necessary. The flavor in fancy buttermilk and mayo salad dressings really comes from the buttermilk; try plain buttermilk and see if you don't agree.

Herb Vinegars

Herb vinegars are a delicious way to store fresh herbs; they add a subtle taste to salads and dressings and are incredibly easy to make. The measurements will vary depending upon the herbs you use.

fresh herbs
vinegar (cider, wine, or malt)

1. Wash and *thoroughly* dry the fresh herbs — make sure there is no water clinging to them as *any* water will cloud the vinegar. Pack the herbs loosely into a glass jar, filling the jar to the top.

2. Heat, but do not boil, the vinegar. As soon as it is fairly hot pour the vinegar over the herbs in the glass jar, filling the jar to the top with vinegar. Cover the jar tightly and leave it in a cool, dark place for at least a month before serving. You can strain before using or leave in the herbs.

Suggested herbs:
Chive blossoms make a lovely, mild, pink vinegar.
Mint is good on fruit salads.
Sweet basil
Tarragon
Thyme

SANDWICHES

Sandwiches make easy pick up and go meals. Pack them for a picnic or to eat at work. I've included slightly complicated sandwich recipes, assuming that somewhere along the line you've learned to make simple sandwiches like cheese or peanut butter and jelly. Please don't neglect simple sandwiches just because they are simple. There's really nothing that can compare with a thick slice of tomato between two slices of fresh, whole wheat bread. Easy, but oh, so delicious!

Use bread from the bread recipes for your sandwhiches, or if that isn't possible, there are now several good, all natural, whole grain breads on the market. If you buy bread, read the labels to make sure the flour is whole grain and the bread does not contain additives or preservatives. Remember, commercial breads do not necessarily contain maximally usable protein; so complement your sandwich with a glass of milk or some cheese.

Reuben Sandwich

1 sandwich

This combination might sound awful, but somehow it comes out absolutely delicious.

*2 slices rye bread	*1 slice Swiss cheese
butter or margarine	1 T. Thousand Island
1-2 T. sauerkraut	dressing

1. Butter one side of each slice of bread. Place one slice, butter side down, on a griddle or frying pan. Spoon sauerkraut onto the bread, cover with cheese, spread salad dressing on top, and cover with the second slice of bread, butter side up.

2. Cook over medium heat until the bottom slice of bread is browned and the cheese melts. With a pancake turner, flip the sandwich over and cook it until the other slice of bread is browned.

1 slice Swiss cheese = 5-8 g.
2 slices rye bread = 2-6 g.
*Total = 7-14 g. usable protein

Peanut Butter Sandwiches

For best quality protein use Complementary Peanut Butter. Spread the peanut butter on whole grain bread and top with one of the following:

sunflower seeds   **cucumber slices**
slices of bananas   **fresh raw greens and**
slices of tomato   **tomato slices**
pickle slices   **raw summer squash slices**
alfalfa sprouts   **other sprouts**
ricotta cheese

1. Cover with a second slice of whole grain bread, or leave the sandwich open-faced if you wish.
2. Experiment with other things you have on hand for toppings.

Broiled Cheese & Tomato Sandwich

1 sandwich

*1 slice whole grain bread   **1 large slice tomato**
*1 slice cheese   **oregano and salt**

1. Toast one side of the slice of bread under the broiler.
2. Turn the bread over. Cover it with the slice of cheese, top with the tomato slice, and sprinkle salt and oregano over all. Return to the broiler and toast until the cheese melts and the tomato sizzles.

VARIATION

Substitute chopped, stuffed olives for the tomato and eliminate the oregano and salt.

1 slice cheese = 5-7 g.
1 slice bread = 1-3 g.
*Total = 6-10 g. usable protein

Grilled Peanut Butter Sandwich

1 serving

*2 slices whole grain bread   butter or margarine
*peanut butter (preferably
  Complementary Peanut
  Butter)

1. Make an ordinary peanut butter sandwich. Butter the outside of the sandwich with butter or margarine.
2. Grill on a hot griddle or frying pan until the bread is toasted and the peanut butter is melting.

1-2 T. Complementary Peanut Butter = 5.5-11 g.
2 slices bread = 2-6 g.
*Total = 7.5-17 g. usable protein

Egg Salad Sandwich

2 open-faced or 1 regular sandwich

A quick and easy, and could be elegant, lunch.

*2 slices whole grain bread   dash dry mustard
*1 hard-cooked egg   dash cayenne
 1 T. yogurt   salt to taste
 3-4 drops Worcestershire
   sauce or tamari

1. Mash the egg with a fork or pastry blender. Stir in the yogurt, Worcestershire or tamari, and the seasonings.
2. Spread the mixture on bread and serve.

2 slices bread = 2-6 g.
1 egg = 6 g.
*Total = 8-12 g. usable protein

Guacamole Cheese Sandwich

1 sandwich

This makes a delicious sandwich. You can also use the filling for a good, mild guacamole sauce.

¼ avocado
*2 T. cottage cheese
¼ t. lemon juice
dash salt
sprinkling paprika

tomato slices, to cover
  the bread
1 or 2 slices whole
  grain bread

1. Mash together the avocado, cottage cheese, lemon juice, salt, and paprika.

2. Place the tomato slices on a slice of bread. Spread the avocado over the tomato and bread. Cover with another slice of bread if you wish.

VARIATIONS

1. Guacamole sauce: Stir diced tomatoes into the mashed avocado mixture. Serve with crackers or chips.

2. For a hotter sauce add a dash of chili powder and a bit of minced chive or scallion.

2 T. cottage cheese = 4 g.
2 slices bread = 2-6 g.
*Total = 6-10 g. usable protein

Swiss Sprout Sandwich

1 serving

The sprouts add a nice crunch, but you can also make a delicious sandwich if you eliminate them.

*2 slices whole grain bread   mung bean or other sprouts
butter   Worcestershire sauce or
*1 slice Swiss cheese   tamari

1. Spread butter on one side of each slice of bread. Place one slice of bread, butter side down, on a griddle or frying pan. Top the bread with cheese, a sprinkling of sprouts, and the other slice of bread, butter side up.

2. Cook over medium heat until the bottom slice of bread is browned; flip the sandwich over. Cook until the other slice of bread is browned and the cheese melts.

3. Sprinkle a few drops of Worcestershire sauce or tamari over the outside of the cooked sandwich and serve.

1 slice cheese = 5-7 g.
2 slices bread = 2-6 g.
*Total = 7-13 g. usable protein

SANDWICH SPREADS

Complementary Peanut Butter

¾ cup

*½ c. peanut butter
*¼ c. instant milk powder
   (3 T. non-instant)

Blend the peanut butter and milk powder together until smooth.

*½ c. peanut butter + ¼ c. milk powder = 42 g. usable protein

Bean and Cheese Spread
1 cup

Good between slices of whole grain bread. Dress it up with a slice of tomato.

*½ c. dry beans, cooked
  tender and mashed
*⅓ c. grated cheddar cheese
1 t. oregano

½ t. sweet basil
dash garlic powder
¼ t. salt or to taste

1. Mash the grated cheese into the mashed beans.

2. Add the seasonings and continue to mash until you have a paste that will hold together fairly well. For smoother spreading blend in a tablespoonful or so of yogurt.

*½ c. beans + ⅓ c. grated cheese = 22 g. usable protein

Ricotta Peanut Spread
½ cup

Sweet and mellow. Good on whole wheat bread, or try it as a dip for raw vegetables.

*¼ c. peanut butter
*¼ c. ricotta cheese

1-3 t. honey
½ t. lemon juice

1. Beat the peanut butter and ricotta cheese together until the mixture is smooth and creamy.

2. Add the honey and lemon juice and beat them in thoroughly.

¼ c. peanut butter + 2 T. ricotta cheese = 21 g.
2 T. ricotta cheese = 2 g.
*Total = 23 g. usable protein

Tahini Ricotta Spread

⅔ cup

*⅓ c. tahini or sesame butter   ⅛ t. dried ginger
*⅓ c. ricotta cheese   ¼ t. tamari
 1 T. lemon juice

1. Beat the tahini and ricotta cheese together until they are fluffy. (The tahini may have to be beaten well beforehand if it has separated.)
2. Add the lemon juice, ginger, and tamari and stir in well. Serve spread on whole grain bread. Keep leftovers in the refrigerator.

⅓ c. tahini + 4 t. ricotta cheese = 15.5 g
¼ c. ricotta cheese = 4 g.
*Total = 19.5 g. usable protein

VEGETABLES

Vegetables taste best when prepared simply and served as close to their natural state as possible. Nearly all vegetables are delicious when eaten raw in salads. If you cook them try steaming, stir-frying, or in some cases, baking. Season steamed vegetables with salt, a little butter, and pepper (black, white, or cayenne). For variety add different herbs, either alone or in combinations, to nearly cooked vegetables.

I haven't used precise measurements in the vegetable recipes because the amounts you eat should depend on your own taste and appetite. I have no trouble eating with relish a whole head of steamed cauliflower or a quart of steamed snap beans, while my sister will eagerly consume two or three medium sized sautéed zucchini in one sitting. You may not have such enthusiasm for any particular vegetable, so prepare the amount you feel like eating and then season according to the suggestions in the recipes. Use your imagination in seasoning — you'll probably come up with combinations you'll just love. When experimenting, start with small amounts of herbs, and add more as you learn which herbs and combinations you like best.

A few suggestions. If you have very hard or very alkaline water add a teaspoonful of milk or lemon juice to your cooking water to prevent the vegetable's discoloring. Certain vegetables discolor easily when exposed to air — dip them in milk or lemon juice before cooking to counteract this tendency. Add salt and other seasonings when the cooking time is over or nearly over, rather than at the beginning, to prevent toughening. Never use soda when cooking vegetables as the soda preserves the color but destroys the vitamins. Proper cooking will preserve most of the color in vegetables. If you have trouble with green vegetables becoming an ugly color while cooking, lift the pot lid 3 or 4 times during the cooking to allow gases to escape.

Remember, for best taste and nutrition undercooking vegetables is better than overcooking. Try adding seasoning to a little stock or butter and gently tossing with the cooked vegetables. Or just sprinkle on seasonings right at the table.

Artichokes, Globe

Wash; trim off stem and any tough leaves. Steam over water, stem side down, until tender, about 20 minutes. Serve with melted butter and lemon juice. Try onion, garlic, celery leaves, bay leaf, or oregano (alone or in combination) in the butter to enhance flavor.

To eat an artichoke, if you've never tried it before, begin at the bottom. Tear off a leaf, dip it in your sauce (melted butter, lemon juice, etc.), then pull the leaf between your teeth, scraping off the "meat." Discard the leaf. Continue this procedure until you get to the center of the artichoke. (When the leaves become paper thin they're generally not worth the effort any more.) Pull off the immature center leaves and scrape off the hairy stuff underneath to expose the artichoke heart. Cut the heart into pieces, dip them in sauce, and savor the taste.

Artichokes, Jerusalem (Sunchokes)

These are really a member of the sunflower family and are eaten much like potatoes. Try baking them in their jackets (see Potatoes) or steaming. When cooked, rub off the peel and use your imagination in seasoning; almost any herb or spice will work well. Try butter, salt, chives, and parsley, or serve them with a cheese sauce (see Cheese Scallopped Potatoes).

Raw Jerusalem artichokes are good in salads, but dip raw artichoke slices in lemon juice before putting them in your salad — especially if you don't plan to eat the salad immediately.

Asparagus

Break off any tough area at the bottom of the stems; they'll snap at the point where they're tender. (Save the tough bottoms for soup stock.) Steam until tender, preferably in a steaming basket, and serve with butter, salt, and lemon juice. Add a little of whatever herb you like. Most herbs go well with asparagus.

Snap Beans
(green or yellow)

Wash the beans and break off the ends. If you like, break or cut the beans into 2 inch pieces or long, thin slices (julienne strips). Steam and serve with salt. Try adding lemon juice, sweet basil, marjoram, summer savory, or onion.

Beans and
Sunflower Seeds

butter	salt, marjoram, thyme,
hulled sunflower seeds	sweet basil, summer
steamed snap beans	savory to taste

1. While the beans are steaming sauté the seeds and seasonings for a few minutes in the butter.
2. Gently toss the seeds and seasonings with the cooked beans.

NOTE: The sunflower seeds taste good and they are a protein source. If you have milk, cheese, or peanuts at the same meal the seed protein will be complemented.

Beans and Mushrooms

When we were little kids my cousin and I liked these beans better than dessert. They're still one of my favorites.

butter	**steamed snap beans**
sliced mushrooms	**salt to taste**

1. Sauté the mushroom slices in butter while the beans are steaming.
2. When the beans are cooked gently toss them with the mushrooms and butter and a little salt.

Bean Sprouts
(and other sprouts)

For optimum nutrition sprouts are best eaten raw. They are rich in vitamins and minerals, some of which are lost in cooking. If you cook them, stir-fry in a little butter and tamari, or add them to Chinese-type dishes with other crisp vegetables.

GROWING SPROUTS

Sprouts are easy and economical to grow at home. Use a large jar. Put the dry seeds in the jar, cover them with water, and let them soak overnight. Cover the jar with a loosely woven fabric (cheesecloth or nylon net) and hold the cloth tightly in place with a rubber band or piece of string. Pour off the soaking water (right through the cloth) and lay the jar on its side in a warm, dark place.

Two or three times a day rinse the growing sprouts by filling the jar with water and then pouring the water off. Don't remove the cloth cover. Pour the water through the cloth, both when pouring in and pouring out. The cloth acts as a strainer. The sprouts must always be moist but never really wet; be sure to use cool water for rinsing the sprouts as hot water will kill them.

In 2-4 days, or when the sprouts are as long as the seeds, they are ready to eat. You can continue to let them grow for a while longer, but eat or refrigerate the sprouts before the leaves become pronounced.

Try sprouting mung beans, soy beans, lentils, alfalfa, wheat berries, rye berries, sunflower seeds, fenugreek seeds, or any other dry bean or seed.

Baked Barbecue Beans

2 servings

These make a terrific side dish with spoonbread, or a fine main dish as long as you remember to include the grated cheese on top. I've suggested dried limas, but use any beans you like. Soybeans will make a dish with even more usable protein.

*½ c. dry limas or other
   beans, cooked tender
1 T. oil
1 small onion, chopped
1 T. molasses
1 T. honey
2 T. catsup
½ t. dry mustard

½ t. summer savory
½ t. salt
¼ t. cinnamon
¼ t. dried ginger
dash cayenne
½ c. stock or water
*⅓ c. grated cheese

1. In a frying pan heat the oil and sauté the onion until soft. One at a time stir in the molasses, honey, catsup, and seasonings. Add the stock and the cooked beans and bring the mixture to a boil.

2. Turn into a well-oiled casserole and bake, uncovered, in a 375⁰ oven for about 45 minutes, or until the amount of liquid is reduced. Reduce the oven temperature to 300⁰. (If it's necessary to keep the dish in the oven longer add more stock as necessary to keep the dish from cooking dry.)

3. About 10 minutes before serving sprinkle grated cheese over the top and return it to the 300⁰ oven until the cheese melts.

½ c. beans + ⅓ c. cheese = 22 g. usable protein

If you've used soybeans the dish will provide:

½ c. soybeans = 20 g.
⅓ c. cheese = 7 g.
*Total = 27 g. usable protein

Lima Beans

Fresh or frozen limas can be cooked by steaming. For dried limas please see the section on cooking dry legumes. Serve with butter and salt, plus parsley, chives, dill, marjoram, savory, or other herbs.

Combine cooked beans and corn in any proportion to make succotash. As beans and corn complement each other this is also a good protein source.

Beets

Leave fresh beets whole and unpeeled. Cut off the tops, leaving about an inch of stem attached to the root. Steam, boil, or pressure cook until tender (about 15 minutes in the pressure cooker). Poke the beets with a fork to see if they're done. When cooked, cut off the stem and tip end and slip the skin off. Cut into chunks or slices, warm for a few minutes, and serve with butter, salt, and pepper. Or you can peel and thinly slice fresh beets. Steam for 6-8 minutes or until crisp and tender, or stir-fry. Try slices of fresh beets in tossed salads. I was amazed when I discovered how good raw beets taste.

Harvard Beets

2 c. cooked beets, sliced or chunked	2 whole cloves
	dash cayenne
1/4 c. cider vinegar	3/4 c. cold stock from the beets
3-4 t. honey	
1/4 t. salt	1-2 T. cornstarch

1. In the top of a double boiler combine all the ingredients except the beets. Cook over boiling water, stirring frequently, until the sauce thickens.

2. Add beets, cover, reduce heat, and simmer for 30 minutes to allow the beets to absorb flavor from the sauce.

Broccoli

The fresher broccoli is, the better it tastes. Wash broccoli in salt water since the salt will kill any cabbage worms and get them out of the vegetable. Break up the head and steam until tender. Serve with salt and a little nutmeg, parsley, dill, or chives. Or serve steamed broccoli with lemon-butter sauce or cheese sauce.

Broccoli and Cheese Casserole

1-2 servings

1 recipe cheese sauce   *partially* **steamed broccoli**

1. Place partially cooked broccoli in an oiled casserole.
2. Pour cheese sauce over the top and bake in a 350⁰ oven for 15-20 minutes or until the casserole is warmed through and lightly browned on top.

VARIATION

Add a little nutmeg to the cheese sauce.

*cheese sauce = 10-14 g. usable protein

Brussel's Sprouts

Prepare and season the same as broccoli.

Cabbage

Raw cabbage is delicious. Try cutting it in wedges and eating it with a little salt. Cooked cabbage is a delicious addition to vegetable soups. To use it as a steamed vegetable cut the head into wedges and wash in salt water. Slice the wedges into 1 inch strips and sauté in a little butter. Do not over-cook cabbage or a strong taste will develop. Serve with a little salt and choose from caraway seeds, dill seeds, thyme, marjoram, chives, onions, or garlic to enhance the flavor.

Sauerkraut

Use commercial sauerkraut or your grandmother's favorite recipe (sauerkraut takes several weeks to make!). Heat by sautéing. Add caraway seeds, dill seeds, and apple chunks if you like.

Carrots

Carrots are delicious when cut into very thin slices and stir-fried for two or three minutes. When cooked this way they require no additional seasoning.

Carrots may also be steamed until tender and served with salt and butter. Nearly any herb can be added. For some unusual treats try mint, cardamom, tarragon, curry powder, or any of your old favorites.

You can also bake carrots in a covered casserole in the oven. Put carrot chunks, butter, salt, herbs, and ½-¾ cup of water in the casserole. Cover and bake in a 350° oven until the carrots are tender (45 minutes-1 hour).

Cauliflower

Cauliflower is terrific when steamed until barely tender and served with just a little salt. Try it raw. You can also cook and season it like broccoli.

Cauliflower with Mushrooms and Cheese Sauce

1-2 servings

steamed cauliflower   ½ c. sliced mushrooms
1 recipe cheese sauce   sautéed in butter

Add the sautéed mushrooms to the cheese sauce and pour the mixture over the steamed cauliflower.

*mushrooms + cheese sauce = 10-14 g. usable protein

Corn

If you've never had corn that was picked, cooked, and eaten all within an hour, then you really don't know what you've missed. The sugar in corn begins to turn to starch a few minutes after picking — the taste changes too. To compensate for the loss of sugar cook corn in boiling water sweetened with a little honey. If you are able to get very fresh corn steam it over plain water until tender. Do not add salt to the cooking water as it will toughen the corn. Serve cooked corn with butter, salt, and pepper.

If you are using corn which has been cut from the cob you can try adding bits of sweet pepper or curry powder. Corn can also be combined with beans to make succotash.

Eggplant

Eggplant has a mild flavor and combines well with other vegetables and/or cheese (see Soybean Creole, Eggplant Parmesan, Ratatouille). It can also be fried and eaten by itself. Since eggplant discolors easily dip peeled eggplant slices in milk or beaten egg. Coat with bread crumbs, flour, or corn-meal, and sauté in butter until golden brown on both sides. Try seasoning the flour with salt and oregano, sweet basil, marjoram, or thyme. Serve with catsup if you like.

A quick and easy way to serve eggplant is to slice it thinly and drop the slices into a cup or two of water with a little lemon juice or vinegar added. Drain the eggplant and steam it over water for 2-3 minutes. Top with Tomato Mushroom Sauce.

Greens

Greens refers to any of a variety of leafy vegetables including spinach, kale, escarole, endive, lettuce, beet greens, etc.

Wash greens thoroughly and remove the midribs from the leaves. Chop the greens; chop stems and midribs separately if you want to eat them. Steam by the sauté method. Cook the stems and midribs first for about 5 minutes, add the chopped leaves, cover the pot, and steam for 2-3 minutes more. Serve with butter, salt, lemon juice or rind, nutmeg, marjoram, or whatever you like.

Don't forget to serve lots of raw greens in salads. Most greens taste better raw anyway, and you don't lose the benefits of vitamins and enzymes which can be destroyed in cooking.

Savory Steamed Greens

You can use this recipe for any greens you want to cook. It's especially good for trying out new ones. When the prolific borage self-sowed all over the garden I used it this way.

raw greens	**tamari soy sauce**
butter	**salt**
chopped scallion	**grated cheese**
or onion	

1. Wash the vegetables. Cut the midribs from the greens and chop them. Sauté the chopped midribs and scallions in a little butter and tamari until they soften.
2. Chop the leafy part of the greens. Add this to the sautéed mixture and grate some cheese over top. Cover and cook (1 or 2 minutes) until the greens wilt and the cheese melts. Salt to taste.

VARIATION

Add any leftover grain to the sautéed mixture and heat for a few minutes before adding the chopped leaves and cheese.

Savory Sautéed Chard

2-3 servings

Substitute other greens if you wish. The flavor of chard really comes out when cooked this way and surprisingly enough, the garlic is very mild.

1 T. oil	**¼ t. salt**
1 clove garlic, minced	**6-8 large leaves Swiss**
¼ t. ground cumin	**chard, stems and**
¼ t. ground coriander	**midribs chopped**
pinch turmeric	**separately from leaves**

1. Over medium-low heat, heat the oil and sauté the minced garlic for 3-5 minutes until it browns lightly. Stir in the seasonings.

2. Add the chopped chard stems and sauté about 3 minutes more.

3. Add the chopped chard leaves and sauté another 3 minutes or until the leaves wilt slightly.

Leeks

Leeks are mild, sweet members of the onion family. They are used extensively in Chinese cooking and in soups. You can also steam them (careful not to over-cook) and serve them with butter, salt, and lemon, or herbs to suit your taste.

Mushrooms

Mushrooms make any meal an elegant event. They are delicious cooked alone, in combination with other foods, or raw in a tossed salad. Sauté them in butter for a tasty side dish that really needs no other seasoning. Besides their delicious taste, mushrooms have the advantage of being high in protein and low in calories.

Stuffed Mushrooms

1 serving

raw mushrooms
bread crumbs
butter

Worcestershire sauce
or tamari

1. Carefully remove the mushroom stems from the caps. Arrange the caps, hollow side up, in an oiled baking dish.

2. Mince the mushroom stems and combine them with an equal amount of bread crumbs. Sauté this mixture in butter and Worcestershire or tamari until the whole mixture is well mixed and warmed through.

3. Fill the mushroom caps with the sautéed mixture. Bake in a 350° oven until warmed through, 15-20 minutes.

Onions

Onions are often considered to be an herb as well as a vegetable. Their flavor, if used sparingly, will enhance the flavor of almost any food. They can be overpowering if used too freely, so use a light hand when adding them to other foods.

Onions can also be served as an individual vegetable by steaming them and serving with butter and perhaps parsley or thyme. Or sauté slices in butter and Worcestershire sauce or tamari. Cook onions slowly over low heat to keep a subtle flavor.

Parsnips

Parsnips make good additions to soups and stews. You may also bake them as you would carrots or sauté them. Serve with butter and salt. Try parsley and rosemary or any of the herbs used for carrots.

Peas

The pea is another vegetable which should be picked, cooked, and eaten all within an hour to be at its best. Add a little honey to compensate for the sugar which has changed to starch since picking. Cook regular peas by steaming and serve with your choice of herbs. Try mint or thyme with a little salt.

Edible pea pods (sugar peas, snow peas) should be cooked by stir-frying in butter with a little soy sauce if you like.

Green Peppers

Green peppers, raw or cooked, combine well with other ingredients. They can also be stuffed and baked. See the stuffed pepper recipes in the section on main dishes. Pepper slices are delicious stir-fried with thin slices of summer squash.

Potatoes

Potatoes are a good, nourishing, staple food and are rich in protein, vitamin C, and minerals. For maximum usable protein be sure to have a glass of milk or its equivalent with each potato. Unless it's absolutely necessary, don't peel potatoes — eat them peel and all. If potatoes *must* be peeled try steaming or gently boiling them until tender, and then slipping the skin off. You'll lose fewer vitamins this way.

Potatoes can be cooked in almost any way you can imagine. If you steam or boil them save the water for making bread. Potato water does wonderful things for bread texture. Cooked potatoes can be seasoned with butter, salt, and pepper, plus almost any herb. Try topping them with butter and parsley, butter and rosemary, cottage cheese mixed with chives or grated fresh ginger, or any kind of grated cheese.

Steamed Potatoes

Potatoes don't have to be fancy to be good. Steam or boil potatoes, slip off the skins, cut into chunks, and serve. Have butter and a variety of seasonings on the table to be added as you please.

Baked Potatoes

Wash potatoes and cut a cross just through the skin or puncture with a fork to keep the potato from bursting and to allow steam to escape. Bake in a 350⁰-400⁰ oven until done, about 1 hour. For nice mealy potatoes please *do not* oil the skins or wrap the potatoes in foil. Top with any seasonings you desire.

For a nourishing meal on a night when you just can't face cooking have baked potatoes topped with cottage cheese and herbs. Have about 4 T. cottage cheese with each potato for about 9 g. usable protein.

Mashed Potatoes

2 medium potatoes   **1 T. butter**
¼ c. milk   **salt and pepper to taste**

1. Steam the potatoes and slip off the skins. Heat the milk and butter.

2. Combine all the hot ingredients and mash until the mixture is thick and creamy. Add salt and pepper and continue to mash. Use a potato masher, pastry blender, or electric mixer to mash the potatoes. If necessary, substitute a fork which will require a little more work than the other utensils. Keep the potatoes warm in a covered casserole in a 200⁰ (or so) oven until ready to serve.

Hash Brown Potatoes

Use grated or diced cooked or raw potatoes. Sauté in butter with a little salt and paprika until the potatoes are cooked through and golden brown. Delicious for breakfast with fried or scrambled eggs.

Paprika Potatoes

Put a little oil in a flat bottomed baking pan. Add chunks of cooked potatoes (leftovers are fine), top with salt, cayenne, and paprika. Stir the potatoes to coat them with oil and seasonings and bake in a 350⁰ oven for 10-15 minutes, or until heated through.

Cheese Scallopped Potatoes

2 servings

*2 potatoes, thinly sliced   **chopped onion, green**
*1 recipe cheese sauce   **pepper, and other**
                                       seasonings to taste

1. Steam the potato slices for about 8 minutes.

2. In an oiled casserole layer the potato slices with cheese sauce and other seasonings as desired. Top with additional grated cheese and bread crumbs if you wish. Bake in a 350⁰ oven for 30-45 minutes.

*2 potatoes + cheese sauce = 12-18 g. usable protein

Sweet Potatoes and Yams

Try serving sweet potatoes with butter, honey or maple syrup, and sweet spices (cinnamon, nutmeg, and cloves). Sweet potatoes may be baked in the same way as regular potatoes. You can steam them, slip the skin off, and sauté the potatoes in butter and honey.

For a more elegant dish steam and peel the potatoes and mash them with honey or maple syrup, salt, and sweet spices. Turn the mixture into an oiled casserole, dot the top with dabs of butter, and bake in a 350⁰ oven until the butter melts and the dish is heated through.

Salsify or Vegetable Oyster

When sautéed, salsify has a taste very similar to oysters, hence its common name. Since it discolors easily, dip slices or strips in milk, then bread crumbs, and sauté in butter. Add a little salt and thyme if you like.

Squash, Summer (yellow, patty-pan, zucchini)

Summer squash taste best when steamed by the sauté method in a little butter and salt. You can season them with nearly any herb. Try adding a drop or two of sesame oil and a tablespoonful of sesame seeds to the butter for sautéing. Sage is also delicious with squash.

For a different dish, sauté chopped onions in butter, add sliced squash (especially zucchini) and sauté for a few minutes more. When the squash is nearly cooked sprinkle Parmesan cheese over all and cover the pan. Allow the dish to cook over low heat for a minute or two more until the cheese has melted.

Summer Squash Bake

2-4 servings

Easy, yummy, and any leftover juice can be used as a base for a delicious minestrone.

2-4 sliced summer squash   1 t. oregano
   (use different kinds   ¼ t. sweet basil
   for color)   ¼ t. honey
1 c. tomato juice   ¼ t. salt
1 T. olive oil

1. Slice the squash into a well-oiled baking dish.
2. Combine all the rest of the ingredients and pour the mixture over the squash.
3. Bake in a 350⁰-400⁰ oven for 30-60 minutes. (The temperature isn't vital — if the rest of the meal requires a higher temperature that's okay.) The squash is ready after 30 minutes, but can wait until the rest of the dinner is done.

Winter Squash and Pumpkin

Winter squash tastes best when served with butter, honey, and sweet spices. All varieties must be split open, seeds scraped out, and baked for 45 minutes to 1 hour. Seasonings should be added for the last 15 minutes of cooking. Pumpkin may be cooked in the same way as any other large winter squash; in fact the two can be used interchangeably for pumpkin bread or pie.

Baked Acorn Squash

2 servings

Acorn squash works best for this because of its size and shape.

1 acorn squash, cut	**2 T. honey**
in half lengthwise	**salt, cinnamon, nutmeg,**
2 T. butter	**cloves, to taste**

1. Scoop the seeds out of the squash and place the halves, cut side down, in a flat baking dish with about ½ inch of water in it. Bake at 350⁰ for 45 minutes.

2. Turn the squash halves cut side up in the baking dish. Fill each hollow with 1 T. butter, 1 T. honey, and the seasonings. Return the squash to the oven and bake for another 15 minutes.

Baked Winter Squash

1-2 servings

1 winter squash, seeds	**honey**
scooped out and squash	**salt, cinnamon, nutmeg,**
cut into large chunks	**cloves, to taste**
butter	

1. Steam the squash chunks for 30-40 minutes or until tender.

2. Peel the steamed squash, then mash or purée it. Stir the seasonings, butter, and honey to taste into the mashed squash.

3. Pour the mixture into an oiled casserole. If you wish, drizzle more honey over top and dot the top with butter. Bake in a 350⁰ oven for 15-30 minutes or until heated through.

Sautéed Candied Winter Squash

Use any amount of squash you like.

steamed and peeled
  winter squash
butter

honey
salt

1. Cut the steamed squash into ¼ inch cubes.

2. In a frying pan melt a tablespoon or two of butter and stir in about an equal amount of honey. Add a little salt.

3. Sauté the squash slices in the butter and honey mixture until the squash is hot and well coated with honey and butter.

Winter Squash Soufflé

2 large servings

Sweet and spicy — this tastes almost like dessert!

2 T. butter
*¼ c. whole wheat flour
*1 c. milk
¼ t. nutmeg
1 t. cinnamon
½ t. salt

¼ c. honey
1 c. mashed or puréed
  winter squash (about ½
  a butternut squash,
  steamed and mashed)
*2 eggs

1. Melt the butter in a saucepan. Add the flour and stir until the flour absorbs all the melted butter. Stir in the milk, seasonings, and honey. Continue to heat over a medium flame, stirring often, until the sauce thickens and boils. Stir in the mashed squash. Remove the pan from the heat.

2. One at a time, beat in the two eggs. Pour the mixture into a well-oiled soufflé dish or 1 quart casserole. Bake in a 350⁰ oven for 30 minutes or until hot and puffy. Serve at once.

¼ c. whole wheat flour + about 2 T. milk = 3.5 g.
⅞ c. milk = 6 g.
2 eggs = 12 g.
*Total = 21.5 g. usable protein

"One-Step" Baked Winter Squash

1-2 servings

You can toss this together, put it in the oven, and pretty well forget it. Yummy too.

raw winter squash	½-1 t. grated fresh ginger
1 T. melted butter	few T. water, if desired
1 T. lemon juice	salt and cayenne
1 T. honey	to taste

1. Cut open the squash, scrape out the seeds, peel the squash, and cut it into slices about ¼ inch thick. Place the slices in a well-oiled casserole.

2. Mix together all the other ingredients, using a little water if you want more liquid. Pour this mixture over the squash slices in the casserole.

3. Cover the casserole and bake in a 350⁰-400⁰ oven for about 1½ hours or until the squash is tender.

Tomatoes

If you've never tasted a homegrown, vine ripened tomato, get yourself a packet of seeds and get growing! Certain varieties have even been bred to grow well in flower pots. Check with your seed catalogue or nursery for the best varieties for your gardening situation. Once you've tasted one of your own delicious, homegrown tomatoes you'll agree that those available at the supermarket are only a pale shadow of the real thing.

Try eating "real" tomatoes raw, in salads, or like an apple, with a little salt. If I'm going to have plain tomatoes I'd much rather have them raw than cooked, but they are good when cooked simply, and delicious when cooked in combination with other foods (spaghetti sauce, vegetable soup, chilis, creoles, the list is limited only by your imagination.)

Broiled Tomatoes

fresh tomatoes　　　　　　**oregano and/or sweet basil**
salt　　　　　　　　　　　**oil**

Cut the tomatoes into chunks, brush with oil and sprinkle with the seasonings. Cook under the broiler for a minute or two until just heated through.

Stewed Tomatoes

fresh tomatoes　　　　　　**sweet basil, oregano,**
salt　　　　　　　　　　　　**thyme, etc.**
honey

1. Pour boiling water over the tomatoes and let them sit in the hot water a minute or two. Drain and slip the skins off. Cut the tomatoes into chunks or mash them.
2. *Slowly* bring the tomatoes to a boil. Simmer for a few minutes and add salt, herbs, and a few drops of honey. Serve in bowls.

Tomatoes and Zucchini

fresh tomatoes　　　　　　**honey**
fresh zucchini, cut　　　　**salt and herbs**
　in chunks　　　　　　　　**to taste**

1. Prepare stewed tomatoes. Combine tomatoes and zucchini in a saucepan.
2. *Slowly* bring the vegetables to a boil and simmer for a few minutes until the squash is tender. Add seasonings and serve in bowls.

Turnips and Rutabagas

Turnips and rutabagas are excellent when eaten raw. When cooked they have a rather strong flavor, so use with discretion when adding them to soups, stews, and other dishes. The peels are rather bitter, so I generally break my own rule and peel them.

When you steam turnips or rutabagas serve them with salt, butter, lemon, and sage, basil, thyme, or sweet spices.

The Germans make a dish called *Himmel und Erde* (Heaven and Earth) by combining mashed turnips, potatoes, and apples in any proportion they happen to have on hand.

Cheese Scallopped Turnips

Substitute sliced turnips for potatoes in the recipe for Cheese-Scallopped Potatoes, substituting ¼ t. nutmeg for the onion and green pepper.

SAUCES

Sauces are a really nice extra with plain vegetables. They really dress things up for company too.

Cheese Sauce

1 cup

Cheese sauce makes a plain vegetable an elegant one. Serve it with plain grains or pasta too.

2 T. butter   ***⅓-½ c. grated cheese**
*1 T. whole wheat flour   **¼ t. salt**
*½ c. milk

1. Melt the butter in a small pan. Sprinkle in the flour and stir until the flour has absorbed all the butter.

2. Keep the pan over medium heat and while stirring constantly add the milk. Continue to stir until the sauce boils and thickens. Add the cheese and salt and continue stirring until the cheese melts.

½ c. milk = 3.5 g.
⅓ c. grated cheese = 7 g.
*Total = 10.5 g. usable protein

White Sauce or Cream Sauce

1 cup

A very basic sauce which you can vary by adding different herbs.

2 T. butter   *½ c. milk
*1 T. whole wheat flour   ¼ t. salt

1. Melt the butter in a small pan. Stir in the flour, stirring until the flour has absorbed all the butter.
2. Keep the pan over medium heat and add the milk while stirring constantly. Continue to stir until the sauce boils and thickens. Serve with vegetables.

VARIATION
Add bay leaf, thyme, oregano, or other herbs to the melted butter.

*½ c. milk = 3.5 g. usable protein
Plus a little protein from the whole wheat flour.

Lemon Butter Sauce

1 cup

Delicious over steamed vegetables. Use the stock from steaming your vegetables in the sauce.

4 T. butter   ⅔ c. water or stock
2 T. lemon juice   ¼ t. salt or to taste
2 T. cornstarch

1. In a small saucepan melt the butter and add the lemon juice. Dissolve the cornstarch in a small amount of *cold* water. Add the cornstarch mixture to the lemon and butter mixture, stirring constantly.

2. When your vegetables are cooked remove about ⅔ c. hot stock from the steaming pan. (If you steam vegetables without a basket you will probably have to add water or other stock to make ⅔ c.) Turn up the heat under the lemon-butter-cornstarch mixture and add the stock. Stirring constantly, bring the mixture to a boil, so that it thickens and then becomes transparent. Pour it into a serving dish and spoon it over your vegetables at the table.

Tomato Mushroom Sauce

1½ c. sauce

This is delicious over plain, steamed eggplant. Try it over steamed summer squash and other vegetables too.

1 T. olive oil	1 t. sweet basil
1 small onion, chopped	¼ t. oregano
1 clove garlic, minced	¼ t. salt
½-¾ c. sliced	dash cayenne
mushrooms	1 T. cornstarch
1½ c. tomato juice	

1. Over a medium flame heat the olive oil and sauté the onion, garlic, and mushrooms until soft.

2. Add 1 cup of tomato juice and the seasonings. Slowly bring the mixture to a boil, stirring often to keep it from sticking.

3. Dissolve the cornstarch in ½ cup of tomato juice and stir this mixture into the hot sauce. Simmer the sauce over low heat, stirring often, until it thickens. Or place the sauce in a 350⁰ oven for about 30 minutes or until it thickens.

Gravy

1 cup

Someone once told me that she wouldn't miss meat at all, but she *had* to have gravy for her potatoes. So, for her, and for you, try this on mashed potatoes or grains.

2 T. butter
3 T. whole wheat flour
1 small onion, chopped

1 c. water or stock
1 T. tamari soy sauce
salt to taste

1. Melt the butter and sauté the onion in it for a few minutes. Stir in the flour, stirring until the flour absorbs all the butter.

2. Add the water or stock and bring the mixture to a boil, stirring often. The gravy will thicken when it boils.

3. Reduce the heat and add the tamari, stirring it in well. Add salt if you wish and serve.

VARIATION

Sauté finely chopped mushrooms in the melted butter before adding the flour.

Easy Herb Sauce

½ cup

This tastes best when made with fresh herbs. Halve the amounts for dried ones. Good on plain, steamed vegetables, and a good way to use the vitamins and minerals from the steaming water.

1 T. olive oil
1 t. chopped fresh basil
½ t. chopped chives
1 T. chopped fresh parsley

few drops lemon juice
dash salt
½ c. hot stock from
  steaming vegetables

1. Combine all the ingredients except the stock and set aside while your vegetables are steaming.

2. When vegetables are cooked, add up to ½ c. hot stock to the herb mixture and spoon the sauce over the vegetables at the table.

Applesauce

2 cups

Serve applesauce as a side dish or try spooning it over grain dishes or vegetables. My grandfather likes it on bread instead of jelly.

2 c. chopped apples,
    peeled and cored
¼ c. water
few drops lemon juice
cinnamon or other sweet
    spices to taste (optional)

honey to taste (the
    amount will depend on
    the tartness of
    your apples)

1. Bring the apples and water to a boil over a medium-high flame. Cover, reduce heat, and simmer for 30 minutes or until the apples are soft.

2. Mash the cooked apples with a spoon, a fork, an electric blender, or a food mill, depending on how fussy you are about applesauce consistency. Add lemon juice, honey, and spices if desired.

NOTE: If you have a food mill there is no need to peel the apples. Core and chop them and cook as above. When you put them through the food mill the skins will be separated from the pulp.

VARIATION

Applebutter: Applebutter is really just spiced applesauce. Make applesauce as above and add spices (cinnamon, nutmeg, cloves) to taste. For real, old-time, thick applebutter you may either:

1. Cook the applebutter over a wood fire, stirring constantly, for 8 hours.

2. Or put the applebutter in a 350⁰ oven and cook it for about 3 hours, or until it is the desired consistency. For most of us these days I think this second method is obviously preferable!

MAIN DISHES

The main dish recipes are a good base for satisfying dinners. Serve them with a steamed vegetable or a salad, homemade bread if you like, and of course, a glass of milk. A dinner which includes a serving of any of the main dishes and a glass of milk will provide one third or more of your daily protein need.

Most of the main dishes use the tested protein complementarity relationships as their protein ingredients. Occasionally I have used a food such as millet, which has not been tested for precise complementary relationships. In these cases I have used combinations which would probably result in complementarity, such as millet with cheese or millet with beans.

Please remember that many of the soup, salad, sandwich, and vegetable recipes contain enough protein to qualify as main dishes. There are always the "perfect protein" egg dishes to fall back on, especially when you're short on time for preparation or cooking.

Most of the recipes in this section make two servings. A few make two to four servings, which means a one dish meal for two which needs no accompaniment, or enough food for four if you round out the menu with steamed vegetables, salads, etc.

LOAVES AND CASSEROLES

Some plain, some fancy, all hearty main dishes. If you have leftovers, cover them with foil to hold in moisture when you reheat them (20-30 minutes at 350º), or try leftovers cold, eaten out of hand or as sandwich fillings.

Herbed Cheese Millet Casserole

2 small servings

Feel free to double this if you're very hungry. Serve with steamed summer squash or a salad.

1-2 T. butter	**½ t. sage**
***¼ c. raw millet**	**2 T. butter**
¼ t. salt	**2 T. milk**
***½ c. grated cheese**	

1. In a saucepan melt a little butter. Sauté the raw millet in the butter until every grain has a light coating of butter, about 5 minutes. Add salt and ½ c. water. Bring to a boil, cover, reduce heat, and simmer until millet is tender, 25-30 minutes.

2. To make the cheese sauce melt 2 T. butter in a pan. Add milk, sage, and grated cheese. Stir over low heat until all the cheese has melted. Stir in the cooked millet.

3. Turn the mixture into an oiled casserole and bake in a 350º oven for 15-20 minutes, until the cheese just begins to brown on top. Or, refrigerate and reheat in a 350º oven for 30 minutes.

¼ c. millet = 2 g.
½ c. grated cheese = 10 g.
*Total = 12 g. usable protein
Plus a little extra protein from the milk and from the cheese complementing the millet.

Lentil Millet Casserole

2 servings

I was surprised the first time I made this. It tastes a little like poultry stuffing.

2 T. butter
*⅓ c. raw millet
*2 T. dry lentils, cooked
*⅔ c. sliced, raw
   mushrooms
1 stalk celery, chopped
1 carrot, thinly sliced

¼ t. onion salt
⅛ t. rosemary
1 t. dried parsley
dash marjoram
sliced mushrooms for
   topping (optional)

1. Heat a small amount of butter in a saucepan. Sauté the raw millet in the butter for a few minutes until each grain is lightly coated with butter. Add ⅔ c. water and bring to a boil, cover, reduce heat, and simmer until the millet is tender, about 30 minutes.

2. In a frying pan melt 1 T. butter. Sauté the vegetables and seasonings in the butter for a minute or two. Add cooked lentils, then cooked millet, and continue to sauté for another minute or so, adding butter if necessary to keep the mixture from sticking.

3. Turn into an oiled casserole. Top with extra mushroom slices and dabs of butter. Bake, covered, in a 350⁰ oven for up to 30 minutes.

⅓ c. millet = 3 g.
2 T. lentils = 2 g.
complementarity = 2-3 g.
⅔ c. mushrooms = 1-2 g.
*Total = 8-10 g. usable protein

Soybean Bulgar Casserole
3-4 servings

I've made this recipe larger than the others because it tastes even better as leftovers than it does the day you make it. Make the leftovers into patties and fry them for a few minutes in a little melted butter.

*¾ c. bulgar, cooked	½ t. salt
*2 T. soybeans, cooked	¼ t. sage
*1 egg	2 t. oregano
½ c. tomatoes, peeled and chopped	2 T. tamari soy sauce
½ c. diced celery	*Parmesan cheese

1. Beat together the egg and tomatoes. Stir in the celery and seasonings, then the cooked soybeans, and finally the cooked bulgar.

2. Turn into an oiled casserole in layers, sprinkling each layer with Parmesan cheese.

3. Cover the casserole and bake at 350° for 25-30 minutes.

¾ c. bulgar + 2 T. soybeans = 16 g.
1 egg = 6 g.
*Total = 22 g. usable protein
Plus protein from the cheese.

Squash and Peanut Stew
2-4 servings

This dish was inspired by the movie Roots—one of the women mentioned something about a stew she was cooking from peanuts and sweet potatoes. I've substituted squash because it's more available where I live than sweet potatoes, and then I added a few touches of my own. It's a rich dish, so serve it with something light like a green salad.

½-⅔ c. peeled and
cubed winter squash
1-2 t. butter
few drops sesame oil
½-1 t. grated fresh
ginger
*½ c. raw brown rice
1 c. water
½ t. salt

¼ c. raisins
1 t. butter
*¼ c. sunflower seeds
*¼ c. peanut butter
*⅓ c. instant milk
powder (¼ c. non-instant)
*a few T. milk
¼ t. salt

1. In a saucepan heat 1-2 t. butter and the sesame oil. Sauté the fresh ginger and squash cubes in the melted butter for a few minutes. Add the rice and sauté for another minute or two. Add water, raisins, and ½ t. salt, bring to a boil, cover, and simmer until the rice is tender.

2. In a frying pan melt 1 t. butter over a medium-low flame. Sauté the sunflower seeds in the butter for a minute or two. Add the peanut butter and continue cooking while stirring until the peanut butter melts. Add the milk powder and enough liquid milk to make a creamy sauce.

3. When the rice mixture is cooked stir it into the peanut sauce. Turn the mixture into an oiled casserole and bake in a 350⁰ oven for 20-30 minutes or until heated through.

VARIATION

Arrange the rice and squash mixture on a serving platter or individual plates. Top with the peanut sauce. This is quicker than the original because there is no baking time.

2 T. peanut butter + ¼ c. sunflower seeds = 13.75 g.
2 T. peanut butter + 1 T. milk powder = 10.5 g.
½ c. rice + 3⅔ T. milk powder = 11.33
1 t. milk powder = 1 g.
few T. milk = 2-3 g.
*Total = 38.5-39.5 g. usable protein

Sweet and Spicy Black Beans

2 servings

Have winter squash or a green vegetable with this dish.

*¼ c. black beans,
   cooked
*⅓ c. bulgar, cooked
*½ c. sliced mushrooms
1 T. butter
1 T. honey

¼ t. cardamom
½ t. salt
dash cayenne
*½ c. yogurt
paprika (optional)

1. In a small pan heat the butter, honey, salt, cardamom, and cayenne until the butter melts and the honey becomes very runny. Pour this mixture over the sliced mushrooms in a small bowl and stir gently until the sauce coats the mushrooms.

2. Drain and rinse the black beans. Add the beans to the mushroom mixture and stir again.

3. Stir the cooked wheat to break up any lumps. Then stir the bulgar and yogurt, gently but thoroughly, into the bean and mushroom mixture.

4. Turn the dish into a well-oiled casserole, sprinkle paprika over the top, and bake at 350° for 20-25 minutes or until the casserole is set.

1 T. beans + ⅓ c. bulgar = 5.75 g.
3 T. beans + 6 T. yogurt = 8.25 g.
2 T. yogurt = 1 g.
½ c. sliced mushrooms = 1-2 g.
*Total = 16-17 g. usable protein

Herbed Bean and Cheese Loaf

2 servings

*½ c. dry beans,
   cooked and mashed
*1 egg, beaten
*⅓ c. instant milk powder
   (¼ c. non-instant)
½ t. salt

½ t. summer savory
1 t. sage
*2 t. brewer's yeast
1 T. tamari soy sauce
*⅓ c. grated cheese

1. Beat the milk powder, seasonings, brewer's yeast, and tamari into the egg. Stir in the grated cheese, and then the mashed beans, mixing all the ingredients thoroughly.

2. Turn into a small (2 or 3 cup), oiled casserole and bake at 350⁰ until firm (30-45 minutes).

VARIATIONS

1. Add a chopped onion to the other ingredients.

2. Slice cold loaf thinly for sandwiches.

½ c. beans + ⅓ c. instant milk powder = 22 g.
⅓ c. grated cheese = 7 g.
1 egg = 6 g.
2 t. brewer's yeast = 1 g.
*Total = 36 g. usable protein

VEGETABLE ENTREÉS

These casseroles use one or more vegetables as their main ingredient. You can reheat them just as you would any other casserole.

Stuffed Winter Squash

2 servings

1 acorn or butternut squash	⅓ c. raisins
*⅔ c. raw brown rice	1 t. + 1 T. honey
*⅓ c. instant milk powder	1 t. butter
(¼ c. non-instant)	½ t. cinnamon
1⅓ c. cold water	¼ t. nutmeg
½ t. salt	dash ground cloves

1. Cut squash in half lengthwise and scrape out seeds and pulp. Steam squash until tender. (Or if your oven is on you may bake the squash, placing it cut side down in a pan with about ½ inch of water in it.) Steam or bake at 350⁰ for about 45 minutes.

2. While the squash is cooking prepare the rice. Dissolve the milk powder in the cold water, add salt, and bring to a boil. Add the rice and raisins, cover, lower heat, and simmer until the rice is tender.

3. When squash and rice are cooked scrape flesh out of the center of the squash, leaving a shell about ⅜ in. thick. Spread about ½ t. butter and ½ t. honey over the inside of each squash shell. Set aside.

4. To the cooked rice add the squash flesh which you scraped out, 1 T. honey, and the seasonings. Mix well.

5. Fill the squash shells with the rice mixture. (The rice will be piled high in the shell, not flush with its top.) Place in a 350⁰ oven for 15 minutes before serving, uncovered for a crunchy surface, covered for a tender surface.

*⅔ c. rice + ⅓ c. milk powder = 15-16 g. usable protein

Rice 'n' Cheese Stuffed Peppers

2 servings

Serve these with steamed green beans or a green salad.

2 raw, green, sweet
   peppers, seeded and
   halved lengthwise
*½ c. + 2 T. raw brown rice,
   cooked with
*1 T. soy grits
1 small onion, chopped
   (2-3 t.)
2 small or 1 large stalk
   celery, chopped

*2 large or 4 small
   mushrooms, sliced
2-3 t. diced green pepper
*2 T. sunflower seeds
¼ t. thyme
¼ t. salt
dash cayenne
2-4 t. oil
*3 T. (or more) grated cheese

1. Heat the oil in a frying pan. Sauté the onion, celery, and
   sunflower seeds until the onion softens and the seeds start
   to brown. Add seasonings, mushrooms, and diced green
   pepper and sauté a minute or two longer. Add cooked rice
   and soy grits and stir thoroughly. Lower the flame and stir
   in the cheese.

2. Fill the green pepper shells with the rice mixture. Bake in a
   covered, oiled casserole at 350° for 30-45 minutes, or until
   pepper shells are tender.

10 T. rice + 1 T. soy grits = 9 g.
2-4 mushrooms = 1-2 g.
2 T. sunflower seeds + 2 t. cheese = 3 g.
2⅔ T. cheese = 3 g.
*Total = 16 g. usable protein

Bean and Cheese Stuffed Peppers

2 servings

2 green peppers, seeded and halved lengthwise	**2 t. cornstarch**
*1/4 c. dry beans, cooked tender	**1 t. salt**
1/2 c. tomatoes, skinned and chopped or canned	**1 t. oregano**
	*1/2 c. grated cheese

1. In a small saucepan dissolve the cornstarch in the tomatoes. Heat over a medium flame, stirring, until the mixture thickens slightly.

2. Stir in salt and oregano, then the cooked beans, and the grated cheese. Reserve a few tablespoons of grated cheese for topping.

3. Spoon the mixture into the green pepper shells and sprinkle the reserved cheese on top.

4. Place the stuffed peppers in an oiled casserole or baking pan. Bake at 350⁰ until the peppers are tender, 30-40 minutes.

Note: If you're using frozen peppers be sure to oil the baking pan especially well. Frozen peppers are too soft to hold the filling well — the finished dish is good, but the pan can be messy. With frozen peppers you can also reduce the baking time to about 20 minutes.

1/4 c. beans + 2²/3 T. cheese = 11 g.
1/3 c. cheese = 7 g.
*Total = 18 g. usable protein

Stuffed Pepper Casserole

2 servings

Fresh from the garden in late summer. Be sure to use olive oil for its unique flavor.

*¼ c. bulgar, cooked with
¼ t. salt
2 large or 4 small
  green peppers, seeded
  and halved lengthwise
1 small summer squash,
  diced
1 t. oregano
1 t. sweet basil

*½ c. grated cheese
  (mild cheddar is good)
1½-2 c. tomatoes,
  skinned and chopped (or
  a combination of toma-
  toes and tomato juice
1 T. olive oil
1 t. sweet basil

1. Stir together the cooked bulgar, raw diced squash, oregano, 1 t. sweet basil, and a small amount of the grated cheese. Spoon this mixture into the raw pepper shells and arrange the stuffed peppers in a baking dish. If you have extra bulgar mixture plop it on top of the peppers in the baking dish.

2. Stir together the tomatoes (or tomatoes and tomato juice), the olive oil, and 1 t. sweet basil. Pour this tomato mixture over the peppers in the baking dish. Sprinkle the rest of the grated cheese over top and cover the casserole. (If you don't have a lid use aluminum foil.)

3. Bake the casserole in a 350⁰ oven for 45 minutes or until the peppers are tender.

Note: Save any juice you have left over to use in soup.

¼ c. bulgar + about 1 T. grated cheese = 4⅔ g.
7 T. grated cheese = 9 g.
*Total = 13⅔ g. usable protein

Eggplant Parmesan
2-4 servings

This makes four average servings, but if two of you are very hungry it isn't hard to finish it all. Serve with a tossed, green salad. This dish can be prepared beforehand and refrigerated until you are ready to bake it. Allow extra baking time to account for the chill from the refrigerator.

1 medium eggplant,
  peeled and sliced
*½ c. whole wheat flour
¼ t. salt, or less
dash cayenne
¼ t. oregano
*1 egg, beaten

1-2 T. butter
*1⅓ c. grated yellow
  cheese (brick, jack,
  or mozzerella)
*small amount grated
  Parmesan cheese

SAUCE:
1 T. butter
3 T. chopped onion
6 or more mushrooms,
  sliced
2 c. tomatoes, peeled
  and chopped or canned
1 12-oz can tomato paste

1 t. oregano
dash thyme
¼ t. sweet basil
1 t. honey
salt to taste

1. On a plate mix together the flour, salt, cayenne, and oregano. In a bowl beat the egg thoroughly. Bread the eggplant slices by dipping them in the egg, then laying them, first on one side and then on the other in the flour mixture.

2. Fry the eggplant slices in hot, melted butter or oil, turning once until they are golden brown on both sides.

3. Arrange eggplant slices in an oiled casserole and top each slice with several spoonsful of grated cheese and a light dusting of Parmesan. Arrange the slices in layers (there will be cheese between the layers).

4. To make the sauce melt butter in a frying pan. Sauté all the ingredients in the order in which they are listed. When the sauce is thick and warm pour it over the eggplant slices in the casserole. Top with a light dusting of Parmesan cheese.

5. Bake in a 350⁰ oven for 25-30 minutes until the cheese melts and the dish is heated through.

½ c. whole wheat flour + 1 T. cheese = 3 g.
1⅓ c. grated cheese = 28 g.
1 egg = 6 g.
*Total = 37 g. usable protein

Soybean Stuffed Eggplant

2 servings

½ eggplant (halved
  lengthwise)
*⅓ c. dry soybeans,
  cooked
1 T. butter
1 clove garlic, minced
  or up to ⅛ t.
  garlic powder

3 scallions or 1
  small onion, chopped
2 t. oregano
2 t. sweet basil
½ t. salt
6 oz. tomato paste
*⅓ c. grated cheese

1. Steam the eggplant for about 5 minutes. Scoop out the pulp leaving a shell about ½ inch thick.

2. In a frying pan melt the butter and sauté the scallions or onions until they soften. Stir in the seasonings and tomato paste. Stir in the cooked soybeans. You may stir in part of the cheese now or save it all for topping.

3. Spoon the sautéed mixture into the eggplant shell. Sprinkle grated cheese over top.

4. Place in a baking dish and bake in a 350⁰ oven for about 20 minutes.

⅓ c. soybeans = 13 g.
⅓ c. grated cheese = 7 g.
*Total = 20 g. usable protein

Stuffed Summer Squash

2-4 servings

This dish has all kinds of benefits. It makes a filling, full meal for 2 hungry people, or a satisfying main dish for 4 when served with a salad and a steamed vegetable or two. It's also a delicious way to use those enormous summer squash gardeners often discover hidden under the squash vines. Use any squash you have, but I think pattypan is the prettiest. I consider an 8 inch diameter pattypan or a 12 inch or longer zucchini to be large.

1 large or 2 medium
  summer squash
*½ c. raw brown
  rice, cooked
1 T. butter
1 t. sesame oil (optional)
*¼ c. sesame seeds
1 small onion, chopped
1 stalk celery, chopped

*about ½ c. sliced
  mushrooms
1 t. grated fresh ginger
½ t. salt
*¼ c. cottage cheese
*1 egg, beaten
dash cayenne
generous sprinkling paprika

1. While the rice is cooking cut the stem and flower ends from the squash and cut the squash in half. (Cut long squash lengthwise, pattypan squash horizontally.) Scrape out the seeds and discard them. Scrape out enough squash flesh to leave a shell ½ inch thick. Chop the squash flesh which you have removed from the shell and set it aside.

2. Prepare the other vegetables and the ginger.

3. Heat the butter and oil in a frying pan. Sauté the sesame seeds, onion, and celery for a few minutes. Add the mushrooms and chopped squash and sauté a few minutes more. Stir in the grated ginger and the salt and remove the pan from the heat.

4. Stir in the cottage cheese, the beaten egg, and the cayenne. Sprinkle paprika generously over all (use as much as you like for color) and stir it in.

5. Spoon the mixture into the bottom squash shell and cover with the other squash shell. Place the stuffed squash in a baking dish or on a cookie sheet (oiled for easier cleaning), and bake in a 400° oven for 45 minutes.

½ c. rice + 2⅔ T. sesame seeds = 8 g.
¼ c. cottage cheese = 7 g.
1 egg = 6 g.
½ c. mushrooms = 1 g.
*Total = 22 g. usable protein

Sage Squash Supreme

2 servings

Try serving this with a dark green vegetable like broccoli or green beans.

*6 T. brown rice or barley, cooked	1 t. sage
*1 c. milk	½ t. salt
*1 egg, beaten	1 summer squash, sliced

1. Beat the milk into the beaten egg. Beat in the sage and salt. Set aside.

2. When the grain has cooked let it cool slightly. Stir the cooked grain and then the squash slices into the egg and milk mixture. Turn the mixture into an oiled baking pan (about 8" × 8").

3. Place the baking pan inside another baking pan with about an inch of water in it. Bake in a 325° oven for about 50 minutes, or until a knife inserted in the center comes out clean.

6 T. rice + ½ c. milk = 8.5 g.
½ c. milk = 3.5 g.
1 egg = 6 g.
*Total = 18 g. usable protein

Vegetable Lasagna
2 servings

Eggplant and zucchini substitute for noodles in this recipe — lots of protein without much starch. Serve with fresh whole grain or muffins to fill out your grain requirement.

½ medium eggplant, thinly sliced
1 medium zucchini, thinly sliced
*1½ c. grated cheese (brick and mozzerella)

SAUCE:

1 T. butter	*1-1½ c. sliced mushrooms
3 scallions or 1	2-3 t. oregano
small onion, chopped	dash thyme, cayenne,
2 small or 1 large	garlic powder
stalk celery, diced	½ t. salt
1 c. tomatoes, skinned	1-2 t. cornstarch
and chopped or canned	

1. In a saucepan melt the butter. Sauté the scallions, celery, and mushrooms for a few minutes until they soften. Add the tomatoes and seasonings and slowly bring the mixture to a boil over medium heat.

2. When the sauce boils dissolve the cornstarch in a few tablespoons of cold water and slowly stir the cornstarch mixture into the hot sauce.

3. In a well-oiled, flat baking dish arrange a layer of zucchini and eggplant slices. (The slices can be either rounds or long thin slices depending on your preference.) Sprinkle grated cheese over the vegetables and then top with the tomato sauce. Arrange another thin layer of zucchini and eggplant over the first, and again top with cheese and sauce. Make a third layer on top, covering it with cheese and sauce, then sprinkle any remaining cheese over all.

4. Bake in a 350° oven for 25-30 minutes or until the eggplant is crunchy-tender.

1½ c. grated cheese = 30 g.
1-1½ c. mushrooms = 2-4 g.
*Total = 32-34 g. usable protein

Carrot Casserole

2-4 servings

*½ c. raw brown rice,
   cooked
1-1½ c. grated carrots
*⅓ c. sunflower seeds
*1 c. milk
*⅓ c. instant milk powder
   (¼ c. non-instant)

*1 egg, beaten
*⅓ c. grated cheese
1½ t. sage
½ t. salt

1. Thoroughly mix together the cooked rice, carrots, and sunflower seeds.

2. In a separate bowl beat together the egg, milk, milk powder, cheese, and seasonings. Add the rice, carrots, and seed mixture and mix together well.

3. Turn the mixture into a well-oiled, flat baking dish or pan. Bake at 325°-350° for 30 minutes, or until the casserole is set. (The lower temperature is preferable but the higher one will work.)

½ c. rice + ⅔ c. milk = 12 g.
⅓ c. sunflower seeds + ⅓ c. milk = 6 g.
⅓ c. milk powder = 7 g.
⅓ c. grated cheese = 7 g.
1 egg = 6 g.
*Total = 38 g. usable protein

Rosemary Casserole
2-3 servings

*¼ c. dry mung beans, cooked (or substitute other beans)	½ medium onion, chopped
*½ c. brown rice, cooked	1 parsnip, sliced
1-2 T. butter	1 carrot, sliced
1-2 t. fresh rosemary (½-1 t. dried)	1 t. dried dill weed
	1 t. salt
	*1 c. yogurt

1. Melt the butter in a small fry pan. Sauté the rosemary and onion in the butter until the onion becomes transparent. Add parsnip and carrot slices and sauté for a few minutes longer. Add dill weed and salt and remove from heat.

2. Gently but thoroughly stir together the cooked rice, cooked beans, and sautéed vegetables. Add the yogurt and mix well.

3. Turn the mixture into an oiled casserole or baking dish and bake at 325⁰ for about 30 minutes or until set.

VARIATION

For a more solid casserole beat an egg into the yogurt before combining it with the other ingredients. This casserole can be cut into squares and eaten out of hand.

⅓ c. brown rice + 2 T. beans = 7.5 g.
2⅔ T. rice + about ¼ c. yogurt = 4 g.
2 T. beans + ¼ c. yogurt = 5.5 g.
½ c. yogurt = 3.5 g.
*Total = 20.5 g. usable protein

QUICHES AND TIMBALES

Cheesy Tarragon Timbale
2 large servings

As far as I can tell the only difference between a quiche and a timbale is that the quiche has a crust. Since I'm trying to be accurate I'll call this flavorful dish a timbale. It needs nothing more than a steamed vegetable or a simple salad for accompaniment.

*¼ c. wheat berries,
  cooked
*¼ c. dry beans (kidney,
  or black for color),
  cooked
1-2 T. oil
1 medium onion, chopped
1 carrot, sliced

*1 egg, beaten
*½ c. milk
*1 c. grated sharp
  cheese
½ t. tarragon
dash cayenne
½ t. salt

1. Sauté the onion and carrot in a little oil until they soften. Set aside.

2. In a bowl beat the milk, grated cheese, and seasonings into the egg. Stir in the sautéed vegetables, wheat berries, and beans.

3. Pour into a well-oiled casserole and bake until set in a 325⁰ oven (about 30 minutes).

4. For ease in cutting let the timbale cool for about 10 minutes before serving.

VARIATION
Substitute triticale berries for the wheat berries.

¼ c. beans + ½ c. milk = 11 g.
¼ c. wheat berries + 1/12 c. cheese = 7 g.
11/12 c. cheese = 19 g.
1 egg = 6 g.
*Total = 43 g. usable protein

Asparagus Timbale

2 small servings

This can make a one dish meal for one or serve it with a yellow vegetable and a salad for two.

1 T. butter	*⅔ grated cheese
1 scallion, chopped	(Swiss or brick)
⅔-1 c. fresh asparagus	*½ c. milk
cut in inch-long slices	¼ t. tarragon
*1 egg, beaten	¼ t. salt

1. In a small frying pan melt the butter and sauté the scallion and asparagus pieces for a few minutes. Place this mixture in the bottom of a well-oiled 1 qt. casserole.

2. In a bowl beat the cheese, milk, salt, and tarragon into the egg. Pour this mixture over the asparagus mixture in the casserole.

3. Bake in a 350⁰ oven for 30-40 minutes or until a knife inserted into the center of the dish comes out clean. For ease in serving let the dish cool for 10 minutes before cutting.

1 egg = 6 g.
⅔ c. grated cheese = 14 g.
½ c. milk = 3.5 g.
*Total = 23.5 g. usable protein

"LAZY" SOUFFLÉS

I call these "lazy" soufflés because I'm too lazy to beat egg whites for ages as you must do with standard soufflés. These aren't quite as delicate, but also not as fussy as soufflés made from beaten egg whites. Like all soufflés though, they are at a peak only for a few minutes — so serve them right at their peak. Don't try to hold or reheat them.

If you must hold a soufflé do so before baking, not after. You can prepare the whole dish and keep it at room temperature for up to half an hour, or hold it in the refrigerator. If you do refrigerate the dish you may have to increase the baking time by 15 minutes or so.

Spoonbread

2 servings

I can't decide whether spoonbread should qualify as a bread or a main dish. The only way I can describe it is as a cornbread soufflé, and like any soufflé it is at its peak of perfection only once and really doesn't make it when served cold or leftover. So serve it at its peak as a main dish, accompanied by a vegetable or two.

*½ c. cornmeal	½ t. salt
*2⅔ T. soy flour	1 T. melted butter
*1 c. milk	*1 egg, beaten
½ t. baking powder	½-1 t. honey

1. In a bowl stir together all the dry ingredients. Add the milk and honey and beat everything together very thoroughly.

2. Add the beaten egg and beat again until the egg is well mixed with the other ingredients.

3. Pour the mixture into a well-oiled small baking dish or soufflé dish. Bake at 350⁰ until golden brown, about 60 minutes.

½ c. cornmeal + 2⅔ T. soy flour + ½ c. milk = 10 g.
½ c. milk = 3.5 g.
1 egg = 6 g.
*Total = 19.5 g. usable protein

Vegetable Soufflé

2-4 servings

For two people serve this alone or with a green salad.

FILLING:

2 T. butter	½ t. salt
1 c. diced mixed	½ t. tarragon
vegetables (peas, carrots	¼ t. summer savory
corn, beans, limas, etc.)	1 T. whole wheat flour
*¾ c. sliced mushrooms	

SAUCE

2 T. butter	1 t. salt
*¼ c. whole wheat flour	½ t. tarragon
*1 c. milk	*2 eggs, at room
*2 c. grated cheese	temperature

1. Prepare filling. Melt the 2 T. butter in a small fry pan. Sauté the mixed vegetables in the butter for a few minutes. Add the mushrooms and seasonings and continue to sauté until the mushrooms soften. Sprinkle 1 T. whole wheat flour over all and sauté about one minute more. Set aside.

2. Melt 2 T. butter in a 2 quart or larger saucepan. Stir in the ¼ c. flour, stirring until the flour absorbs all the butter. Add the milk. Over a medium-high heat stir the mixture until it thickens and then boils. Stir in the cheese and the seasonings. When the cheese melts remove the mixture from the heat and beat in the eggs, one at a time.

3. Oil a 1 qt. casserole or soufflé dish. Pour half of the cheese mixture into the casserole, spread the vegetable filling over top, then add the rest of the cheese mixture, spreading it over the vegetables.

3. Bake in a 400⁰ oven for 25-30 minutes or until golden brown and puffy. Serve immediately.

¼ c. whole wheat flour + ⅛ c. milk = 3.5 g.
⅞ c. milk = 6 g.
2 c. grated cheese = 42 g.
¾ c. sliced mushrooms = 2 g.
2 eggs = 12 g.
*Total = 65.5 g. usable protein

Millet Soufflé

2-4 servings

This is the most delicious way I know to eat millet.

*½ c. raw millet,
 cooked with
½ t. salt
1 T. butter
1 scallion, sliced
*½-¾ c. sliced mushrooms
*2 T. butter
*¼ c. whole wheat flour

*1 c. milk
*1 c. grated cheese
½ t. nutmeg
½ t. Worcestershire sauce
 or tamari
dash cayenne
*2 eggs

1. Melt 1 T. butter and sauté the scallion and mushrooms in it until they soften. Set aside.
2. In a saucepan melt the 2 T. butter. Stir in the whole wheat flour, stirring until the flour absorbs all of the butter. Slowly stir in the milk. Continue cooking over a medium flame, stirring constantly until the mixture thickens and then boils.
3. Stir the cheese into the sauce, stirring until the cheese melts. Stir in the seasonings, cooked millet, and sautéed vegetables. Remove from heat. Beat in the two eggs, one at a time.
4. Pour the mixture into a well-oiled 1 qt. casserole or soufflé dish. Bake at 425° for 25 minutes, or until puffed and golden brown. Serve immediately.

VARIATION

Triticale Soufflé: Substitute ½ c. raw triticale berries for the raw millet. The amount of usable protein in the dish will increase to about 55 grams.

½ c. millet = 4 g.
¼ c. whole wheat flour + ⅛ c. milk = 3.5 g.
⅞ c. milk = 6 g.
1 c. grated cheese = 21 g.
¾ c. sliced mushrooms = 2 g.
2 eggs = 12 g.
*Total = 48.5 g. usable protein

PASTA

Use whole wheat or wheat-soy noodles if you can get them. To cook noodles boil a quart or more of salted water, pour in a teaspoon of oil to keep the noodles from sticking together, then add the dry noodles. Boil, uncovered, for about 10 minutes, or until the noodles are tender.

Macaroni and Cheese

2 servings

Make it plain—make it fancy with the mushrooms and sunflower seeds. Round out the meal with a couple of steamed or sautéed vegetables.

½ c. whole wheat macaroni, cooked
1 T. butter
2 scallions, chopped
1 c. sliced mushrooms (optional)
⅓ c. sunflower seeds (optional)

*½ c. milk
*1 c. grated cheese
1 t. Worcestershire sauce or tamari
¼ t. salt
dash cayenne

1. In a saucepan melt the butter and sauté the scallions, sunflower seeds, and mushrooms. Stir in the milk, cheese, and seasonings. Stir until the cheese melts. Finally, stir in the cooked macaroni.

2. Turn the mixture into a well-oiled 1 quart casserole and bake at 350⁰ for 20-30 minutes.

½ c. macaroni + ½ c. milk = 14 g.
1 c. grated cheese = 21 g.
1 c. mushrooms = 2-3 g.
⅓ c. sunflower seeds complemented by 2 T. of the cheese = 4 g.
*Total = 41-42 g. usable protein

Macaroni and Beans

2 servings

This is a good quick dish, takes less than 15 minutes to prepare
if you have some pre-cooked soybeans in the freezer.

*½ c. whole wheat
   macaroni, cooked
*2 T. soybeans, cooked
1 T. butter
1 small onion, chopped
½-1 c. sliced mushrooms
1 T. tamari soy sauce

½ t. oregano
1 c. tomatoes, skinned and
   chopped or canned
salt to taste
*grated Parmesan cheese
   (optional)

1. In a frying pan melt the butter and sauté the onion and
   drained soybeans until the onion softens. Add mushrooms
   and sauté a minute or two longer.

2. Stir in tamari, oregano, and tomatoes. Add salt and drained
   macaroni, stirring thoroughly.

3. Serve with a sprinkling of grated cheese on top if you like.

VARIATION (or to reheat leftovers)

Pour dish into oiled casserole, top with cheese, and heat in a
350⁰ oven until the casserole is warmed through or the cheese
is melted.

½ c. macaroni + 2 T. soybeans = 16 g. usable protein
Plus extra protein from the optional cheese.

Spaghetti Sauce

4 servings

This recipe makes enough sauce for two meals; so freeze half of the sauce, either alone, mixed with cooked noodles, or as lasagna in an oiled casserole. On a hungry night when you don't have time to cook, just put the casserole in a cold oven, turn to 350⁰ and reheat for about 30 minutes.

1-2 T. oil
1 small onion, chopped
1 clove garlic, minced
1 stalk celery, diced
¼ c. green pepper, diced
*½-1 c. sliced mushrooms
*¼-½ c. soy grits
1 c. tomatoes, skinned
   and chopped or canned

6 oz. tomato sauce
½ t. salt
1 bay leaf
½ t. oregano
½ t. sweet basil
½ t. honey
1-2 T. cornstarch (if
   needed for thickening)

1. In a large pot heat the oil and sauté the vegetables in the order in which they are listed. Feel free to adjust the amounts of vegetables to suit your own taste. I love the mushrooms and generally include as many as I can. The green pepper is delicious, but can be expensive when not in season. Use your own judgement — the finished sauce will always be delicious.

2. When the vegetables begin to soften add the soy grits and sauté for a minute or two longer.

3. Stir in the tomatoes, seasonings, honey, and tomato paste. Bring to a slow boil over medium heat, cover, and simmer for at least 30 minutes (the longer the better).

4. When it's time to eat, check the sauce. If it seems too "runny" thicken it with cornstarch. Dissolve the cornstarch in a little cold water first and pour the solution into the hot sauce while stirring. Just dumping dry cornstarch into hot liquid is a fantastic way to get lumpy, not thick, sauce.

5. Serve on cooked whole wheat noodles and sprinkle grated cheese over all. The cheese will complement any noodles not already complemented by the soy grits.

VARIATION

Use the spaghetti sauce to make lasagna. Use 4 oz. noodles and half the spaghetti sauce recipe for 2 people. In a baking pan make layers of cooked noodles, ricotta or cottage cheese, grated yellow cheese, and spaghetti sauce. Bake in a 350° oven for 20-40 minutes or until the dish is heated through and the cheese melts.

*The amount of protein in this dish depends on the final amount of noodles and cheese which you use. The soy grits complement the wheat noodles, and the more cheese you use, the more usable protein there will be in the dish. There are about 8-12 g. usable protein per serving.

Macaroni 'n' Cheese 'n' Tomatoes

2 servings

*½ c. whole wheat
  macaroni, cooked
1-3 t. oil
1-2 tomatoes, skinned
  and chopped
1 small onion, chopped

½ clove garlic, minced
  or a dash or two
  of garlic powder
½ t. oregano
¼ t. salt
*⅓ c. grated cheese
  (brick and Parmesan)

1. Sauté the onion and garlic in the oil until the onion softens. Add the tomatoes and seasonings and cook for a few minutes over low heat until the flavors mingle.

2. In a well-oiled casserole arrange the food in layers — a thin layer of macaroni, topped by ⅓ of the tomato mixture, topped by ⅓ of the grated cheese. Repeat the layers twice more, ending with the cheese on top.

3. Bake in a 325° oven until the casserole is warmed through and the cheese is melted.

½ c. macaroni + 2 ⅔ T. cheese = 14 g.
2 ⅔ T. cheese = 4 g.
*Total = 18 g. usable protein

STOVE-TOP MAIN DISHES

These dishes range from the very simple to the rather complex. They all provide significant amounts of usable protein, and since they require no baking time they are fairly quick to prepare.

Creamy Curried Vegetable Sauce on Bulgar

2 servings

*⅔ c. bulgar, cooked
   with ¼ t. salt
1-2 T. butter or oil
½ t. curry powder
dash cayenne and salt
2 scallions or 1 small
   onion, chopped

2 stalks celery, chopped
¼-½ c. sliced
   mushrooms
*½ c. or more yogurt

1. In a frying pan heat the oil or butter and the seasonings for a minute or two to develop the flavor of the curry.

2. Sauté the vegetables in the seasoned oil in the order in which they are listed. Sauté until the vegetables are warmed through.

3. When the vegetables are cooked turn off the heat and stir in the yogurt. (If the heat is on the yogurt will curdle when you stir it in.) Serve the sauce over the cooked bulgar.

⅔ c. bulgar + 7 T. yogurt = 11.5 g.
1 T. yogurt = .5 g.
*Total = 12 g. usable protein

Nasi Goreng

2 servings

This is a variation on an Indonesian dish which is traditionally made with pork. It's a very hot dish so serve it with cool fruits, like pineapple, tomatoes, pickles, and mango chutney. Sambal Oelek is a *very* hot pepper sauce made in Holland for Indonesian food. Use it (carefully!) if you can find it. If not, substitute another hot pepper sauce.

*2 T. dry soybeans, cooked
*2 T. wheat berries
*¼ c. brown rice
1 small onion, chopped
1-3 T. butter
1 T. tamari sauce

½ t. Sambal Oelek or
  slightly more tobasco
  sauce
*1 egg
salt to taste
*2-4 eggs (for topping)

1. Cook the grains by adding the wheat berries to boiling water, covering, and simmering for ½ hour. Add the rice, cover again, and simmer until the grains are tender.

2. Melt the butter in a frying pan. Add the onions and sauté until they soften. Add the cooked soybeans, tamari, and Sambal Oelek, and sauté until everything is heated through.

3. Add an egg and salt, stirring constantly to scramble and break up the egg.

4. Add the cooked grains, stirring to distribute the flavorings and beans throughout the grains.

5. Serve with fried or scrambled eggs on top.

VARIATION
Substitute triticale berries for the wheat berries.

2 T. soybeans + 2 T. wheat berrries + ¼ c. rice = 10 g.
1 egg = 6 g.
if topped with 1 egg per serving, 2 eggs = 12 g.
*Total = 28 g. usable protein

Bean Stroganoff

2-4 servings

Depending upon the amount of noodles this recipe will make a dinner for two or a small dinner party. If you don't have noodles you might want to substitute up to 2½ c. wheat berries or up to 4 cups bulgar for the noodles. Serve the stroganoff with colorful vegetables.

1 T. butter	½ t. Worcestershire
2 scallions or one	sauce or tamari
small onion, chopped	dash dry mustard
*1-1½ c. sliced mushrooms	2 T. red wine
*½ c. dry garbanzo	*1 c. yogurt
beans, cooked	*up to 10 oz. whole
½ c. stock or water	wheat noodles (about
¼ t. nutmeg	2½ cups)
½ t. salt	

1. In a frying pan melt the butter and sauté the onion and mushrooms until soft. Add the drained garbanzo beans and sauté for another minute or two.

2. Add the stock, all of the seasonings, and the wine. Bring to a slow boil. Reduce the heat and simmer for 10-15 minutes, until the flavors mingle and the amount of liquid is reduced.

3. Remove the pan from the heat and stir in the yogurt. Serve immediately over the cooked noodles.

NOTE: If you reheat this — make it into a casserole. Put the noodles on the bottom, stroganoff sauce over the top, and heat it in the oven at about 350⁰. Don't try to reheat it on top of the stove or it will curdle.

VARIATION

Green Bean Stroganoff: Add fresh snap beans to the sautéed vegetables in step 1 before continuing on with the rest of the recipe.

6 oz. noodles + ½ c. garbanzo beans = 46 g.
4 oz. noodles + 1 c. yogurt = 28 g.
1 c. sliced mushrooms = 2-3 g.
*Total = 76-77 g. usable protein

Soybean Creole

2 servings

Please do not omit the green pepper, as this is what gives the dish its "creole" flavor. Serve with steamed snap beans and/or a salad.

*¼ c. brown rice	¼ t. salt
*2 T. wheat berries	¾ c. water

SAUCE:

1 T. butter	6 oz. tomato paste
1 small onion, chopped	dash thyme
¼ c. chopped celery	1 t. sweet basil
¼ c. diced green pepper	½ t. honey
*2 T. dry soybeans, cooked	salt to taste
½ c. tomatoes, skinned and chopped or canned	

1. Cook the grains. Bring salted water to a boil, add wheat berries and cover. Reduce heat and simmer ½ hour. Add rice, cover again and simmer until the grains are tender.

2. Melt the butter in the frying pan. Sauté the vegetables and soybeans in the butter in the order in which they are listed. Add the tomatoes and tomato paste, stirring constantly. Add seasonings and honey and mix well. Reduce heat and simmer the sauce for about 10 minutes.

3. Serve the sauce over the cooked grains.

VARIATION

1. Add ⅔ to ¾ c. diced eggplant and/or zucchini to the sautéing vegetables before adding the tomatoes, etc.

2. Substitute triticale berries for the wheat berries.

*¼ c. rice + 2 T. wheat berries + 2 T. soybeans = 10 g. usable protein

Sweet and Sour Lentils

2 servings

*¼ c. raw lentils, cooked	dash cayenne
*⅔ c. brown rice, cooked	dash ground cloves
1 T. oil	1 t. lemon juice
2 T. honey	½ t. fresh ginger
3 T. cider vinegar	1 apple, cut in chunks
¼ t. onion salt	½ t. cornstarch and
	a few t. water

1. In a frying pan combine oil, honey, vinegar, seasonings, lemon juice, and grated ginger. Heat gently, stirring often, for about 5 minutes.

2. Dissolve the cornstarch in a little cold water. Add this slowly to the hot mixture, stirring constantly. The sauce should thicken only slightly.

3. Drain the cooked lentils. Rinse and drain again if you wish. Add them to the sauce and continue cooking for a few more minutes.

4. Stir in the raw apple chunks and cook just long enough to warm the apple. Serve the sauce over cooked rice.

VARIATION

Substitute other dry beans for the lentils.

*¼ c. lentils + ⅔ c. rice = 15 g. usable protein

Curried Bulgar and Garbanzos

2 servings

Serve this flavorful dish with a steamed vegetable or a cool, yogurt salad.

1 T. oil	1 t. curry powder
¼ t. curry powder	2 scallions, chopped
*10 T. bulgar	*¼ c. garbanzo beans, cooked
1⅜ c. water	chopped celery (optional)
½ t. salt	½ t. salt
1 T. oil	*½ c. yogurt

1. Heat 1 T. oil and ¼ t. curry powder in a saucepan. Sauté the bulgar in the seasoned oil. Add water and ½ t. salt, bring to a boil, cover, and simmer until tender.

2. In a frying pan, heat 1 T. oil and 1 t. curry powder. Sauté the scallions, garbanzos, and celery until the vegetables soften and the beans brown slightly. Add ½ t. salt and the cooked bulgar. Remove from the heat and stir in the yogurt.

VARIATIONS

1. Don't stir the bulgar into the bean mixture. Stir the yogurt into the beans to make a sauce and serve over the bulgar.

2. Casserole: Turn the entire mixture into an oiled casserole and bake in a 350⁰ oven until the casserole is set.

10 T. bulgar + 2 T. beans = 11.5 g.
2 T. beans + ¼ c. yogurt = 5.5 g.
¼ c. yogurt = 2 g.
*Total = 19 g. usable protein

Sweet Vegetable Curry

2 large servings

This *really* is a one dish meal. It needs nothing to accompany it, except perhaps some iced tea or a little yogurt to cool the tongue.

*¼ c. dry soybeans, cooked
*¼ c. wheat berries, cooked
*½ c. brown rice, cooked with ½ t. salt
1 T. oil
1 t. curry powder

¼ c. chopped onion or scallion
2 carrots, sliced
½ c. raisins
1 c. water or stock
1 small summer squash, sliced
½ t. salt or to taste

1. In a saucepan heat the oil and sauté the curry powder, onions, and carrots until the onion softens and the carrot slices are coated with oil. Add the cooked soybeans, water, and raisins, and bring to a boil. Cover, reduce heat, and simmer until the carrots are tender, about 25 minutes.

2. Stir in the squash slices for the last 4-5 minutes of cooking time. Add the salt and if necessary raise the heat so that most of the water boils away or is absorbed by the vegetables and raisins.

3. Stir together the cooked rice and wheat berries. Serve the curry over the grains.

VARIATION

Substitute triticale berries for the wheat berries.

*¼ c. soybeans + ¼ c. wheat berries + ½ c. brown rice = 20 g. usable protein

Garbanzo Curry

2 servings

Accompany this dish with a raw salad and, for coolness, a little yogurt. It is hot but so delicious.

*¼ c. garbanzos, cooked
*⅔ c. brown rice, cooked
   with ½ t. salt
1-2 T. oil
⅓ c. chopped scallion
   or onion
⅓ c. diced green pepper

1 t. curry powder
1 c. tomatoes, skinned
   and chopped or canned,
   or tomato juice
½ t. salt
1-2 t. cornstarch (optional,
   if needed for thickening)

1. In a frying pan heat the oil and sauté the curry powder, onions, and green pepper until the onion softens. Add the cooked, drained garbanzos and sauté for a few more minutes. Add the tomato juice or tomatoes and slowly bring the mixture to a boil. Reduce heat, cover, and simmer for about 30 minutes.

2. Check the sauce. Thicken with a little cornstarch if thin. Dissolve the cornstarch in a little cold water and add the solution to the sauce while stirring. Add the salt and serve over the cooked rice.

*¼ c. garbanzo beans + ⅔ c. brown rice = 15 g. usable protein

Chili

2 servings

*¼ c. dry kidney
  beans, cooked
*5 T. bulgar
1-3 T. oil
1 small onion, chopped
2 T. chopped celery
  (optional)

½ t. chili powder
¼ t. salt
dash cayenne
1 c. tomatoes, skinned
  and chopped or canned
*2 T. instant milk powder
  (1½ T. non-instant)

1. Over a medium flame toast the bulgar in a dry saucepan, stirring constantly to keep it from getting too dark. Add oil, onions, and celery and sauté for a few minutes until the onions soften. Stir in all the seasonings.

2. In a bowl or large measuring cup mash the tomatoes slightly. Add the milk powder and stir until the milk is completely dissolved in the tomatoes.

3. Stir the tomato mixture into the bulgar and vegetables. Cover and simmer until the bulgar is tender, 15-20 minutes.

VARIATIONS

1. Serve over bulgar wheat (up to 1¼ c. + 3 T. uncooked). The beans and milk will complement the extra wheat. This will give up to 21 g. usable protein, but it makes enough food to serve 4 or 5 people.

2. Eliminate bulgar from the sauce recipe and serve the sauce over bulgar (up to 1¾ c. uncooked).

1 T. beans + 5 T. bulgar = 5.75 g.
3 T. beans + 2 T. milk powder = 8.25 g.
*Total = 14 g. usable protein

Survival Stew

2-4 servings

This is a plain, hearty stew — very filling so serve it on a night when you've worked or played hard. It's named Survival Stew because nothing in it (except the optional tomato juice) requires refrigeration. A good dish for camping.

*2 T. soybeans, cooked
*½ c. wheat berries
oil for sautéing
1 medium onion, chopped
2 carrots, thickly sliced
*1 large potato, cut
  in chunks
1½ c. water
½ t. each thyme, mar-
  joram, and summer
  savory

1 T. tamari soy sauce
  or miso
½ c. tomato juice or water
*⅓ c. instant milk powder
  (¼ c. non-instant)
½ t. salt or to taste
cornstarch to thicken
  (optional)

1. Sauté the onion in the oil until the onion becomes transparent. Add carrots and potato chunks and sauté a few more minutes. Add wheat berries and sauté until the grain is coated with oil.

2. Add 1½ c. water and bring to a boil, reduce heat, add herbs and tamari or miso (dissolve miso in a little warm water first), and cooked soybeans. Cover and simmer until the wheat berries are tender, 1-1½ hours.

3. Beat the milk powder into the tomato juice or water. Add this mixture to the stew. Add salt to taste. If you wish, thicken the stew with a little cornstarch.

4. Serve with fresh bread or a green salad — depending on how hungry you are.

½ c. wheat berries + 2 T. soybeans = 16 g.
1 potato + ⅓ c. milk powder = 9 g.
*Total = 25 g. usable protein

Soybean Patties
6 patties

*¼ c. soybeans,
  cooked and drained
1 T. tamari soy sauce
¼ t. salt
	½ t. oregano
	*1 egg
	*oatmeal and wheat
	  germ to bind

1. Mash the soybeans thoroughly. Mix well with all the other ingredients, adding enough grain so that the mixture holds together.

2. In a frying pan heat a small amount of butter or oil. Drop heaping tablespoons of the soybean mixture into the hot fat. Flatten the patties slightly with the back of a spoon. Fry over a medium low heat until the patties are heated through and are holding together fairly well. Flip and fry on the other side for a minute or two, or until both sides are golden brown. Serve with catsup.

VARIATIONS

1. Soybean loaf: Press the mixture into a small oiled casserole and bake until set at 350⁰ (30-40 minutes).

2. Simple patties: Eliminate egg and substitute a pat of butter. Reduce the amount of grain used for binding and shape the patties with your hands. Makes 2 large patties.

¼ c. soybeans = 10 g.
1 egg = 6 g.
⅓ c. oatmeal + 2 T. wheat germ = 5 g.
*Total = 21 g. usable protein

The total grams of usable protein depends upon the amount of grain used for binding.

STIR-FRIED VEGETABLES WITH GRAINS

These are some of my favorite recipes. The possible variations are endless — see if you can invent some of your own. Stir-fried vegetables are an excellent means for trying out unfamiliar seasonings. The vegetables are always crunchy-good, so even if you aren't crazy about the new flavor you will probably still like the dish. These dishes are also terrific for throwing together at the last minute. Prepare the vegetables while the grains are cooking, then cook quickly, and serve at once.

Crunchy Vegetables with Barley I

2-3 servings

*½ c. + 2 T. raw barley,
   cooked with
*1 T. soy grits, and
½ t. salt
2 scallions or 1 leek,
   sliced
¾ c. sliced carrots
1 stalk celery, sliced

2 T. green pepper,
   chopped
*¾ c. sliced mushrooms
2-3 T. oil or butter
¼ t. salt
¼ t. dill weed
1 t. ground cardamon

1. Chop all the vegetables very thinly (⅛ in. thick or less) for stir-frying.

2. When the barley is cooked, and you're just about ready to eat, heat the oil with ¼ t. salt and the herbs over a medium flame. Add the vegetables to the hot oil in the order they are listed, stirring constantly. As soon as one vegetable is coated with oil stir in the next. The whole process should take less than 5 minutes.

3. Finally stir in the cooked barley, distributing the oil and cooked vegetables throughout the barley. Serve at once.

10 T. barley + 1 T. soy grits = 9 g.
¾ c. mushrooms = 2-3 g.
*Total = 11-12 g. usable protein

Crunchy Vegetables with Barley II

2-3 servings

*10 T. barley
¼ t. salt
*1 T. soy grits
2-3 scallions or
   1 leek, sliced
1 carrot, sliced

1-2 stalks celery, sliced
1 c. sliced mushrooms
1-3 T. oil or butter
¼ t. ground cumin
¼ t. salt

1. Slice all the vegetables thinly for stir-frying.
2. Cook the barley with ¼ t. salt and soy grits. When the barley is cooked, and you're just about ready to eat, heat the oil, cumin, and ¼ t. salt over a medium heat. Stir-fry the vegetables in the order listed, adding the next vegetable as soon as the previous one is coated with oil.
3. Stir in the cooked barley and stir to distribute the vegetables and seasonings throughout the grain. Serve at once.

10 T. barley + 1 T. soy grits = 9 g.
1 c. mushrooms = 2-3 g.
*Total = 11-12 g. usable protein

Crunchy Tarragon Vegetables and Bulgar

2-3 servings

*¾ c. bulgar, cooked with
*2 T. soy grits and
½ t. salt
1-2 T. butter
½ t. tarragon

¼ t. salt
2 scallions, chopped
1 stalk celery, sliced thin
2 carrots, sliced thin
¾-1 c. sliced mushrooms

1. Melt the butter with the tarragon and ¼ t. salt in a frying pan. Stir-fry the vegetables in the order in which they are

listed. As soon as one vegetable is coated with melted butter add the next vegetable. It should take no longer than 5 minutes.

2. Add the cooked bulgar and soy grits, stirring constantly to distribute the herbed butter and vegetables throughout the grain. Serve at once.

¾ c. bulgar + 2 T. soy grits = 16 g.
¾ c. - 1 c. sliced mushrooms = 2-3 g.
*Total = 18-19 g. usable protein

Sweet-Spice Vegetables and Bulgar

2-3 servings

*¾ c. bulgar, cooked with
*2 T. soy grits and
½ t. salt
1-2 T. butter
1 t. ground coriander
¼ t. salt

2 scallions, sliced
1 carrot, sliced
¼ lb. snowpeas
½ green pepper, diced
¾-1 c. sliced mushrooms

1. In a large frying pan heat the butter with the coriander and ¼ t. salt. Stir-fry the vegetables in the order in which they are listed. As soon as one vegetable is coated with butter add the next. The whole process should take less than 5 minutes.

2. Serve the vegetables over the cooked bulgar.

¾ c. bulgar + 2 T. soy grits = 16 g.
¾-1 c. mushrooms = 2-3 g.
*Total = 18-19 g. usable protein

Crunchy Vegetables on Wheat Berries

2 servings

*2 T. dry soybeans, cooked
*½ c. wheat berries
butter or oil for sautéing
1 small onion, chopped
1 carrot, thinly sliced
1 stalk celery, thinly sliced

*¾-1 c. sliced mushrooms
1 T. tamari soy sauce
¼ t. marjoram
¼ t. sage
salt to taste

1. In a saucepan sauté the onion in a little oil or butter. Add the raw wheat berries and sauté for a few minutes more. Add 1 c. hot water, bring to a boil, cover, and simmer until the wheat is tender, about 1 hour.

2. Prepare all the other vegetables. When the wheat berries are cooked you are ready to finish cooking the meal.

3. In a large pan heat a little oil or butter, the tamari, and all the other seasonings. Sauté the drained, cooked soybeans until they are heated through.

4. Stir-fry the other vegetables in the order in which they are listed. As soon as one vegetable is coated with oil add the next. Serve over the cooked wheat berries.

VARIATION

Substitute triticale berries for the wheat.

2 T. soybeans + ½ c. wheat berries = 16 g.
¾-1 c. mushrooms = 2-3 g.
*Total = 18-19 g. usable protein

Summer Stir-fry

2-3 servings

Crunchy and colorful. For a pretty dish cut some of the vegetables on the diagonal, others in rounds, and cut the green peppers in long, thin strips. This really is yummy, so you may want to make a larger quantity of rice and soy grits and treat yourself to a big dinner. Serve with a big glass of buttermilk.

*10 T. raw brown rice
*1 T. soy grits
¼ t. salt
1-2 T. butter or oil
¼ t. salt
dash cayenne
dash thyme
1 small onion, chopped
1 carrot, sliced

1 stalk celery, sliced
½ green pepper, sliced
3 large leaves Swiss
   chard, stems and leaves
   chopped separately
1-2 small summer squash,
   sliced (A yellow squash
   is good for color. Add a
   zucchini too if you like.)
tamari soy sauce

1. Cook the brown rice with the grits and ¼ t. salt.

2. Melt the butter or heat the oil and add ¼ t. salt, cayenne, and thyme. Stir-fry the vegetables in this order: onion, carrot, celery and chard stems, green pepper, and squash. Add the next vegetable as soon as the previous one is coated with oil. Stir in the Swiss chard leaves and remove from heat immediately.

3. To serve, make a bed of rice on each plate and top the rice with the vegetable mixture. Sprinkle tamari over top.

*10 T. rice + 1 T. soy grits = 9 g. usable protein

PILAFS

The original pilaf was made with cracked wheat. Rice is commonly used today. Yankee ingenuity has given us pilafs made from other grains as well. Feel free to interchange the grains, vegetables, and seasonings in any way you wish; just be sure to include the proper amount of soy grits for best quality protein. For more protein top each serving with a big spoonful of cold, fresh yogurt. Serve pilafs as main dishes or side dishes with beans or cheese.

Wheat Pilaf

2 servings

*⅜ c. bulgar
*1 T. soy grits
1-2 T. oil
1 scallion, sliced
1 stalk celery, chopped
*½-1 c. sliced mushrooms

¼ t. thyme
½ t. salt
dash cayenne
dash oregano
¾ c. water

1. Heat the oil in a saucepan. Sauté the vegetables in the order in which they are listed. Add seasonings, bulgar, and soy grits and sauté for about 5 minutes, until everything is coated with oil.

2. Add ¾ c. water and bring to a boil. Cover, reduce heat, and simmer until the bulgar is tender.

⅜ c. bulgar + 1 T. soy grits = 8 g.
½-1 c. mushrooms = 1-3 g.
*Total = 9-11 g. usable protein

Millet Pilaf

2 servings

*⅓ c. raw millet
*2 t. soy grits
1 T. oil
1 scallion, sliced
*½-¾ c. mushrooms, sliced

½ t. sage
½ t. salt
dash oregano
dash cayenne
⅔ c. water

1. Sauté the scallion, then the mushrooms in the oil until they soften. Add seasonings, millet, and soy grits. Sauté for about 5 minutes.
2. Add ⅔ c. water and bring to a boil. Cover, reduce heat, and simmer until the millet is tender, 25-30 minutes.

⅓ c. millet = 3 g.
2 t. soy grits = 1 g.
complementarity = 1 g.
½-¾ c. mushrooms = 1-2 g.
*Total = 6-7 g. usable protein

Kasha

2 servings

If you like buckwheat breakfast cereal omit the vegetables and herbs and serve with milk and honey.

*⅜ c. buckwheat groats	¼ t. salt
*1 T. soy grits	1 T. dried parsley
1-2 T. oil	dash thyme and cayenne
1 scallion, sliced	¾ c. water
1 small stalk celery, chopped	

1. In a saucepan heat the oil and sauté the scallion and celery until the onion softens. Add the buckwheat groats and soy grits and sauté for a few minutes more.
2. Add the water and seasonings and bring to a boil. Reduce heat, cover, and simmer until the grain is tender, about 30 minutes.

*⅜ c. buckwheat groats + 1 T. soy grits = 9 g. usable protein

COMPANY'S COMING

When you have guests for dinner try one of the company main dishes which look and taste as though you'd spent all day in the kitchen, but really aren't at all difficult to prepare. You may also use any of the other main dish recipes, doubling, tripling, or whatever, the measurements. When doubling recipes season to taste; often twice as much food can be seasoned perfectly with a little less than twice as much seasoning.

If you're really into entertaining you'll find that the sandwich fillings, spread on crackers or rye crisps, will make delicious hors d'oeuvres. Raw vegetables can be dipped in a mustard sauce (yogurt with Dijon mustard). Garnish dips and canapés with fresh parsley, alfalfa sprouts, or slices of stuffed olives. For an appetizer, serve tomato juice or one of the lighter soups.

If you find yourself with an impromptu dinner party on your hands — some old friends and their six kids are moving from Nome to Atlanta and just had to stop to see you on their way south — try expanding one of the stir-fry recipes. Mix soy grits with grains in the proper proportions. While the grains are cooking put everyone old enough to use a knife to work chopping vegetables. The result will be so delicious and so much fun that you might even decide to plan your next dinner party this way.

A meal for company doesn't have to be ornate and complicated. Serve foods that you make well and that look well together. Then relax and enjoy — your guests will too.

Chow Mein

4 servings

Serve this with a salad of dark greens and sprouts. To round out the meal you can also have fresh bread or rolls, a steamed vegetable, and something dairy-rich like fruit and yogurt or ice cream for dessert.

*1¼ c. raw brown rice
*2 T. soy grits
½ t. salt
1-2 T. oil
3 scallions or 1 leek, chopped
1-2 t. grated fresh ginger
2 carrots, sliced
2 stalks celery, sliced

*½ lb. mushrooms, sliced
1-1½ c. snow peas
1 c. bean sprouts
1-1½ c. water
1 T. tamari soy sauce
3 T. sherry
1 T. cornstarch
½ t. salt

1. Cook the brown rice with the soy grits and ½ t. salt.

2. Prepare the vegetables while the rice is cooking. When the rice is done heat the oil in a soup pot, frying pan, or wok and sauté the vegetables in the order in which they are listed. Add each vegetable as soon as the previous one is coated with oil. Scoop the vegetables out of the pan and set them aside.

3. To the oil remaining in the pan add water, tamari, sherry, and salt and bring to a boil. Dissolve the cornstarch in a little cold water and slowly stir this into the boiling mixture. Continue boiling and stirring until the mixture thickens.

4. Return the stir-fried vegetables to the hot sauce and keep cooking and stirring for about 30 seconds to rewarm the vegetables. Serve at once over the cooked rice.

1¼ c. brown rice + 2 T. soy grits = 18.5 g.
½ lb. mushrooms, about = 9 g.
*Total = 27.5 g. usable protein

Ratatouille

4-8 servings

This will serve 4 to 8 people depending on the amount of rice. If you have a garden you may find all the ingredients free for the picking in your backyard. Reheat leftovers in a covered casserole in the oven, at 350°, and feel free to add extra touches of your own. Mushrooms might be nice, or grated cheese sprinkled over each serving. This recipe is for eight people; use half the amount of rice and grits to serve four.

*2½ c. raw brown rice	1 clove garlic, minced
*¼ c. soy grits	3 or more tomatoes, chopped
1 t. salt	handful of dried parsley
1 eggplant, chopped	1 t. oregano
1-3 zucchini, chopped	1 t. sweet basil
1-4 onions, chopped	½ t. salt
1 sweet green pepper,	2-3 T. oil
chopped	6 or 12 oz. can tomato paste

1. Cook the rice with the grits and 1 t. salt. Put all the chopped vegetables and seasonings in a large saucepan or Dutch oven. In a separate pan heat the oil. Pour the hot oil over the vegetables and stir to distribute the oil.

2. Bring the mixture to a boil over medium heat. Cover and simmer for 1½-2 hours.

3. Add tomato paste for the last ½ hour of cooking. Serve over cooked rice, or other grains cooked with soy grits.

*2½ c. brown rice + ¼ c. soy grits = 37 g. usable protein

Zucchini and Onion Quiche

10 in. quiche

Serve this quiche with a steamed vegetable and a raw green salad. If you have leftovers they're good straight from the refrigerator. Cool but nourishing on a hot summer day.

*1 10 in. unbaked whole wheat pie shell
*3 eggs, beaten
*1 c. milk
½ t. salt
*1½ c. grated cheese (mostly Swiss with some brick)
1 T. butter

1 small onion, finely chopped
1 medium zucchini, sliced in ¼ inch half rounds
pinch thyme
¼ t. sage
dash salt

1. Prepare cheese mixture. Beat eggs, milk, and ½ t. salt together. Stir in the grated cheese.

2. In a frying pan melt the butter. Sauté the onions until they are transparent and soft, but not browned. Add thyme, sage, dash salt, and zucchini. Sauté, uncovered, until the zucchini softens and is slightly reduced. Keep the heat at medium-low until the zucchini juices are released, then turn the heat higher to reduce the amount of liquid.

3. Line the bottom of the pie shell with the zucchini-onion mixture. Pour the cheese mixture over the vegetables, trying to cover evenly.

4. Bake the quiche at 350° for 30-40 minutes, or until a knife inserted in the center comes out clean.

5. Allow the quiche to cool for about 10 minutes for ease in cutting.

1 whole wheat pie shell = 16 g.
3 eggs = 18 g.
1 c. milk = 7 g.
1½ c. grated cheese = 31 g.
*Total = 72 g. usable protein

Tomato and Bean Quiche or Timbale

10 in. quiche

A beautiful and elegant dish to serve for company. Not difficult either. Serve with a steamed green vegetable and a raw salad.

*½ c. dry garbanzos,
  cooked
1 T. oil
1 clove garlic, minced
1 large onion, chopped
2 c. tomatoes, peeled
  and chopped or canned
dash cayenne
1 t. oregano

1 t. sweet basil
*3 eggs
*1 c. milk
*1 c. grated cheese
¼ t. salt
Parmesan cheese for
  topping
whole wheat pie shell
  (optional)

1. In a large frying pan heat the oil and sauté the garlic and onion until soft. Stir in the tomatoes, cayenne, oregano, sweet basil, and the cooked garbanzos. Bring the mixture to a boil over medium heat. Reduce heat and continue to simmer while you prepare the rest of the dish.

2. In a bowl beat the eggs, and then beat in the milk. Grate the cheese and stir it into the egg mixture. Add the salt. Slowly stir in the tomato mixture.

3. If you are not using a pie shell, oil your pie plate well. Turn the mixture into the oiled pie plate or pie shell. Sprinkle Parmesan cheese over top. Bake in a 350⁰ oven for 30 minutes, or until a knife inserted in the center of the quiche comes out clean. Let cool for 5 or 10 minutes before cutting and serving.

NOTE: If necessary you may bake this ahead of time and return it to a 350⁰ oven for about 15 minutes to reheat it.

½ c. garbanzo beans + 1 c. milk = 22 g.
3 eggs = 18 g.
1 c. grated cheese = 21 g.
*Total = 61 g. usable protein
If you use a whole wheat pie shell add 14-16 g.

Cheese and Nut Surprise

6-8 servings

This is a beautiful casserole for company. The cashews give it a nutty sweetness, and any leftovers can be refrigerated and eaten chilled. Accompany the casserole with steamed artichokes, asparagus, or snap beans and a raw green salad. Cake would be good for dessert.

*1 c. raw wheat berries,
  cooked
*3 eggs
*1 c. cottage cheese
*1 c. milk
dash cinnamon

dash cayenne
few gratings fresh ginger
¼ t. salt
*raw cashews
*toasted wheat germ

1. Beat the eggs and beat in the cottage cheese, milk, and seasonings.

2. Choose a pretty casserole (a soufflé dish is nice) and oil it well. Assemble the casserole in three layers. Spread a layer of wheat berries over the bottom of the dish and cover them with about ⅓ of the egg mixture. Top the layer with a scattering of raw cashews. Assemble the second and third layers in the same manner and sprinkle the top of the dish with wheat germ.

3. Bake in a 350⁰ oven for 45 minutes or until a knife in the center of the casserole comes out clean.

1 c. wheat berries + 1 c. milk = 28 g.
3 eggs = 18 g.
1 c. cottage cheese = 28 g.
*Total = 74 g. usable protein

Vegetable Pie

10 in. pie

A pretty, colorful dish. You can prepare it beforehand and bake it while you socialize with your guests. A big tossed salad goes well with this dish, as does almost any steamed vegetable. Have something creamy and dairy-rich for dessert.

*¼ c. dry soybeans, cooked
*¼ c. raw wheat berries, cooked
*½ c. raw brown rice, cooked
1 T. oil
1 leek or 2 scallions, chopped
2 carrots, thinly sliced
1 small zucchini, quartered lengthwise and sliced

2 small stalks celery, sliced
*5 mushrooms, sliced
1 c. tomatoes, skinned and chopped or canned
1 t. sweet basil
1 T. tamari soy sauce
½ t. salt
*2 eggs
*1 c. grated cheese
sesame seeds

1. After the grains and soybeans have cooked sauté the soybeans and all the vegetables except the tomatoes in the oil. Mash the tomatoes slightly and add the sweet basil, tamari, and ¼ t. salt. Stir this tomato mixture into the other vegetables and remove them from the heat.

2. Beat one of the eggs. Stir this egg and ¼ t. salt into the wheat berries and rice. Spread the egg and grain mixture over the bottom of a well-oiled 10 inch pie plate. Sprinkle the grated cheese over the top.

3. Beat the other egg and stir it into the vegetable mixture (step one). Spread the vegetable mixture over top of the grated cheese and sprinkle with sesame seeds.

4. Bake the pie in a 325° oven for 40 minutes, or until a knife inserted in the center comes out clean. Let cool for a few minutes before cutting and serving.

¼ c. soy beans + ¼ c. wheat berries + ½ c. rice = 20.5 g.
2 eggs = 12 g.
1 c. grated cheese = 21 g.
5 mushrooms = 2-3 g.
*Total = 55.5-56.5 g. usable protein

Many of the regular main dishes can also be used for company. In most cases you will just need to fill out the meal by adding a salad and a steamed vegetable or two and perhaps muffins or freshly baked bread. To feed four people try any or the following:

Soybean Bulgar Casserole

Squash and Peanut Stew: With small servings it can stretch to serve 4.

Eggplant Parmesan

Carrot Casserole: Makes 4 small servings.

Stuffed Summer Squash

Cheesy Tarragon Timbale: Double the amounts of wheat berries and beans and leave everything else the same to make this serve 4.

Vegetable Soufflé

Millet Soufflé

Spaghetti or Lasagna

Sweet Vegetable Curry: Will stretch to serve 3.

All of the stir-fry dishes can easily be expanded to serve as many as you like. Just add more vegetables and adjust the seasonings.

BREAD

Bread has been called "the staff of life," and properly made, it really can support life by itself. Unfortunately, the stuff the supermarkets try to push on us as bread can hardly be said to deserve the name. If you've never tasted fresh, homemade whole grain bread before, you're in for a real treat.

The bread recipes each make one loaf; if you're really into lots of bread feel free to double the recipes whenever you like. I prefer to make smaller amounts of bread more often so the bread will get eaten while it is still really fresh. To store fresh bread wait until the loaf has cooled completely, then wrap it in a plastic bag or tinfoil and store it in your bread box or drawer (*not* in your refrigerator — it dries out more quickly in there). You may also freeze bread for longer storage. Let it cool, frozen bread slices about as easily as a brick, and slice it so that you can remove a slice or two at a time. Wrap the loaf in plastic or foil and freeze. Freezing bread is an especially good idea if you occasionally want a sandwich or toast but otherwise aren't much of a bread eater. Thaw slightly before slicing.

If you've never made bread before ask a more experienced friend to help the first time you bake. Certain steps in making bread are judged by the way things feel, and you'll learn to judge them almost immediately with a friend's help. It will take a little longer when you're learning from a book.

Some people complain that making yeast breads just takes too much time to be practical. It is true that you have to plan to be around for a couple of hours, but only a few minutes of those hours are actually spent working with the bread. One day I timed myself and found that the actual working time for making a loaf of bread was about 15 minutes. That's not even as much time as it takes to whip up a super-instant quick bread mix from the supermarket. While you're waiting for the bread to do its thing there are all kinds of lovely things *you* can be doing. A long, leisurely bath, a good book, a time to meditate, to paint, to sew — the list is endless. Finally, heaven itself, you can just sit and smell your delicious bread baking!

BASIC YEAST BREAD BAKING INSTRUCTIONS

1. The yeast must be dissolved in a warm liquid. Temperature is *very* important to the success of the bread. Active dry yeast must be dissolved in liquid between 105° and 115° F; cake yeast requires liquid between 80° and 90° F. Some type of sugar must then be added to feed the yeast — nourishment and warmth are vital if the yeast is to grow, and the yeast must grow if the bread is to be light. I usually add the oil or other fat to the rest of the liquid ingredients at this point. The liquid can then sit for up to five minutes to give the yeast a chance to start growing.

2. Most of the dry ingredients will now be stirred into the wet and the whole mixture beaten about 150 strokes to develop the gluten. Gluten is a form of protein found in wheat. It is necessary for the proper texture in a loaf of bread. Cornmeal, rye, buckwheat, and other flours have little or no gluten and so must be combined with wheat flour to make good bread. *Don't* eliminate the salt from the dry ingredients. It's needed to control the rising of the bread. You want it to rise, but only a certain amount.

3. Gradually, flour must now be added until the dough can be kneaded. Begin by stirring in the additional flour until the dough gets too stiff to stir, then use your hands. A "kneadable dough" is a very precise consistency — it is dry enough not to stick to your hands, but moist enough so that if you fold it in half and press the halves together the seam will quickly disappear. An experienced friend can help judge this consistency for the first time, but after that you'll recognize it when you see it. Remember, the least flour makes the lightest bread.

4. On a floured surface, or in a big bowl, knead the dough. Lift one edge and fold the dough over. Press down on the dough with the heel of the hand, and give the dough a quarter turn; repeat the whole process until the dough becomes "elastic." Add extra flour while you're kneading if the dough becomes too sticky. You'll know when you've done enough kneading — the dough will seem to come alive in your hands and when you press it, it will spring back. It's fun to play with at this stage, but since the authorities differ on how much kneading is good for the bread, it's probably a good idea to avoid getting too carried away with your new toy.

5. After the dough is kneaded put it back in the bowl. Cover it with a clean towel, put it in a warm place, and let the dough rise until it has doubled in bulk.

6. When the dough is done rising, punch it down with your fist. Knead the dough for a minute or two to knock most of the air out of it. Shape the dough into a loaf or loaves by patting and pushing until you get the shape you want. Place the loaf in a greased pan or on a greased baking sheet, brush the loaf with oil or butter for a soft crust, cover, and let rise again until the dough has nearly doubled in bulk.

7. When the loaf has finished rising you're ready to bake it. If you want a hard, shiny crust, brush the loaf with beaten egg white before baking.

8. The loaf is done baking if it sounds hollow when you tap it with your fingernail. If the loaf is getting a very brown crust, but still doesn't sound hollow, cover it with foil or lower the oven heat and continue baking until the bread is done. ENJOY!

Basic Whole Wheat Bread

1 loaf

1 c. warm water
  or stock
2 t. (1 pkg.) active
  dry yeast
1 T. honey
1 T. oil

*¾ c. instant milk powder
  (9 T. non-instant)
½ t. salt
*2½-3 c. whole wheat
  flour

1. Combine the wet ingredients and the yeast. Allow them to sit for a few minutes.

2. Measure and stir together the milk powder, salt, and 1 c. of whole wheat flour in a separate bowl.

3. Add the dry mixture to the wet and beat about 150 strokes.

4. Add enough flour to make a kneadable dough. Knead the dough on a well-floured surface until the dough comes alive (about 5 minutes). Cover and let rise in a warm place until double (45 min.-1 hour).

5. Punch down dough and shape it into a loaf. Place the loaf in a well-greased loaf pan or on a greased cookie sheet. Oil the top of the loaf, cover it, and let it rise in a warm place until it is almost double, about 45 minutes.

6. Bake in a 350⁰ oven for about 30 minutes, or until the loaf is done.

VARIATION

Triticale Bread: Add 1 c. triticale flour in step 4 and reduce the total amount of whole wheat flour by 1 c. This makes a finely grained sweet loaf which is easy to slice thin.

6⅔ T. milk powder + 2½ c. whole wheat flour = 35 g.
⅓ c. milk powder = 7 g.
*Total = 42 g. usable protein

High-Rising Egg Bread
1 loaf

This is an incredibly light loaf, especially if you are careful to use the very least amount of flour necessary to make a kneadable dough.

1 c. warm water
2 t. (1 pkg.) active
   dry yeast
1-2 T. honey
1 T. oil
*1 egg
*¼ c. soy flour

*¾ c. instant milk powder
   (9 T. non-instant)
½ t. salt
*2½-3 c. whole wheat
   flour
pinch saffron (optional)

1. Dissolve the yeast, honey, and oil in the warm water. Set aside.

2. In a separate bowl stir together the soy flour, milk powder, salt, and 1 c. whole wheat flour.

3. Beat the egg into the liquid ingredients. Add the dry mixture and beat 150 strokes.

4. Add enough whole wheat flour to make a kneadable dough. Knead the dough until it becomes elastic, 5-10 minutes. Cover and let rise until double, 1-1¼ hours.

5. Punch the dough down, shape into a loaf, cover, and let rise again until nearly double, about 45 minutes.

6. Bake in a 350° oven until done, about 30 minutes.

¼ c. soy flour + 1 c. whole wheat flour = 16 g.
1½ c. whole wheat flour + ¼ c. milk powder = 21 g.
½ c. milk powder = 10 g.
1 egg = 6 g.
*Total = 53 g. usable protein

Milk and Honey Bread

1 loaf

1 c. warm water
or stock
2 t. (1 pkg.) active
dry yeast
3 T. honey
1 T. oil

*1 c. instant milk powder
(¾ c. non-instant)
½ t. salt
*2½-3 c. whole
wheat flour

1. Dissolve the yeast, honey, and oil in the warm water. Set aside for a few minutes.

2. In a separate bowl stir together the milk powder, salt, and 1 c. whole wheat flour. Add this mixture to the liquid ingredients and beat 150 strokes to develop the gluten.

3. Add enough whole wheat flour to make a kneadable dough. Knead the dough on a floured surface until the dough becomes elastic.

4. Cover the dough, set it in a warm place, and allow it to rise until double, about 1 hour.

5. Punch down the dough, shape it into a loaf, cover, and allow it to rise again until nearly double (about 1 hour).

6. Bake in a 350⁰ oven for 30-35 minutes or until done.

3 c. whole wheat flour + ½ c. milk powder = 40.5 g.
½ c. milk powder = 10 g.
*Total = 50.5 g. usable protein

Whole Wheat Soy Bread

1 loaf

This loaf seems to be really foolproof. The first time I made it, an emergency came up during the second rising and I forgot all about the bread until about 4 hours later. I baked it anyway, and to my surprise, it worked! And turned out to be delicious too. I may have just been lucky that time, so I wouldn't advise baking that way normally. But, as you can see, even a big goof doesn't necessarily mean a failure.

*1 c. milk or	1 T. honey
1 c. warm water and	1 T. oil
⅓ c. instant milk powder	*½ c. soy flour
(¼ c. non-instant)	½ t. salt
2 t. (1 pkg.) active	*2½-3 c. whole
dry yeast	wheat flour

1. If you are using regular milk scald it and let it cool until it is just warm, about 110⁰.
2. To the warm milk or water add the yeast, honey, and oil. Set aside.
3. In a separate bowl stir together the soy flour, salt, 1 c. whole wheat flour, and milk powder if you have used water in Step 2. Add this to the yeast mixture and beat 150 strokes to develop the gluten in the wheat flour.
4. Add enough whole wheat flour to make a kneadable dough and knead the dough until it becomes elastic, 5-10 minutes. Cover and let rise in a warm place until double, about 1 hour.
5. Punch the dough down, shape it into a loaf and place it in a well-greased loaf pan. Cover and let it rise again until nearly double.
6. Place the loaf in a cold oven and turn the heat to 375⁰. Bake for 20 minutes, then turn the oven down to 350⁰. Continue baking until done, about 15 more minutes.

½ c. soy flour + 2 c. whole wheat flour = 32 g.
½ c. milk + 1 c. whole wheat flour = 14 g.
½ c. milk = 3.5 g.
*Total = 49.5 g. usable protein

Whole Wheat Bran Bread

1 loaf

So good fresh and hot from the oven! The bran provides extra fiber and also some extra protein which should be complemented by the milk powder.

1 c. warm water	½ c. bran
or stock	*¼ c. soy flour
2 t. active dry yeast	½ t. salt
1-2 T. honey	*1 egg
1 T. oil	*2½-3 c. whole
*1 c. instant milk powder	wheat flour
(¾ c. non-instant)	

1. Dissolve the yeast in the warm water. Add honey and oil and set aside.

2. In a separate bowl stir together the milk powder, bran, soy flour, salt, and 1 c. whole wheat flour. Add the dry ingredients and the egg to the yeast mixture and beat 150 strokes to develop the gluten in the wheat.

3. Add enough whole wheat flour to make a kneadable dough and knead the dough until it becomes elastic, about 5-10 minutes.

4. Cover the dough and let it rise in a warm place until double, about 1 hour.

5. Punch the dough down, shape it into a loaf, and place the loaf in a well greased pan. Cover and let rise again until nearly double, about 1 hour.

6. Bake the loaf in a 350⁰ oven for about 30 minutes or until done.

1 c. whole wheat flour + ¼ c. soy flour = 16 g.
2 c. whole wheat flour + ⅓ c. milk powder = 28 g.
⅔ c. milk powder = 14 g.
1 egg = 6 g.
*Total = 64 g. usable protein

Cracked Wheat Bread

1 loaf

1 c. warm water or stock	*1 egg
2 t. active dry yeast	*1 c. instant milk powder
*½ c. cracked wheat	(¾ c. non-instant)
*2 T. soy grits	½ t. salt
1 T. honey	*2½-3 c. whole wheat flour
1 T. oil	

1. Dissolve the yeast in the warm water. Beat in the cracked wheat, soy grits, honey, oil, and ½ c. whole wheat flour. Allow the mixture to sit in a warm spot for about 15 minutes, until the wheat and soy grits soften.

2. Beat the egg into the liquid.

3. In a separate bowl stir together the milk powder, salt, and about ½ c. whole wheat flour. Add this mixture to the liquid and beat 150 strokes.

4. Add enough whole wheat flour to make a kneadable dough. Turn the dough out onto a well-floured surface and knead until the dough becomes elastic.

5. Cover the dough and let it rise in a warm place until double, about 1 hour.

6. Punch the dough down, shape it into a loaf, and place it in a well-greased pan. Cover and let rise until nearly double, about 45 minutes.

7. Bake in a 350⁰ oven until done, about 30 minutes.

½ c. cracked wheat + 4 t. soy grits = 10⅔ g.
⅓ c. whole wheat flour + 2 t. soy grits = 5⅓ g.
2⅔ c. flour + about 7 T. milk powder = 37 g.
9 T. milk powder = 10 g.
1 egg = 6 g.
*Total = 69 g. usable protein

Oatmeal Bread

1 loaf

1 c. warm water	½ t. salt
or stock	*¾ c. instant milk powder
2 t. active dry yeast	(9 T. non-instant)
1 t. honey	*½ c. rolled oats
1 T. oil	*2-3 c. whole wheat flour

1. Dissolve the yeast and honey in the warm water. Add the oil.

2. In a separate bowl stir together the salt, milk powder, and 1 c. whole wheat flour. Stir this dry mixture into the wet ingredients and beat 150 strokes to develop the gluten.

3. Add the rolled oats and enough whole wheat flour to make a kneadable dough. Knead the dough on a well-floured surface until the dough becomes elastic.

4. Cover the dough and let it rise in a warm place until double.

5. When the dough has doubled in bulk punch it down and form it into a loaf. Place the loaf in a greased pan, cover, and allow it to rise until almost double.

6. Bake in a 350⁰ oven for 30-35 minutes or until done.

6⅔ T. milk powder + 2 c. flour + ½ c. rolled oats = 35 g.
⅓ c. milk powder = 7 g.
*Total = 42 g. usable protein

Cornmeal-Soy Grits Bread

1 small loaf

A mellow loaf with an interesting texture.

1 c. warm water	*½ c. cornmeal
1 T. active dry yeast	*⅓ c. instant milk powder
1 T. oil	(¼ c. non-instant)
1 T. honey	½ t. salt
*3⅓ T. soy grits	*1½-2 c. whole wheat flour

1. Dissolve the yeast in the warm stock. Add the oil and honey and set aside.

2. In a separate bowl stir together the soy grits, cornmeal, milk powder, salt, and 1 c. whole wheat flour. Stir these dry ingredients into the yeast mixture and beat 150 strokes to develop the gluten in the wheat.

3. Add enough whole wheat flour to make a kneadable dough and knead the dough until it becomes elastic. Cover and set in a warm place to rise until double, about 1 hour.

4. Punch the dough down, shape it into a loaf, place the loaf in a well-greased pan, cover, and let rise until nearly double, about 1 hour.

5. Bake in a 350⁰ oven until done, about 30 minutes.

½ c. cornmeal + 1⅓ T. soy grits + 2⅔ T. milk powder = 10 g.
1 c. whole wheat flour + 2 T. soy grits = 16 g.
1 c. whole wheat flour + 2⅔ T. milk powder = 14 g.
*Total = 40 g. usable protein

Wheat Germ-
Soy Grits Bread
1 loaf

1 c. warm water or stock	*2 T. soy grits
2 t. active dry yeast	½ t. salt
1 T. honey	*½ c. toasted wheat germ
1 T. oil	*1½-2 c. whole wheat flour
*½ c. instant milk powder	
(6 T. non-instant)	

1. Dissolve the yeast and honey in the warm water. Add the oil.

2. In a separate bowl stir together the milk powder, soy grits, salt, and 1 c. whole wheat flour. Add this dry mixture to the wet ingredients and beat 150 strokes to develop the gluten.

3. Add the wheat germ and enough flour to make a kneadable dough. On a floured surface knead the dough until it becomes elastic, about 5 minutes.

4. Cover the dough and let it rise until double, about 1 hour.

5. When the dough has doubled in bulk punch it down and form it into a loaf. Place the loaf in a well-greased loaf pan and let it rise until almost doubled, about 1 hour.

6. Bake in a 350⁰ oven for 35-40 minutes or until the bread is done.

1 c. whole wheat flour + 2 T. soy grits = 16 g.
1 c. flour + 2⅔ T. milk powder = 14 g.
⅓ c. milk powder = 8 g.
½ c. wheat germ = 8 g.
*Total = 46 g. usable protein

Rye Bread

1 loaf

1 c. warm water	*¼ c. instant milk powder
or stock	(3 T. non-instant)
2 t. active dry yeast	½ t. dill seed
1 T. molasses	½ t. caraway seed
1 T. oil	*1½-2½ c. whole
½ t. salt	wheat flour
*3 T. soy flour	*½ c. rye flour

1. Mix together the stock, yeast, molasses, and oil. Set aside.

2. In a separate bowl stir together the salt, soy flour, milk powder, rye flour, and ½ c. whole wheat flour. Add this dry mixture to the yeast mixture and beat 150 strokes to develop the gluten.

3. Add dill and caraway seeds and enough whole wheat flour to make a kneadable dough. On a well floured surface knead the dough until it becomes elastic, 5-10 minutes.

4. Cover the dough and let it rise in a warm place until doubled, 1½-2 hours.

5. Punch the dough down and shape it into a loaf. Place the loaf in a greased baking pan. Cover and let rise until almost double, 1¼ hours.

6. Bake in a 350⁰ oven for 30-40 minutes or until done.

3 T. soy flour + ¾ c. whole wheat flour = 12 g.
¼ c. milk powder + 1½ c. flour = 21 g.
*Total = 33 g. usable protein

Herbed Four Grain Bread
1 loaf

For an even more flavorful loaf substitute the leftover juice from pickles for part or all of the stock.

1 c. warm water	*¼ c. rye flour
or stock	*¼ c. corn meal
4 t. yeast (2 pkg.)	*¼ c. rolled oats
1 T. honey	½ t. salt
1 T. oil	¼ t. dill weed
*¼ c. + 2 t. soy grits	¼ t. celery seed
*⅓ c. instant milk powder	*2½-3 c. whole wheat flour
(¼ c. non-instant)	

1. Dissolve the yeast in the warm water. Add the honey, oil, and soy grits, stir, and set aside for about 5 minutes.

2. In a separate bowl, stir together the milk powder, rye flour, cornmeal, rolled oats, salt, dill weed, celery seed, and 1 c. whole wheat flour. Stir this mixture into the yeast mixture and beat 150 strokes to develop the gluten in the wheat.

3. Add enough whole wheat flour to make a kneadable dough and knead until the dough becomes elastic, 5-10 minutes. Cover and let rise in a warm place until double, about 1 hour.

4. Punch the dough down, shape it into a loaf, cover and let rise again until nearly double, about 1 hour.

5. Bake the loaf in a 350⁰ oven for 30 minutes or until done.

¼ c. cornmeal + 2 t. soy grits + 1⅓ T. milk powder = 5 g.
¼ c. rye flour + ¼ c. rolled oats + ½ c. whole wheat flour + 2 T. soy grits = 16 g.
1 c. whole wheat flour + 2 T. soy grits = 16 g.
1 c. whole wheat flour + 2⅔ T. milk powder = 14 g.
1⅓ T. milk powder = 2 g.
*Total = 53 g. usable protein

Super Seedy Sesame Bread

1 loaf

A yummy, nutty tasting loaf. It tastes just like a "super" bread should!

1 c. warm water	*¼ c. soy flour
1 T. yeast	*⅓ c. instant milk powder
1 T. honey	(¼ c. non-instant)
1 T. oil	½ t. salt
*½ c. sesame seeds	*2-2½ c. whole wheat flour

1. Dissolve the yeast in the warm water. Add the honey and oil and let the mixture sit for a few minutes. Stir in the sesame seeds.

2. In a separate bowl stir together the soy flour, milk powder, salt, and 1 c. whole wheat flour. Stir this mixture into the liquid mixture and beat 150 strokes to develop the gluten.

3. Add enough whole wheat flour to make a kneadable dough and knead the dough until it becomes elastic. Cover and let rise in a warm place until double, about 1 hour.

4. Punch the dough down, shape it into a loaf, and place the loaf in a well-greased pan. Cover and let rise again until nearly double, about 45 minutes.

5. Bake the loaf in a 350⁰ oven. After 30 minutes turn the oven down to 300⁰ and continue baking for another 10-15 minutes.

1⅝ c. whole wheat flour + ¼ c. soy flour + ¼ c. sesame seeds = 28.5 g.
¼ c. sesame seeds + about 1 T. milk powder = 6.25 g.
⅞ c. whole wheat flour + 2⅓ T. milk powder = 12.25 g.
2 T. milk powder = 2-3 g.
*Total = 49-50 g. usable protein

Yeast Raised Coffeecake with Raisin Filling

1 ring

DOUGH:

¼ c. warm water
*½ c. milk, scalded and
   cooled to warm
2 t. active dry yeast
3-4 T. oil, butter, or
   a combination of the two

⅓ c. honey
*1 c. instant milk powder
   (¾ c. non-instant)
*2-2½ c. whole wheat flour
½ t. salt

FILLING:

1 T. butter
⅓ c. honey

1 t. cinnamon
½ c. or more raisins

ICING

*⅓-½ c. milk powder
1 T. honey

milk (enough to make
   pourable icing)

1. Dissolve the yeast and honey in the warm water and milk. Add the oil or butter.

2. In a separate bowl stir together the milk powder, salt and one cup of flour. Add this to the liquid and beat 150 strokes.

3. Add just enough flour to make a kneadable dough. Knead the dough until it is smooth and elastic. Oil the ball of dough, cover it, and let it rise in a warm place until double, about 1 hour.

4. Punch the dough down, knead it a few times, re-cover, and let rise until double again, 45 min.-1 hour.

5. Punch the dough down and knead it a few times. On a flat, floured surface use a rolling pin to roll the dough into a flat sheet ¼ in. thick and about 13 in. long and 9 in. wide.

6. Prepare the filling by heating the butter, honey, and cinnamon. Drizzle this over the surface of the dough and sprinkle the raisins over top.

7. Starting at a 13 in. side, roll up the dough with the filling inside. Place the roll, seam side down, on a greased baking sheet. Shape the roll into a ring using your fingers to press the ends together and seal them.

8. Using a sharp knife or scissors make cuts halfway through the ring at 1 in. intervals all the way around the ring. Oil the surface of the ring. Cover and let rise until double.

9. Bake in a 350⁰ oven, lowering the heat to 300⁰ after 25 minutes. Continue baking until done, 35-45 minutes.

10. When the cake has cooled drizzle icing over the top.

VARIATIONS

1. In step 3 substitute 1 c. triticale four for 1 c. whole wheat flour. This makes an even sweeter cake.

2. Spiced Apple Filled Coffeecake: Substitute applebutter for raisin filling.

2 c. whole wheat flour + ⅓ c. milk powder = 28 g.
1 c. milk powder = 21 g.
½ c. milk = 4 g.
***Total = 53 g. usable protein**

Fruit Topped Coffeecake

1 cake

Use the dough for the Yeast Raised Coffeecake with Raisin Filling. After the second rising divide the dough into 20-24 parts. Roll each part between your hands until you have a "rope" about 10 inches long. Use 2 ropes for each roll. Twist the 2 ropes around each other, then arrange them in a heap, tucking the ends under. On a greased baking sheet arrange the heaps with one in the center, the others surrounding the center roll, and all the rolls touching. Cover and let rise until double. Bake as usual.

When the baked cake has cooled ice it with powdered milk icing and top each roll with a spoonful of fruit jelly or preserves.

***Total = 53 g. usable protein**

Sun-Seedy Raisin Bread
1 loaf

Nutty and sweet, this loaf has all the good things anyone could want.

1 c. warm water or stock	*¼ c. sesame seeds
1 T. yeast	*½ c. sunflower seeds
1-2 T. honey	½ t. salt
1 T. oil	*2½-3 c. whole
*1 egg	wheat flour
*¼ c. soy flour	½ c. raisins
*⅓ c. instant milk powder	
(¼ c. non-instant)	

1. Dissolve the yeast in the warm water. Beat in the honey, oil, and egg and set aside.

2. In a separate bowl stir together the soy flour, milk powder, sesame seeds, sunflower seeds, salt, and 1 c. whole wheat flour. Stir this mixture into the yeast mixture and beat 150 strokes. Thoroughly stir in the raisins.

3. Add enough whole wheat flour to make a kneadable dough and knead until the dough becomes elastic, about 5 minutes. Cover and let rise in a warm place until double, about 1 hour.

4. Punch the dough down, shape it into a loaf, cover, and let it rise again until nearly double, about 1 hour.

5. Bake in a 350° oven for about 30 minutes or until done.

VARIATION

In step 3 substitute 1 c. triticale flour for 1 c. whole wheat flour.

1⅝ c. whole wheat flour + ¼ c. soy flour + ¼ c. sesame
seeds = 28.5 g.
½ c. sunflower seeds + about 2 T. milk powder = 12.5 g.
2⅔ T. milk powder + 1 c. whole wheat flour = 14 g.
1 egg = 6 g.
*Total = 61 g. usable protein

QUICK BREADS

Quick breads are more like extra rich cakes than regular yeast breads. Because they are made without active yeast there is no rising time involved, hence the name "quick breads." Rising in quick breads results from chemical activity from baking soda or baking powder. For most healthful results please use a baking powder (such as Rumford brand) which is double acting and aluminum free.

Quick breads and rolls make delicious additions to lunches or dinners when you've run out of yeast bread. Sometimes you may want fresh from the oven bread for dinner and are too hungry to wait for yeast bread to rise. The sweet loaves and coffeecakes can also be used as a central food for breakfast, a pleasant afternoon tea, or evening coffee hour.

Quick Wheat-Soy Bread

1 loaf

¼ c. oil	*½ c. soy flour
¼ c. honey	*2 c. whole wheat flour
*1 egg	½ t. salt
*1 c. milk	1 T. baking powder

1. Beat together the oil and honey. Beat in the egg and the milk.

2. In a separate bowl stir together all the dry ingredients. Blend the dry ingredients into the wet ones.

3. Turn the mixture into a greased and floured loaf pan and bake at 350° for about 45 minutes, or until a toothpick inserted in the center of the loaf comes out clean.

2 c. whole wheat flour + ½ c. soy flour = 32 g.
1 c. milk = 7 g.
1 egg = 6 g.
*Total = 45 g. usable protein

Basic Baking Soda Muffins or Shortcake

12 muffins

Great spread with butter or as dessert with fruit topping.

¼ c. butter
¼ c. honey
*1 egg
*1 c. yogurt or buttermilk

2 t. baking soda
1 t. baking powder
*¼ c. soy flour
*1½ c. whole wheat flour

1. Cream together the butter and honey. Beat in the egg and yogurt or buttermilk.
2. Beat in all the dry ingredients.
3. Pour into well-oiled muffin tins, filling each cup about ⅔ full.
4. Bake at 350° for 20 minutes or until lightly browned and a toothpick inserted in the center of a muffin comes out clean.

¼ c. soy flour + 1 c. whole wheat flour = 16 g.
¼ c. yogurt + ½ c. whole wheat flour = 7 g.
¾ c. yogurt = 6 g.
1 egg = 6 g.
*Total = 35 g. usable protein

Cornmeal Muffins

16 muffins

¼ c. oil
2 T. honey (or more)
*2 eggs
*1 c. milk
*1 c. cornmeal
*⅓ c. soy flour

*1 c. whole wheat flour
*⅓ c. instant milk powder
(¼ c. non-instant)
2 t. baking powder
½ t. salt

1. Cream the oil and honey together. Beat in the eggs and then the milk.

2. In a separate bowl stir together all of the dry ingredients. Stir the dry ingredients into the liquid ones, stirring just until all the dry ingredients are moistened.

3. Pour the mixture into well-oiled muffin tins, filling each cup about ⅔ full.

4. Bake in a 375⁰ oven for 20 minutes or until a toothpick inserted in the center of a muffin comes out clean.

VARIATION

Cornbread: Pour the batter into a well-oiled 8″ x 10″ or 9″ x 9″ baking pan. Bake at 350⁰ for 30 minutes or until the bread tests done with a toothpick.

1 c. cornmeal + ⅓ c. soy flour + 1 c. milk = 20 g.
1 c. whole wheat flour + 2⅔ T. milk powder = 14 g.
2⅔ T. milk powder = 3.5 g.
2 eggs = 12 g.
*Total = 49.5 g. usable protein

Bran Muffins

12 muffins

Easy, light muffins. Yummy, and high in fiber too.

*1 egg	½ t. salt
*1 c. milk	2 t. baking powder
¼ c. oil	½ c. miller's bran
¼ c. honey	*1 c. whole wheat flour

1. Beat the egg and beat the milk into it. Beat in the honey and oil.
2. Add all the other ingredients and stir them into the liquid.
3. Pour the batter into well-oiled muffin tins, filling each cup about ⅔ full.
4. Bake in a 350⁰ oven for 20 minutes or until the muffins test done with the toothpick test.

VARIATION

Triticale Muffins: Substitute ½ c. triticale flour for the bran and increase baking time by about 5 minutes if necessary. This may add an extra gram or two of usable protein.

½ c. milk + 1 c. whole wheat flour = 14 g.
½ c. milk = 3.5 g.
1 egg = 6 g.
½ c. bran = 4 g.
*Total = 27.5 g. usable protein

Apple Muffins

12 muffins

Not highly recommended for dieters — it's too easy to sit down and polish off the whole dozen by yourself! Spicey, moist, and delicious.

*1 egg	½ t. cinnamon
2 T. oil	¼ t. salt
2 T. honey	*¼ c. soy flour
*¾ c. buttermilk	*1 c. whole wheat flour
½ t. baking soda	1 med. apple, peeled and
1 t. baking powder	diced (½-⅔ c.)

1. Beat the egg, then one at a time beat in the oil, honey, and buttermilk.

2. In a separate bowl stir together the dry ingredients. Stir them into the egg mixture, stirring just enough to moisten the dry ingredients. Finally, fold in the raw apple pieces.

3. Spoon the batter into a well-oiled muffin tin, filling each cup about ⅔ full.

4. Bake in a 400⁰ oven for 18-20 minutes, or until the muffins test done with the toothpick test. Serve hot, or allow to cool before serving.

VARIATION

Pear Muffins: Substitute a raw pear for the apple and use coriander instead of cinnamon.

1 egg = 6 g.
1 c. whole wheat flour + ¼ c. soy flour = 16 g.
¾ c. buttermilk = 6 g.
*Total = 28 g. usable protein

Orange Sunflower Muffins

12 muffins

¼ c. butter	½ t. salt
½ c. honey	2 t. baking powder
*1 egg	*1⅔ c. whole wheat flour
½ c. orange juice	*¼ c. soy flour
1 T. grated orange rind	*⅓ c. instant milk powder
(rind of one orange)	(¼ c. non-instant)
¼ t. ground coriander	*⅓ c. sunflower seeds

1. Cream together the butter and honey. Beat in the egg. Add the orange juice, orange rind, coriander, salt, and baking powder. Stir well.

2. In a separate bowl stir together all the remaining dry ingredients. Blend the dry ingredients into the wet ones using as few strokes as possible. The batter will be fairly stiff.

3. Spoon the batter into well-oiled muffin tins, pressing the batter into the cups and filling the cups nearly full.

4. Bake in a 375⁰ oven for 12-15 minutes or until a toothpick inserted in the center of a muffin comes out clean.

1 c. whole wheat flour + ¼ c. soy flour = 16 g.
⅔ c. whole wheat flour + 5⅓ t. milk powder = 9⅓ g.
⅓ c. sunflower seeds + 2 T. milk powder = 6 g.
4⅔ t. milk powder = 2 g.
1 egg = 6 g.
*Total = 39⅓ g. usable protein

COFFEECAKES

Coffeecake is so delicious for breakfast. Mix it up the night before for a no preparation breakfast in the morning. The coffeecake recipes also make delicious quick desserts or evening snacks; if guests drop in unexpectedly you can throw one together in about 45 minutes from the cracking of the first egg to removing the finished cake from the oven.

Sesame Spice Coffeecake

9" x 9" cake

¼ c. oil
¼ c. honey
*2 eggs
*⅓ c. sesame seeds
1 t. ground coriander
1 t. cinnamon
½ t. nutmeg
*1 c. yogurt or buttermilk

*¼ c. soy flour
*⅓ c. instant milk powder
   (¼ c. non-instant)
*2 c. whole wheat flour
1 t. baking soda
1 t. baking powder
½ t. salt
¼-½ c. raisins

ICING:
*⅓ c. milk powder
1-2 T. honey

liquid milk

1. Cream together the oil and honey. Beat in the eggs, then the sesame seeds, spices, and yogurt or buttermilk.

2. In a separate bowl stir together all the other ingredients, mixing them thoroughly. Add these dry ingredients to the wet ingredients; stir only until all the ingredients are *just* blended.

3. Turn the mixture into a greased and floured baking pan. Bake at 325⁰ for 30 minutes, or until it tests done with the toothpick test.

4. To make icing combine milk powder, honey, and enough milk to make a thin icing. Add the liquid a drop at a time until you get the right consistency. When the cake is cool drizzle the icing over the cake.

1 c. whole wheat flour + ¼ c. soy flour = 16 g.
1 c. whole wheat flour + ½ c. yogurt = 14 g.
⅓ c. sesame seeds + ¼ c. yogurt = 7 g.
¼ c. yogurt = 2 g.
2 eggs = 12 g.
⅓ c. milk powder = 7 g.
*Total = 58 g. usable protein
If iced, add 7-8 g. for the milk and milk powder in the icing.

Sunflower Topped Coffeecake

9" x 9" cake

CAKE:

¼ c. oil	*⅓ c. instant milk powder
¼-¾ c. honey	(¼ c. non-instant)
*2 eggs	*2 c. whole wheat flour
*1 c. milk	2 t. baking powder
*¼ c. soy flour	½ t. salt
	2 t. ground coriander

TOPPING:

*⅓ c. sunflower seeds	2 T. honey
2 T. butter	1 t. cinnamon

1. Cream together the oil and honey. Beat in the eggs and milk. Set aside.

2. In a separate bowl stir together all the dry ingredients. Set aside.

3. Prepare the topping in a small frying pan. Melt the butter and add the honey and cinnamon. Stir in the sunflower seeds and continue to cook over low heat for a minute or two. Set aside.

4. Add the dry ingredients (from step 2) to the egg and milk mixture (from step 1). Stir just enough to blend and moisten the dry ingredients. Turn into a greased and floured baking pan.

5. Drizzle the sunflower seed topping over the cake. Bake at 325° for 30 minutes or until a toothpick inserted in the center of the cake comes out clean.

1 c. whole wheat flour + ¼ c. soy flour = 16 g.
1 c. whole wheat flour + ½ c. yogurt = 14 g.
⅓ c. sunflower seeds + ¼ c. yogurt = 7 g.
¼ c. yogurt = 2 g.
2 eggs = 12 g.
⅓ c. milk powder = 7 g.
*Total = 58 g. usable protein

Feel free to increase the amount of sunflower seeds in the topping, there is plenty of extra milk to complement them.

Orange Coffeecake

9"x 9" cake

CAKE

¼ c. oil	1 t. vanilla
¼-¾ c. honey	*2 c. whole wheat flour
*2 eggs	*¼ c. soy flour
grated rind of one orange (1 T.)	*⅓ c. instant milk powder (¼ c. non-instant)
*juice of one orange, plus enough milk to make 1 c. liquid	1 t. baking soda
	1 t. baking powder
	½ t. salt

TOPPING:

1 T. butter	1 t. orange rind
1 T. orange juice	1 T. honey

1. Beat together the oil and honey. Beat in the eggs, orange juice, milk, and vanilla.

2. In a separate bowl stir together the dry ingredients. Stir the dry ingredients into the wet ones with as few strokes as possible. Pour the mixture into a greased and floured baking pan.

3. Prepare the topping by melting 1 T. butter in a small pan, adding the honey, orange juice, and rind, and heating until the mixture is runny. Drizzle topping over the unbaked cake.

4. Bake at 325⁰ for 30 minutes or until done.

¼ c. soy flour + 1 c. whole wheat flour = 16 g.
1 c. whole wheat flour + 2⅔ T. milk powder = 14 g.
2⅔ T. milk powder = 4 g.
⅔-¾ c. milk = 5-6 g.
2 eggs = 12 g.
*Total = 51-52 g. usable protein

SWEET LOAVES

These are all rich and delicious, especially when spread with creamy butter, ricotta, or cream cheese.

Pumpkin Bread

1 loaf

⅓ c. oil
⅔ c. honey
*2 eggs
1 c. puréed pumpkin
  or winter squash
½ t. each nutmeg
  and cinnamon
¼ t. each cloves and salt

grated fresh ginger,
  up to 1 t.
*½ c. instant milk powder
  (6 T. non-instant)
*2 c. whole wheat flour
1 T. baking powder
¾-1 c. raisins

1. Cream together the oil and honey. Add eggs, pumpkin, and fresh ginger and beat until fluffy.

2. In a separate bowl stir together the dry ingredients, except for the raisins. Stir the dry ingredients into the wet ones. Add the raisins.

3. Turn the mixture into a greased and floured 9x5x3 in. loaf pan. Bake in a 325⁰ oven for 1 hour, or until the loaf tests done with a toothpick.

VARIATION

Add ½-1 c. chopped nuts to the recipe.

2 c. whole wheat flour + ⅓ c. milk powder = 28 g.
2⅔ T. milk powder = 3.5 g.
2 eggs = 12 g.
*Total = 43.5 g. usable protein

Zucchini Bread

9x5x3 in. loaf

In the summer when you or your gardening friends find your-
selves inundated with zucchinis you'll appreciate this tasty
way to use them up.

¼ c. oil
½ c. honey
*2 eggs
1 medium zucchini or
    yellow squash, grated,
    about 1¼ cups
*½ c. instant milk powder
    (6 T. non-instant)

*½ c. sunflower seeds
*2 c. whole wheat flour
1 t. ground coriander
½ t. cinnamon
¼ t. nutmeg
1 t. vanilla
1 T. baking powder

1. Cream the oil and honey together. Beat in the eggs and the
   grated squash.

2. In a separate bowl stir together the milk powder and whole
   wheat flour. Stir the flour mixture and all the other ingredients into the liquid mixture. Turn the batter into an oiled
   and floured loaf pan.

3. Bake the loaf in a 350⁰ oven for 50 minutes or until the loaf
   tests done with a toothpick. If necessary reduce the oven
   heat to 325⁰ near the end of the baking time if the top of the
   loaf gets too brown before the loaf is done inside.

2 eggs = 12 g.
2 c. whole wheat flour + ⅓ c. instant milk powder = 28 g.
½ c. sunflower seeds + about 2 T. milk powder = 12.5 g.
*Total = 52.5 g. usable protein

Banana Bread

9x5x3 in. loaf

The riper your bananas, the sweeter this loaf will be.

*⅓ c. instant milk powder
   (¼ c. non-instant)
*¼ c. soy flour
*2 c. whole wheat flour
1 T. baking powder
½ t. salt
½ t. ground coriander

¼ c. oil
¾ c. honey
1 c. mashed banana
   (3 small bananas)
*3 eggs
2 t. vanilla
*¼ c. milk

1. In one bowl stir together all the dry ingredients.

2. In a separate bowl beat together the oil and honey. Beat in the eggs, banana, vanilla, and milk.

3. Stir the dry mixture into the wet mixture, stirring until well blended.

4. Pour the mixture into an oiled and floured loaf pan and bake in a 325⁰ oven for one hour or until the loaf tests done with the toothpick test.

5. Cool the baked loaf for a few minutes before removing it from the loaf pan. Serve warm or cool completely before serving.

1 c. whole wheat flour + ¼ c. soy flour = 16 g.
1 c. whole wheat flour + 2⅔ T. milk powder = 14 g.
2⅔ T. milk powder = 3.5 g.
¼ c. milk = 2 g.
3 eggs = 18 g.
*Total =53.5 g. usable protein

Raisin-Nut Bread

9x5x3 in. loaf

Luscious bread, packed with protein.

¼ c. oil	¼ t. coriander
¼ c. honey	1 T. baking powder
*3 eggs	1 t. vanilla
*1 c. milk	*3 c. whole wheat flour
*⅔ c. instant milk powder	*1 c. chopped nuts
(½ c. non-instant)	(walnuts or a
1 t. salt	combination)
	½ c. raisins

1. Cream the oil and honey together. Beat in the eggs and milk. Stir in the vanilla.

2. In a separate bowl stir together all the other ingredients except the nuts and raisins. Stir these dry ingredients into the wet ones until all the dry ingredients are moistened. Fold in the chopped nuts and raisins.

3. Turn the batter into an oiled and floured loaf pan. Bake the loaf in a 350⁰ oven for one hour or until it tests done with a toothpick.

VARIATION

Substitute chopped dates, dried apricots, apples, figs, pineapple, etc. for the raisins.

3 eggs = 18 g.
1 c. milk = 7 g.
3 c. whole wheat flour + ½ c. milk powder = 42 g.
2⅔ T. milk powder = 4 g.
*Total = 71 g. usable protein
Plus protein from the chopped nuts.

Carob Fruit and Nut Bread

1 high 9x5x3 in. loaf

The different fruit flavors in this go amazingly well with the carob flavor. The thought of fruit with "chocolate" flavor worried me before I tasted it, but it really works!

*¼ c. soy grits	1 t. baking soda
1 c. orange juice	1 t. baking powder
¼ c. oil	½ t. salt
½ c. honey	1 t. vanilla
*2 eggs	*1 c. chopped nuts
*2 c. whole wheat flour	½ c. chopped, pitted dates
⅓ c. carob powder	½ c. chopped, dried apricots

1. Pour the orange juice over the soy grits and let the mixture sit for a few minutes until the soy grits soften. Beat in the honey and oil, and finally the eggs.

2. In a separate bowl stir together the whole wheat flour, carob powder, baking soda, baking powder, and salt. Blend this dry mixture into the moist ingredients.

3. Blend in the vanilla, chopped nuts, and dried fruit.

4. Pour the batter into a greased and floured loaf pan and bake the loaf in a 325° oven for about 1¼ hours, or until the loaf tests done with the toothpick test. Let the loaf cool at least slightly before slicing and serving.

¼ c. soy grits + 2 c. whole wheat flour = 32 g.
2 eggs = 12 g.
*Total = 44 g. usable protein
Plus protein from the chopped nuts.

Pineapple-Raisin Nut Bread
1 medium sized loaf

Chunks of dried pineapple make for a delicious taste difference in this loaf.

¼ c. oil
½ c. honey
*1 egg
*½ c. buttermilk
*⅓ c. instant milk powder
   (¼ c. non-instant)
*1½ c. whole wheat flour
1 t. baking soda

1 t. baking powder
½ t. salt
2 t. vanilla
½ t. coriander
½ c. dried pineapple,
   chopped
½ c. raisins
*¾ c. chopped nuts

1. Beat the oil and honey together until they are smooth. Beat in the egg, then the buttermilk.

2. In a separate bowl stir together the milk powder, whole wheat flour, baking soda, baking powder, and salt. Blend this dry mixture into the moist ingredients.

3. Stir in the vanilla and coriander, and finally the chopped nuts and dried fruit.

4. Turn the mixture into a greased and floured loaf pan and bake the loaf in 325⁰ oven for one hour or until it tests done with a toothpick. Let cool slightly before slicing and serving.

1½ c. whole wheat flour + ¼ c. instant milk powder = 21 g.
1⅓ T. instant milk powder = 2 g.
½ c. buttermilk = 3.5 g.
1 egg = 6 g.
*Total = 32.5 g. usable protein
Plus protein from the nuts.

DESSERTS

Desserts need not be sugar-filled, empty caloried extravaganzas which fill you up, fatten you up, and generally lower the quality of your health. Desserts based on fresh fruits, dairy products, honey, and whole grains can satisfy your sweet tooth while providing a nutritional boost to your daily diet.

Many of the dessert recipes are high in usable protein. Others are lower in protein but are good sources of vitamins and minerals. In any dessert recipe where any protein occurs I have tried to make sure that it is complemented, high quality protein, even if very little is present in each serving.

The dessert recipes range from very simple to rather complex. For a simple, but delicious, dessert serve fruit and cheese, the way the Europeans do. And nothing tastes better for dessert than a bowl of fresh fruit, sweetened with honey, and topped with a dollup of whipped cream, fresh yogurt, or a little sweet milk.

Hard as it may be for even *you* to believe, if you've used wholesome ingredients, those goodies that taste so sinfully yummy are actually good for you!

Baked Apples
1 serving

Adjust this recipe to suit the size and number of servings you want. Some people like a one apple serving, some a two apple serving, so make as many as you want.

1 apple, cored but
  unpeeled
¼ t. butter
1-2 t. raisins

dash nutmeg
⅛ t. cinnamon
1-3 t. honey

1. Leave the apples whole and cut out the core and any bad spots.
2. Set the apples in a well-greased baking dish. Fill the core holes with the butter, followed by the raisins, the spices, and finally the honey.
3. Bake in a 350⁰-400⁰ oven for 30 minutes to 1 hour, or until the apples are tender.

Fruit Soup
2½ cups

This is a very basic recipe for an easy dessert. Feel free to vary it with whatever dried or fresh fruits you may have around.

*¼ c. chopped nuts
¼ c. raisins
1 slice dried pineapple,
  diced
4 dried apricots, diced
4 dried prunes, pitted
  and diced

¼ c. diced dried apple
1-3 t. honey
2 c. water
1-2 whole cloves
1-3 t. cornstarch

1. In a saucepan combine the nuts, fruit, honey to suit your sweet tooth, cloves, and 1½ c. water. Over medium heat bring the mixture to a slow boil and simmer until the fruits are softened.

2. Dissolve the cornstarch (use more or less depending on how thick you want the soup) in ½ cup of water. Slowly stir the cornstarch into the hot soup and continue to cook until the mixture thickens.

3. Keep the soup warm over a very low flame and serve it hot, or allow it to cool and then serve it.

Baked Fruit Delight

2 cups

This should serve 4, but it tastes so good it may only serve 2, or even 1. Easy too.

2 apples, peeled, cored, and sliced	**2 t. cornstarch**
¼ c. dried apricots, diced	**1 c. orange juice**
¼ c. raisins	**2 T. honey**

1. Gently combine the apples, apricots, and raisins, mixing them together thoroughly. Pour the honey over the fruit mixture.

2. Dissolve the cornstarch in the orange juice. Pour the orange juice solution over the fruit and honey and stir gently to distribute the juice and honey throughout the fruit.

3. Pour the mixture into a well-oiled 1 quart baking dish and bake in a 350⁰ oven for 45 minutes. Let cool slightly before serving.

Grandma's Rice Pudding

4 servings

*¼ c. raw brown rice
¼ t. salt
3 T. honey
¼ t. cinnamon
dash nutmeg
¼ t. vanilla

*⅓ c. instant milk powder
   (¼ c. non-instant)
1 c. water
*1 c. milk
*1 egg

1. Combine all the ingredients except the milk, milk powder, and egg. Bring to a boil, cover, reduce heat, and simmer for 1 hour.

2. In the top of a double boiler beat the milk, milk powder, and egg together. Gradually stir the hot mixture (from step 1) into the egg and milk. Pour very slowly so the egg does not curdle.

3. Cook in the top of a double boiler, over, not in, simmering water for 1 hour or until set.

¼ c. rice + ⅓ c. milk = 5⅔ g.
⅓ c. milk powder = 7 g.
⅔ milk = 5 g.
1 egg = 6 g.
*Total = 23⅔ g. usable protein

Tapioca Pudding

4-5 servings

*2 eggs
*⅓ c. instant milk powder
   (¼ c. non-instant)
*2 c. milk

3 T. quick cooking tapioca
3-4 T. honey
¼ t. salt
½-1 t. vanilla

1. In the top of a double boiler beat together all the ingredients.

2. Cook the mixture over, not in, rapidly boiling water for 7 minutes without stirring.

3. Stirring constantly, continue cooking over rapidly boiling water for another 5 minutes.

4. Remove the cooked pudding from the heat, pour it into individual dishes if you wish, and cool or chill. Serve still warm or well chilled.

2 eggs = 12 g.
⅓ c. milk powder = 7 g.
2 cups milk = 14 g.
*Total = 33 g. usable protein

Baked Custard

4-5 servings

This is an easy dessert to prepare beforehand and serve at your leisure. Keep leftovers in the refrigerator for tomorrow's dessert.

*2 eggs	**¼ t. salt**
*2 c. milk	**½ t. vanilla**
¼ c. honey	

1. Beat the eggs, and then beat in all the other ingredients. Pour the mixture into a well-oiled casserole or individual custard cups.

2. Place the casserole or custard cups in a pan containing about one inch of hot water. Bake in a 300⁰ oven for 1-1½ hours (a little less for custard cups) until a knife inserted in the center of the custard comes out clean.

3. Serve hot or refrigerate until well chilled.

VARIATIONS

You can use any of the custard-type pie fillings to make a similar dessert. Just mix the filling according to the pie recipe, pour it into a well-oiled baking dish or custard cups, and bake as directed above.

2 eggs = 12 g.
2 c. milk = 14 g.
*Total = 26 g. usable protein

Fruit Freeze

2½ cups

This tastes like fresh, homemade ice cream, but is much easier and better for you than regular ice cream. Use your favorite ice cream fruit flavors, or try vanilla, carob, or instant coffee for flavoring. One warning — this is *very* cold, but it also melts very quickly; so don't waste any time between serving and eating.

1 c. sliced fruit	***yogurt for blending**
***1 c. yogurt**	**(up to ½ c.)**
1-2 T. honey	**ice cubes (optional)**

1. Put 1 c. of yogurt, the fruit, and the honey into the blender and process until smooth. Pour into an ice cube tray and freeze until solid (2-24 hours).

2. When you're ready to serve dessert put a tablespoon or two of yogurt, and a few ice cubes into your blender. Begin processing on a low speed, adding frozen yogurt cubes one at a time. Continue adding cubes until you have the amount of fruit freeze you want, adding a little plain yogurt if the mixture becomes too thick to blend. You do want a fairly thick mixture though, so go easy on the extra yogurt.

3. Serve at once. Refreeze any unused yogurt cubes to make more fruit freeze later.

1 c. yogurt = 7-9 g.
few T. yogurt = 1 or more g.
***Total = 8-9 g. usable protein**

FRESH AND EASY DESSERTS

Three easy variations on a theme. Perfect healthful, hot weather desserts. Adjust the amounts to suit your appetite and the number of people you are feeding.

Yogurt Parfait

fresh fruit, washed   **lemon juice**
  and sliced   ***yogurt**
honey

1. Pour a little honey and a few drops of lemon juice over the fruit. Let the mixture sit, stirring occasionally, until a syrup forms.
2. Stir a little honey into the plain yogurt if you like.
3. In parfait glasses layer the fruit and syrup with the yogurt, making each layer thick enough for contrast and appeal.
4. Top with whipped cream and one piece of fresh fruit.

*4-8 g. usable protein per serving

Yogurt Sundae

1. Follow steps 1 and 2 in the directions for Yogurt Parfait.
2. Put a heap of yogurt in a bowl or sundae glass and top with fruit syrup. Add whipped cream if you like.

*4-8 g. usable protein per serving

Boston Cooler

1 serving

slices of cantalope   **honey**
***½ c. yogurt**   **fresh blueberries**

1. Scoop the seeds out of the cantalope.
2. Put a scoop of yogurt on the cantalope, drizzle honey over top, and sprinkle blueberries over all.

*½ c. yogurt = 4 g. usable protein

PIES AND PIE DOUGHS

For me, making pie crusts has always been a bit of a hassle. I don't have a natural knack for pies, so I've had to do a lot of learning along the way — learning which I will pass on to you. As with yeast breads, the best way to learn to make good pie crust is with an experienced friend at your side. If you can't press anyone into service just be very watchful in combining ingredients and rolling the dough and you should do just fine on your own.

When you make a pie crust, the less water you use, the flakier the finished crust will be. Of course, if you don't use enough water the crust will fall apart when you put it in the pie plate. If your crust does fall apart you can "glue" it back together with water and your fingertips.

To roll out the pie crust, flour your working surface *very* well. Place a ball of dough on the surface and flatten the ball slightly with your hands. Rub a little flour on your rolling pin and sprinkle flour over the surface of the dough. Start with the rolling pin in the center of the ball of dough and roll toward the edge. Keep rolling from the center to the edges until the crust is about ⅛ inch thick and large enough to cover the pie plate. Fold the pie crust in half, then in half again, so that you have a wedge shape. Place the point of the wedge in the center of the pie plate and unfold the dough so that it covers the whole pie plate. Cut away the excess dough from around the pie plate. If this is to be a single crust pie decorate the rim of the crust by pinching with your fingers or pressing on the edge of the dough with the tines of a fork.

For a two crust pie decorating the edge will come later. Prepare the bottom crust, add the filling, and pat a little water over the rim of the pie crust. Roll out a second crust, fold it, then unfold it over the pie. Cut away excess dough, then press and pinch the two crusts together all the way around the rim of the pan. This also adds the decorative edging. Poke several small holes in the top crust before baking.

To bake a bottom crust by itself for filling later, just prepare it as you normally would. Prick little holes all over the bottom with a fork. Bake the shell in a 400° oven for about 20 minutes, or until it is golden brown. This works well for any pie which you don't want to or can't bake — fill the shell with ice cream, for example, and keep it in the freezer until ready to serve.

Complementary Pie Crust

two 9 in. crusts

½ t. salt
*⅓ c. instant milk powder
  (¼ c. non-instant)
*2 c. whole wheat pastry
  flour

¾ c. butter or shortening
  (or combination of the two)
*1 egg, beaten
6-10 T. icewater

1. Stir together the salt, flour, and milk powder. Cut in the butter or shortening with a pastry blender or two knives. Continue cutting in until the mixture has the consistency of cornmeal.

2. Add the beaten egg and use a fork to toss the flour mixture with the egg (toss as you would a salad). Continue tossing until the egg is well incorporated.

3. Continue tossing while adding water, 1 tablespoonful at a time. Use only enough water to get the dough to hold together.

4. Divide the dough in 2 parts and roll out each part for one pie crust.

2 c. whole wheat flour + ⅓ c. milk powder = 28 g.
1 egg = 6 g.
*Total = 34 g. usable protein

Wheat-Soy Pie Crust

1 crust

*1 c. whole wheat pastry flour	¼ t. salt
	6 T. butter
*¼ c. soy flour	6-7 T. ice water

1. Stir together the flours and salt. Cut in the butter until the mixture has the consistency of cornmeal.
2. Toss the dough with a fork while you add water a little at a time. Add just enough water to get the dough to hold together.
3. Roll the dough out to make one pie crust.

*1 c. whole wheat pastry flour + ¼ c. soy flour = 16 g. usable protein

Sweet and Crumbly Crust

1 crust

You can use this whenever a graham cracker crust is called for. Vary the amount of honey to suit your own sweet tooth.

*1 c. whole wheat pastry flour	¼ t. salt
	1-2 T. honey
*2⅔ T. instant milk powder (2 T. non-instant)	¼ c. oil
	2-3 T. water

1. Stir together the flour, milk powder, and salt. Drizzle the honey and the oil over top and mix it in using a fork and a tossing motion.
2. Add the water a little at a time, tossing the mixture with a fork, until the mixture begins to hold together.
3. Use your fingers or the back of a spoon to press the mixture into a pie plate. Fill the crust with your favorite filling.

*1 c. whole wheat pastry flour + 2⅔ T. milk powder = 14 g. usable protein

Pastry Tarts

When you make a pie there is always some leftover pastry. Use this recipe to use up the leftovers.

scraps from pie crust recipe
raisins or other dried
fruit

honey
cinnamon and/or other
spices to taste

1. Roll out the pastry, then cut it into 3 inch circles using a drinking glass or cookie cutter.
2. On each circle place 4 or 5 raisins, ¼ t. or less of honey, and a dash of cinnamon. Fold the circle in half, enclosing the raisins, and press the edges together using the tines of a fork.
3. Place the tarts on an ungreased baking sheet and bake at 350⁰ for 15 minutes.

Easy Fruit Pies

1 pie

*2 whole wheat pie
crusts, unbaked
peeled and chopped
fresh fruit

¼-¾ c. honey
dash salt and sweet
spices

1. Prepare the bottom crust and fill it with the fresh fruit. Sprinkle seasonings over the fruit and then drizzle honey over all.
2. Prepare the top crust and place it on top of the pie. Pinch the two crusts together all the way around the pie. Prick lots of holes in the top crust and bake the pie in a 350⁰ oven for 30-40 minutes or until the crust is golden brown.

VARIATION

For a thicker filling mix 2 T. cornstarch into the honey before drizzling it over the fruit. Bake as above.

*2 whole wheat pie crusts = 32-34 g. usable protein

Pumpkin Pie

two 9 inch pies

Feel free to halve this recipe. Pumpkin pie never lasts long enough in our house to make baking one pie worth the trouble. It's really no harder to make two.

*2 Complementary Pie Crusts, unbaked	¼ t. ground cloves 1 t. salt
*4 eggs	*1 c. instant milk powder
3 c. puréed pumpkin or winter squash	(¾ c. non-instant)
	*3 c. milk
2 t. cinnamon	1-1½ c. honey
½ t. nutmeg	

1. In a large bowl, beat the eggs. Gradually beat in all the other ingredients in the order in which they are listed.

2. Pour the filling into the two pie crusts.

3. Bake at 400⁰ for 15 minutes. Reduce the heat to 350⁰ and continue baking for another 45 minutes, or until a knife inserted in the center of the pie comes out clean.

2 Complementary Pie Crusts = 34 g.
4 eggs = 24 g.
1 c. milk powder = 21 g.
3 c. milk = 21 g.
*Total = 100 g. usable protein

Buttermilk Pie

1 pie

In spite of the fact that it's full of things that are good for him, my dessert loving grandfather was crazy about this pie.

*1 whole wheat pie crust, unbaked	1 t. grated lemon rind ½ t. vanilla
*3 eggs	¼ t. salt
*2 c. buttermilk	½ c. honey
2 T. lemon juice	

1. Beat the eggs thoroughly. Beat all the other ingredients, in the order in which they are listed, into the eggs. Pour the filling into the unbaked pie crust.

2. Bake the pie at 350° for 1 hour, or until a knife inserted in the center of the pie comes out clean.

3. Allow the pie to cool slightly before serving.

1 whole wheat pie crust = 17 g.
3 eggs = 18 g.
2 c. buttermilk = 14 g.
***Total = 49 g. usable protein**

Frozen Yogurt Pie

1 pie

*1 whole wheat pie
  crust, baked
*2 c. yogurt
1 c. fruit or fruit juice

¼ c. honey (or more
if your fruit is
very tart)

1. In the blender buzz together the yogurt, fruit, and honey. Pour the mixture into an ice cube tray and freeze until solid.

2. Put the yogurt cubes into the blender and process again for about 5 minutes. Pour the mixture back into the ice cube tray and freeze again.

3. Repeat step 2.

4. Repeat step 2 again, only this time pour the processed mixture into the baked, cooled pie shell. Freeze until solid and serve.

VARIATION

Make the filling as directed but don't bother with the pie shell. Serve the frozen yogurt as you would ice cream.

1 whole wheat pie crust = 16 g.
2 c. yogurt = 16 g.
***Total = 32 g. usable protein**

Carob Cream Pie

1 pie

A three-year-old I know told me that her mommy was going to make a carob pie. I think mommy really intended to make a carob cake, but a pie sounded as though it might work out really well, as you can see it did.

*1 whole wheat pie
  crust, unbaked
½ c. carob powder
½ c. honey
*2 eggs
*2 c. milk

*1 c. instant milk powder
  (¾ c. non-instant)
1 t. coriander
½ t. cinnamon
¼ t. nutmeg

1. Stir the carob powder into the honey and heat them over low heat until the carob powder dissolves completely.

2. In a bowl beat the eggs. Beat in all the other ingredients in the order listed. Finally beat in the carob-honey mixture, pouring slowly while beating constantly.

3. Pour the mixture into an unbaked pie shell and bake at 350° for 45 minutes, or until a knife blade inserted in the center of the pie comes out clean. Let cool slightly before serving.

1 whole wheat pie crust = 17 g.
2 eggs = 12 g.
2 c. milk = 14 g.
1 c. milk powder = 21 g.
*Total = 64 g. usable protein

Cheesecake

1 cake

This cheesecake has all the rich flavor of regular cheesecake, but far fewer calories and far more protein than cheesecake made with cream cheese. It's most easily made in a blender, but you can use an electric mixer or a wire whisk and lots of elbow grease if necessary.

*1 Sweet and Crumbly
　Crust
*1 c. creamed cottage
　cheese
*1 c. ricotta cheese
*1 c. milk
　½ c. honey

grated rind of one
　lemon (about 1 t.)
juice of one lemon
　(about 2 T.)
½ t. vanilla
¼ t. salt
2 large eggs

1. Put the cottage cheese in the blender and process until the cheese is smooth, or beat until it is smooth. Add the ricotta cheese and the milk. Process again.

2. Add the honey, lemon rind and juice, vanilla, and salt, and process again. Finally add the eggs and process until the eggs are well beaten into the mixture.

3. Pour the mixture into the pie crust shell and bake the cake in a 350⁰ oven for 1¼ hours, or until a knife inserted in the center of the cake comes out clean.

4. Refrigerate until well chilled.

1 c. cottage cheese = 28 g.
1 c. ricotta cheese = 21 g.
1 c. milk = 7 g.
2 eggs = 12 g.
1 Sweet and Crumbly Crust = 14 g.
*Total = 82 g. usable protein

Fruit Cobbler
2-6 servings

If you have a sweet tooth this yummy dessert should satisfy it; it has all the taste of a fruit pie with practically none of the work. Use whatever fruits are in season, even "apple drops" (those found on the ground) and just cut away any bad parts.

1 qt. fresh fruit, washed and sliced	*½ c. rolled oats
2 T. or more honey	*¼ c. soy flour
½ t. ground coriander	1 t. baking powder
1 t. cornstarch	¼ t. salt
1-2 T. water	¼ c. butter
*½ c. whole wheat flour	¼ c. honey

1. Prepare the fruit by sprinkling it with the coriander and 2 T. honey. Stir. Dissolve the cornstarch in a little cold water and stir this into the fruit mixture. Pour the fruit mixture into a well-oiled 9x9 in. baking pan.

2. To prepare the topping stir together all the remaining dry ingredients. Melt the butter in a saucepan. Stir the honey into the warm butter and continue to heat for just a minute or two longer, until the mixture is very runny. Stir the butter and honey into the dry ingredients until they are well moistened.

3. Drop the topping by teaspoonsful over top of the fruit mixture in the baking pan, until the fruit is fairly well dotted with topping. The topping will run together as it bakes. It isn't necessary to try to make a solid topping.

4. Bake the cobbler in a 325⁰ oven for 30 minutes. Serve while still warm with milk, ice cream, or yogurt.

Note: If you don't have much of a sweet tooth reduce the amount of honey and coriander you use in the fruit mixture. Feel free to add other touches of your own. Lemon juice or rind is good with blueberry filling; apples taste best with a sprinkling of cinnamon and nutmeg and a dash of cloves.

*½ c. whole wheat flour + ½ c. oatmeal + ¼ c. soy flour = 16 g. usable protein

Fruit Shortcake

1 serving

Use seasonal fresh fruits or your own home-frozen fruit for this yummy dessert. Double, quadruple, or whatever, to suit the number of people you plan to serve.

1 muffin (Basic Baking Soda Muffin or Shortcake) ¼-½ c. sliced fruit	honey to taste sprinkling of coriander (optional)

1. Prepare the fruit by sprinkling a little ground coriander over it and pouring honey over top. Stir the mixture. Allow it to sit, stirring occasionally, until the fruit produces juice. Check the sweetness and add more honey if you wish.

2. Assemble the dessert by breaking the shortcake in half and spooning the fruit and honey mixture over top. Serve plain or add milk, yogurt, ice cream, or whipped cream.

The total amount of protein will depend upon how you eat the dessert. The muffin provides at least 2 grams of usable protein. Milk, yogurt, or even ice cream will add more protein.

CAKE AND FROSTING

"Cake and Coffee" is always a good dessert for family, or if friends drop in. A piece of cake can also go into a brown bag lunch to be eaten wherever you wish. The cakes and frostings can be interchanged in other ways, and don't forget that the coffeecake recipes make good dessert cakes too. You can even frost them with one of the frostings listed here if you like.

All of the frosting recipes make enough to frost the top of the cake comfortably. If you want to remove the cake from the pan and frost the sides too, you should probably double the frosting recipe unless you're an absolute whiz at spreading frosting thinly, something which I definitely am not! With all the frosting recipes, feel free to add extra milk powder if they aren't thick enough for you.

Fruit and Nut Cake

1 small cake

A super rich dessert. Have it hot from the oven, either plain, spread with butter, or topped with whipped cream.

*1 egg
*½ c. buttermilk
*1 c. whole wheat flour
1 t. baking soda
¼ c. honey
1-2 T. oil

*½ c. mixed, chopped
  nuts and seeds
1 dried fig, finely chopped
1 slice dried pineapple,
  finely chopped
½ c. raisins
up to ¼ t. coriander

1. Beat the egg and beat in the buttermilk. Add the flour, baking soda, honey, and oil and mix thoroughly.

2. Fold in the chopped nuts and seeds, dried fruit, and coriander.

3. Pour the mixture into a well greased 1 quart casserole or baking dish and bake in a 325° oven for 1-1¼ hours, or until the cake tests done with the toothpick test.

4. Let the cake cool for a few minutes before removing it from the casserole. If it sticks to the dish gently loosen it with a knife.

1 egg = 6 g.
½ c. buttermilk + 1 c. whole wheat flour = 14 g.
*Total = 20 g.
Plus protein from the seeds and nuts.

Carob Cake with "Butter Cream" Icing

9" x 9" in. cake

CAKE:

*¼ c. butter
½ c. honey
*2 eggs
*1 c. milk
½ c. carob powder
*⅓ c. instant milk powder
  (¼ c. non-instant)

*2 c. whole wheat flour
½ t. salt
2 t. baking powder
1 t. cinnamon
½ t. allspice
1 t. vanilla

ICING:

2 T. butter, melted
¼ c. honey
*⅓-½ c. milk powder

few drops vanilla
few drops milk

1. Cream together the butter and honey listed in the cake ingredients. Beat in the eggs, milk, and carob powder.

2. In a separate bowl stir together all the dry ingredients. Stir the vanilla and the dry ingredients into the wet ones, using as few strokes as possible.

3. Turn the mixture into a greased and floured baking pan and bake at 350° for 30 minutes or until done (use the toothpick test). Cool and frost with butter cream icing.

4. To make the icing mix together the melted butter, honey, and milk powder. Add vanilla and enough milk to make a spreadable icing. It should be fairly thick. Add extra milk powder if necessary.

2 c. whole wheat flour + ⅓ c. milk powder = 28 g.
1 c. milk = 7 g.
2 eggs = 12 g.
⅓-½ c. milk powder = 7-10 g.
*Total = 54-57 g. usable protein

Vanilla Buttermilk Cake with Carob Frosting

9" x 9" in. cake

CAKE:

*2 eggs	½ t. salt
*1 c. buttermilk	1 t. baking soda
¼-½ c. oil	1 t. baking powder
½ c. honey	*2¼ c. whole wheat flour
*¼ c. soy flour	2 t. vanilla

FROSTING:

¼ c. butter	¼ c. honey
¼ c. carob powder	*½ c. or more milk powder

1. Beat the eggs and thoroughly beat the buttermilk into them. Beat in the oil and then the honey.

2. In a separate bowl stir together all the dry ingredients. Blend the dry ingredients and the vanilla into the egg mixture.

3. Pour the batter into a greased and floured baking pan. Bake in a 350⁰ oven for about 30 minutes or until the cake tests done with a toothpick. (If you've used the larger amount of oil this cake will be moister, but it may take a little longer to bake.)

4. Cool the cake and frost with carob frosting.

5. To make the frosting melt the butter and stir in the carob powder. Continue to heat until the carob is completely dissolved. Stir in the honey and remove from heat.

6. Beat in the milk powder. Use a spatula to spread the frosting over the cake.

2 eggs = 12 g.
¼ c. soy flour + 1 c. whole wheat flour = 16 g.
½ c. buttermilk + 1 c. whole wheat flour = 14 g.
¼ c. whole wheat flour + 1 T. buttermilk = 3.5 g.
3 T. buttermilk = 1.5 g.
½ c. milk powder = 10 g.
*Total = 57 g. usable protein

Lemon Cake with Lemon Butter Cream Frosting

9" x 9" cake

A mildly lemon flavored cake with delicious tart-sweet frosting.

CAKE:

¼ c. oil	½ t. grated lemon peel
½ c. honey	2 t. vanilla
*2 eggs	2 T. lemon juice
*1 c. milk	*⅓ c. instant milk powder
1 T. baking powder	(¼ c. non-instant)
¼ t. salt	*2 c. whole wheat flour
¼ t. coriander	

FROSTING:

¼ c. butter	½ t. vanilla
2-3 T. honey	*⅓-½ c. milk powder
1 T. lemon juice	

1. Cream together the oil and honey. Beat in the eggs, then the milk. Stir in the baking powder and all the seasonings including the lemon juice.

2. In a separate bowl, stir together the milk powder and whole wheat flour. Stir the flour mixture into the liquid mixture. Turn the batter into a greased and floured 9" x 9" in. pan.

3. Bake in a 350⁰ oven for about 35 minutes, or until the cake tests done with the toothpick test. Frost when cool.

4. To make the icing cream together the butter and honey until they are fluffy. Beat in all the other ingredients using enough milk powder to make a thick frosting.

2 eggs = 12 g.
1 c. milk = 7 g.
2 c. whole wheat flour + ⅓ c. milk powder = 28 g.
½ c. milk powder = 10 g.
*Total = 57 g. usable protein

COOKIES

Cookies made from nutritious, natural ingredients make delicious, satisfying snacks or desserts. They are the perfect added touch of sweetness in a bag lunch and a terrific "pick-me-up" with a glass of milk or even a cup of coffee during that late afternoon slump time.

When you bake your own cookies you can control what goes into them. Using wholesome, natural ingredients will allow you to satisfy your sweet tooth with a nourishing snack rather than with a lot of empty calories in overprocessed goodies from the supermarket. You also have the chance to eat a few (or many) fresh and hot from the oven — a real taste treat which no one has yet found a way to package.

For ease in baking, all the cookie recipes are for either bar or drop cookies. Bar cookies are baked in a pan and cut into squares when cooled. To make drop cookies use two spoons, one to scoop up a spoonful of batter, the second to scrape that batter off onto a cookie sheet. Use a spatula or pancake turner to slide the baked cookies off the cookie sheet.

Store cooled, baked cookies in a cookie jar or other airtight container. A wedge of raw apple in the cookie jar will help to keep the cookies soft and fresh.

Old-fashioned Oatmeal Raisin Cookies

3 dozen

½ c. butter	¼ t. salt
½ c. honey	½ t. cinnamon
*1 egg	¼ t. nutmeg
*1 c. whole wheat flour	pinch ground cloves
*⅓ c. instant milk powder	*5 T. milk
(¼ c. non-instant)	*1 c. oatmeal
¼ t. baking soda	½ c. raisins
1 t. baking powder	½ c. chopped nuts (optional)

1. Cream together the butter and honey. Add the egg and beat until fluffy.

2. Stir together the whole wheat flour, milk powder, soda, baking powder, salt, and spices.

3. Alternately add the dry mixture and the milk to the creamed mixture. Stir in the oatmeal, raisins, and nuts.

4. Drop by teaspoonsful several inches apart on an ungreased cookie sheet.

5. Bake 10-12 minutes at 375⁰.

1 c. whole wheat flour + 1 c. oatmeal + ⅓ c. milk powder = 28 g.
1 egg = 6 g.
5 T. milk = 2 g.
*Total = 36 g. usable protein

Carob Cookies

40 cookies

½ c. honey	1 t. vanilla
½ c. butter	1 t. baking powder
½ c. carob powder	¼ t. salt
*1 egg	*½ c. soy flour
*½ c. milk	*2 c. whole wheat flour

1. Cream together the butter and honey. Beat in the carob powder, then the egg and milk.

2. Stir in all the other ingredients. The batter will be fairly stiff.

3. Drop by heaping teaspoonsful on an ungreased baking sheet.

4. Bake at 350⁰ for 10 minutes or until crisp on the surface.

½ c. soy flour + 2 c. whole wheat flour = 32 g.
1 egg = 6 g.
½ c. milk = 3.5 g.
*Total = 41.5 g. usable protein

Grandma's Orange Cookies
4 dozen

COOKIES:

½ c. honey
½ c. butter
*6 T. buttermilk or yogurt
½ t. baking soda
*1 egg

*1¾ c. whole wheat flour
*¼ c. soy flour
¼ t. salt
juice and grated rind
of ½ orange

1. Cream together the honey and butter. Add buttermilk and egg and beat thoroughly.

2. In a separate bowl stir together the dry ingredients. Add them to the wet ingredients, beating thoroughly. Add orange juice and rind and beat again.

3. Drop by teaspoonful on an ungreased baking sheet. Bake for 10-12 minutes at 325^0.

ICING:

*⅓ c. instant milk powder
1 T. honey
1 T. melted butter

grated rind of ½ orange
few t. orange juice

1. Combine the first 4 ingredients. Add enough orange juice to make a spreadable, but rather thick icing.

2. When the cookies are cool, top each one with a dab of icing. Allow the icing to harden before storing the cookies.

1 c. whole wheat flour + ¼ c. soy flour = 16 g.
⅜ c. buttermilk + ¾ c. flour = 10.5 g.
1 egg = 6 g.
⅓ c. milk powder = 7 g.
*Total = 39.5 g. usable protein

Peanut Butter-Sunflower Seed Cookies

40 cookies

*½ c. peanut butter
½ c. honey
1 T. butter
*1 egg
*½ c. milk
2 t. baking powder

¼ t. salt
2 t. vanilla
*2 c. whole wheat flour
*2 T. soy flour
*½ c. sunflower seeds

1. Cream together the peanut butter, butter, and honey. Beat in the egg and the milk.

2. Add the salt, baking powder, and vanilla. Stir in the flours. The mixture will be very stiff.

3. Fold in the sunflower seeds, distributing them through the batter as much as possible.

4. Drop by heaping teaspoonful on an ungreased baking sheet. The cookies don't spread much so you can place them fairly close together.

5. Bake at 350⁰ for 10 minutes or until lightly browned.

¼ c. peanut butter + ½ c. sunflower seeds = 27.5 g.
¼ c. peanut butter + 2 c. whole wheat flour + 2 T. soy flour = 41.5 g.
½ c. milk = 3.5 g.
1 egg = 6 g.
*Total = 78.5 g. usable protein

Familia Cookies

40 cookies

If you use the familia recipe from the breakfast section you'll find that each cookie will have a slightly different taste because of all the different goodies in the familia. You can substitute commerical familia, but you might want to reduce the amount of honey in the recipe slightly.

½ c. butter
½ c. honey
*1 egg
*½ c. milk
1 t. baking powder
½ t. salt

2 t. vanilla
*¼ c. soy flour
*⅓ c. instant milk powder
   (¼ c. non-instant)
*½ c. familia
*1½ c. whole wheat flour

1. Cream together the butter and honey. Beat in the milk and egg, then the baking powder, salt, and vanilla.

2. In a separate bowl stir together the soy flour, milk powder, familia, and whole wheat flour.

3. Stir the dry ingredients into the wet ones. Drop the batter by heaping teaspoonsful onto an ungreased baking sheet.

4. Bake in a 350⁰ oven for 10 minutes or until lightly browned.

1 c. whole wheat flour + ¼ c. soy flour = 16 g.
½ c. whole wheat flour = 1⅓ T. milk powder = 7 g.
4 T. milk powder = 6 g.
1 egg = 6 g.
½ c. milk = 3.5 g.
½ c. familia = 4.5 g.
*Total = 43 g. usable protein

Cowboy Cookies (Chocolate Chip)

4 dozen

I don't know why these are called cowboy cookies, but they are good.

½ c. butter
½ c. honey
*1 egg
*1 c. whole wheat flour
*¼ c. soy flour
*⅓ c. instant milk powder
(¼ c. non-instant)

1 t. baking powder
¼ t. salt
1 t. vanilla
*1 c. rolled oats
*5 T. milk
1½ c. chocolate or
carob chips

1. Cream together the butter and honey. Beat in the egg and beat until the mixture is fluffy.

2. Beat in all the other ingredients in the order listed.

3. Drop the batter by heaping teaspoonsful onto an ungreased baking sheet. Bake at 350⁰ for 12 minutes.

1 c. whole wheat flour + ¼ c. soy flour = 16 g.
1 c. rolled oats + 2⅔ T. milk powder = 14 g.
2⅔ T. milk powder = 4 g.
1 egg = 6 g.
5 T. milk = 2 g.
*Total = 42 g. usable protein

Easy Almond Cookies

5 dozen

Easy to put together and pretty enough for company.

½ c. butter
½ c. honey
*1 egg
*½ c. buttermilk
*⅓ c. instant milk powder
    (¼ c. non-instant)
*2 c. whole wheat flour

¼ t. salt
1 t. baking soda
1½ t. vanilla
½ t. almond extract
    (optional)
whole almonds for topping

1. Cream the butter and honey together until fluffy. Beat in the egg and buttermilk.

2. In a separate bowl stir together the milk powder, whole wheat flour, salt, and baking soda. Beat this mixture and the vanilla and almond extracts into the creamed mixture.

3. Drop the batter by heaping teaspoonful onto an ungreased cookie sheet and press a whole almond into the top of each cookie.

4. Bake in a 325° oven for 10-12 minutes or until golden brown.

1 egg = 6 g.
⅓ c. milk powder + 2 c. whole wheat flour = 28 g.
½ c. buttermilk = 3.5 g.
*Total = 37.5 g. usable protein

Carrot Cookies

5 dozen

Spicy and scrumptious!

½ c. butter
½ c. honey
*1 egg
1 c. grated carrot
*½ c. buttermilk
*⅓ c. instant milk powder
   (¼ c. non-instant)
*1½ c. whole wheat flour

1 t. baking soda
1 t. cinnamon
½ t. nutmeg
¼ t. cloves
⅛ t. salt
*½ c. sunflower seeds
½-¾ c. raisins

1. Cream the butter and honey together until they are fluffy. Beat in the egg, then the grated carrot and buttermilk.

2. In a separate bowl stir together all the dry ingredients except the sunflower seeds and raisins. Beat the dry mixture into the liquid one until smooth.

3. Fold in the sunflower seeds and raisins.

4. Drop the batter by heaping teaspoonsful onto an ungreased cookie sheet and bake in a 350⁰ oven for about 12 minutes or until golden brown.

1 egg = 6 g.
1½ c. whole wheat flour + 4 T. milk powder = 21 g.
1⅓ T. milk powder = 2 g.
½ c. sunflower seeds + ½ c. buttermilk = 12 g.
*Total = 41 g. usable protein

Lemon Sesame Drops

5 dozen

Yummy!

½ c. butter
½ c. honey
*1 egg
*¼ c. milk
grated rind of one
   lemon (1 t.)
juice of one lemon (2-3 T.)

*1½ c. + 1 T. whole
   wheat flour
*¼ c. soy flour
*½ c. sesame seeds
1 t. baking soda
⅛ t. salt
2 t. vanilla

1. Cream the butter and honey together until fluffy. Beat in the egg, milk, lemon juice, and lemon rind until smooth.

2. Beat in all the other ingredients until the dry ones are moistened.

3. Drop the batter by heaping teaspoonsful onto an ungreased baking sheet. Bake in a 350⁰ oven for 10 minutes or until golden brown.

12 T. whole wheat flour + 2 T. soy flour + 2 T. sesame seeds = 14.25 g.
⅓ c. sesame seeds + ¼ c. milk = 8 g.
½ c. whole wheat flour + 2 T. soy flour = 8 g.
1 egg = 6 g.
*Total = 36.25 g. usable protein

Coffee Bars

15 bars

If you wish to double this recipe you may do so without adding an extra egg.

COOKIES:
2 T. butter
6 T. honey or
 ½ c. brown sugar
*1 egg
¼ c. hot coffee
*3 T. soy flour
*¾ c. whole wheat flour

¼ t. baking powder
¼ t. baking soda
¼ t. cinnamon
¼ c. raisins
¼ c. chopped walnuts
 (optional)

ICING:
*⅓ c. instant milk powder
1 T. honey

liquid milk

1. Cream together butter and honey (or sugar). Add egg and beat thoroughly. Add hot coffee gradually, mixing well.

2. In a separate bowl combine dry ingredients (except raisins and nuts) and mix thoroughly. Add the dry mixture to the wet and stir until the dry particles are moistened. Add raisins and nuts and stir to distribute them through the mixture.

3. Pour the mixture into a well-greased 9"x9" in. pan and bake at 350⁰ for 15-20 minutes. Use the toothpick test to determine when it's done. Frost cake while still warm, not hot.

4. To make the icing, combine the milk powder, honey, and enough liquid milk to make a spreadable icing.

5. Cut into squares when cool.

3 T. soy flour + ¾ c. whole wheat flour = 12 g.
1 egg = 6 g.
⅓ c. milk powder = 7 g.
*Total = 25 g. usable protein

Carob Sunflower Seed Brownies

9"x9" in. pan

Yummy with a glass of cold milk.

BROWNIES:

½ c. butter	1 t. baking powder
½ c. honey	½ t. salt
⅓ c. carob powder	½ t. coriander
*2 eggs	1 t. vanilla
*¼ c. instant milk powder	*1 c. whole wheat flour
(3 T. non-instant)	*⅔ c. sunflower seeds
*¼ c. soy flour	*¼ c. milk

1. Cream together the butter and honey. Beat in the carob powder until all the lumps are gone. Beat in the eggs.

2. One at a time, beat in all the other ingredients in the order in which they are listed.

3. Turn the mixture into a greased and floured baking pan. Bake in a 325° oven for 25 minutes or until a toothpick tester comes out clean. Cool before frosting or cutting.

ICING:

3 T. melted butter	2-3 T. honey
¼ c. carob powder	few t. liquid milk
*⅓ c. instant milk powder	

1. Melt the butter and while it is hot stir in the carob powder. Beat until all the lumps of carob are dissolved.

2. Beat in the honey, milk powder, and enough liquid milk to make a spreadable icing. Frost the brownies with the icing while it is still warm.

VARIATION

If you like you can substitute chopped walnuts for the sunflower seeds. The protein content of the brownies will diminish somewhat.

¼ c. milk powder + ⅔ c. sunflower seeds = 16 g.
1 c. whole wheat flour + ¼ c. soy flour = 16 g.
2 eggs = 12 g.
¼ c. milk = 2 g.
⅓ c. milk powder = 7 g.
*Total = 53 g. usable protein

Honey Peanut Bars

3 dozen bars

The peanuttiest!

½ c. honey
*½ c. peanut butter
   (smooth or crunchy)
*1 egg
*¼ c. milk
*1 c. whole wheat flour
*1 T. soy flour

*2 T. instant milk powder
   (1½ T. non-instant)
1 t. baking powder
1 t. vanilla
⅛ t. salt
*¼ c. sunflower seeds
*¼ c. chopped nuts

1. Cream together the honey and peanut butter until the mixture is smooth. Beat in the egg and the milk.

2. Add all the other ingredients except the seeds and nuts and beat until the dry ingredients are well moistened. Finally stir in the sunflower seeds and chopped nuts.

3. Turn the mixture into a greased and floured 9x9 in. pan. Bake in a 325⁰ oven for 25 minutes, or until the bars test done with a toothpick.

4. When cool, cut into 1 inch square bars.

1 egg = 6 g.
¼ c. milk = 2 g.
1 c. whole wheat flour + 2 T. peanut butter + 1 T. soy flour = 20 g.
2 T. peanut butter + ¼ c. sunflower seeds = 13.75 g.
¼ c. peanut butter + 2 T. milk powder = 10.5 g.
*Total = 52.25 g. usable protein
Plus protein from the nuts.

Gingery Tahini Cookies

3 dozen

¼ c. oil
*¼ c. tahini
½ c. honey
*1 egg
*2 T. soy grits
*1½ c. + 2 T.
  whole wheat flour

¼ t. baking soda
½ t. baking powder
¼ t. salt
*6 T. milk
1 T. fresh ginger, grated

1. Cream together the oil, tahini, and honey. Add the egg and beat until fluffy.

2. Add the dry ingredients and milk to the creamed ingredients and mix well. Stir in the grated ginger.

3. Drop the batter by heaping teaspoonsful onto an ungreased baking sheet. Bake in a 350⁰ oven for about 10 minutes or until done.

2 T. tahini + 2 T. soy grits + 1½ c. + 2 T. whole wheat flour = 28.5 g.
2 T. tahini + 3 T. milk = 6 g.
1 egg = 6 g.
3 T. milk = 1 g.
*Total = 41.5 g. usable protein

Prune, Date, or Fig and Nut Bars

3 dozen bars

The larger amount of dried fruit makes for a chewier bar; the smaller amount a cakier bar. Either way, they're delicious.

*2 eggs
½ c. honey
*2 T. soy flour
*½ c. whole wheat flour
1 t. baking powder

1 t. vanilla
⅛ t. salt
*½-1 c. chopped nuts
1-2 c. pitted and chopped
  prunes or dates or figs

1. Beat the eggs. Trickle the honey into the eggs while constantly beating. Continue beating until the mixture is fluffy.

2. Beat the flours, baking powder, vanilla, and salt into the egg-honey mixture.

3. Finally stir in the chopped nuts and dried fruit. Turn the mixture into a greased and floured 9x9 in. pan. Bake in a 325° oven for 25 minutes, or until the bars test done with the toothpick test.

4. When cool, cut into 1 inch square bars. If you aren't a natural foods purist you might want to roll the finished bars in powdered sugar, but they really don't need it.

2 eggs = 12 g.
2 T. soy flour + ½ c. whole wheat flour = 8 g.
*Total = 20 g. usable protein

Lemon-Apricot Bars

3 dozen

Fruity and delicious.

*2 eggs
½ c. honey
grated rind of 1 lemon
**   (about 1 t.)**
juice of 1 lemon
**   (2-3 T.)**
*¾ c. whole wheat flour

*3 T. soy flour
1 t. baking soda
1 t. vanilla
⅛ t. salt
¾ c. diced dried apricots
½ c. raisins

1. Beat the honey into the eggs until the mixture is fluffy. One by one, beat in all the other ingredients in the order listed.

2. Turn the batter into a greased and floured 9x9 in. baking pan.

3. Bake in a 325° oven for 30 minutes or until the bars test done with the toothpick test. Cut into bars when cool.

2 eggs = 12 g.
¾ c. whole wheat flour + 3 T. soy flour = 12 g.
*Total = 24 g. usable protein

BEVERAGES

No matter how your taste runs in beverages you should be able to find something here that will satisfy. From thick and creamy, to light and refreshing, to hot drinks made to warm up your insides — all of them rich in yummy, natural ingredients.

A blender is a real help in making beverages. If you don't have one you can still make most of the recipes by stirring the ingredients together with a spoon or wire whisk. The finished drink may not be as smooth as it would be if made in a blender.

Don't forget some of the easiest beverages of all, herb teas.

Health-Nut Smoothie

1 serving

*1 c. yogurt
5-6 strawberries
½ orange, peeled
*1 T. brewer's yeast

*1 T. wheat germ
1-3 t. honey, or to taste
ice cubes (optional)

Buzz everything together in a blender until fairly smooth. There will be some noticeable pulp from the orange. Serve in a tall glass.

1 c. yogurt = 7-9 g.
1 T. brewer's yeast = 1.5 g.
1 T. wheat germ = 1 g.
*Total = 9.5-11.5 g. usable protein

Buttermilk

1 quart

1 qt. water
1⅓ c. instant milk powder
  (1 c. non-instant)

½ c. commercial butter-
  milk (or ½ c. left from
  your last batch)

1. Thoroughly mix together all the ingredients and set the mixture in a warm place overnight until the milk clabbers.
2. Refrigerate until you are ready to use it.

Orange Pineapple Supreme

1 serving

*1 c. yogurt or buttermilk
¼ c. pineapple chunks

¼ c. orange juice
1-3 t. honey

Process everything in the blender until smooth. Serve in a tall glass.

*1 c. yogurt = 7-9 g. usable protein

Orange Lassi

1 serving

*1 c. yogurt or buttermilk   1 T. honey
½ c. orange juice

Process all the ingredients in a blender until smooth or stir
together until well blended.

*1 c. yogurt = 7-9 usable protein

Peach Lassi

1 serving

1 peach, peeled and   *1 c. yogurt
   chopped, *or* ½ c. frozen   1-3 t. honey
   peaches

Process everything in a blender until smooth. If you use frozen
peaches this makes a super-cold refreshing summer drink.

*1 c. yogurt = 7-9 g. usable protein

Apricot Lassi

1 serving

⅓ c. apricot nectar   1 t. honey, or to taste
*1 c. yogurt

Stir or blend together all ingredients until smooth. Serve in a
tall glass.

*1 c. yogurt = 7-9 g. usable protein

Purple Passion
1 serving

There are lots of variations on this drink. For best results use grape juice diluted half-and-half with water.

½ c. grape juice (¼ c.
  grape juice, ¼ c. water)
*½ c. or more yogurt

½ c. pineapple or orange
  juice

1. Stir together the juices.
2. Add the yogurt; stir it into the juices or leave as is to be eaten with a spoon.

VARIATIONS

1. Substitute a scoop of vanilla ice cream for the yogurt, or try pineapple or orange sherbet.
2. Purple Passion Spritzer: Add ½ c. or more of club soda for a "fizzy" drink.

*½ c. yogurt = 4 g. usable protein

Spiced Hot Carob "Cocoa"
2 servings

This will warm up your insides on a cold winter night:

*2 c. milk
2 T. carob powder

2-3 t. honey
dash cinnamon (optional)

1. Beat together 1 c. milk, the carob powder, and the honey. Heat over a medium flame, stirring occasionally, until the carob dissolves.
2. Add another cup of milk and a sprinkling of the optional cinnamon. Stir and continue heating just until the mixture is hot enough to drink.

*2 c. milk = 14 g. usable protein

Hot Mulled Fruit Juices

1 serving

1 c. apple juice or cider,   2 or 3 whole cloves
    orange juice, or pineapple   dash cinnamon
    juice

1. Combine all ingredients in a sauce pan and heat until steaming.
2. Cover and simmer for a few minutes to blend the flavors. Remove cloves if you wish and serve.

Russian Tea

2 servings

1 c. orange juice   3 or 4 whole cloves or
1 c. hot black tea   ⅛ t. ground cloves
1 t. lemon juice   ¼ t. ground cinnamon
1 t. honey

1. Make the black tea and set it aside to steep.
2. Combine all the other ingredients in a saucepan and heat until steaming. Cover and simmer for about 5 minutes.
3. Add the tea and remove the whole cloves if you wish.

Apricot Apple Drink

1 serving

½ c. apricot nectar   ½ c. apple juice

Stir together and serve cold. You can vary this by using different amounts of the two juices for very subtle flavor changes.

Summer Cooler
1 serving

⅓ c. apple juice   ⅓-⅔ c. strained and cooled
⅓ c. pineapple juice   lemon balm tea

Stir everything together and serve with a couple of ice cubes.

Fall Refresher
1 serving

⅓ c. orange juice   ⅓ c. apple juice or cider
⅓ c. grapefruit juice

Stir together and serve. The sweet and tart flavors in this really bring out the best in each other.

Lemonade
1 serving

1 c. cold water   1 t. honey or more to taste
2 T. lemon juice

Stir everything together until the honey dissolves. Add more honey if necessary to satisfy your sweet tooth. Garnish with a sprig of fresh mint.

Juicerless Juices

Even if you don't own a juicer you can still have fresh squeezed juices at home, if you make the juices in your blender. Use any juicy fruits and remove any parts (rinds, seeds etc.) which you don't want in the finished juice. Put the fruit, either singly or in any combination you like, in your blender and process until the mixture is liquified.

Suggested fruits for juicing:

apples
apricots
grapefruit
grapes
melon
oranges
papaya

peaches
pineapple
raspberries and
   blackberries
strawberries
tomatoes

Blend banana and/or avocado with other juices. You can skin tomatoes before blending, but don't worry about the seeds. They add a texture to the juice that doesn't effect the taste.

HERB TEAS

In addition to flavoring other foods herbs can be used to make herb teas or tisanes. Start with 1-1½ teaspoons of dry herbs (or twice as much of fresh herbs) for each cup of tea. Put the herbs in a warmed teapot and pour boiling water over them. Let the tea steep for three to five minutes; strain the tea and serve it with a little honey or lemon. To make one cup of tea at a time use a special tea strainer, tea "egg," or slotted tea spoon. For iced tea use twice as much of the herbs as for hot tea and pour the steeped tea over ice cubes in a tall glass.

ICED TEA:

lemon balm (The *very* best iced tea herb!)
mints

HOT TEAS:

catnip
chamomile
comfrey
lemon balm
lemon grass
maté

mints
mullein
rose hips
sage
strawberry leaves

The suggested tea herbs are ones which you should be able to obtain without too much difficulty. With the exceptions of maté and lemon grass, which come from tropical or semi-tropical areas, you can grow most of them yourself. Several companies package herb teas, either as single herbs or as delicious blends. Do try some of the herb teas for a healthful, delicious change from ordinary coffee and tea.

Herb Tea Blends

Each of these recipes will make about one teapot (about four cups) of tea. Use spearmint, peppermint, or applemint when mint is called for. If necessary you may interchange lemon grass and lemon balm, with a slight change in flavor. Stir all the ingredients together well. Brew as you would any tea.

HERB TEA BLEND #1

2 t. ground, dried
   rose hips
2 t. dried lemon grass

1 t. dried mint
⅛ t. ground cloves

HERB TEA BLEND #2

1 t. dried mint
2 t. dried lemon grass

2 t. dried chamomile
   flowers

HERB TEA BLEND #3

1 t. dried comfrey leaf
2 t. dried lemon balm

½ t. dried mint
½ t. dried catnip

HERB TEA BLEND #4

3 t. dried catnip
1 t. dried lemon balm

1 t. dried chamomile
   flowers

HERB TEA BLEND #5

½ t. dried sage
3 t. dried mint

½ t. dried lemon balm

HERB TEA BLEND #6

1 t. dried sage
2 t. dried lemon balm

1 t. dried comfrey

Try experimenting to find some of your own favorite herb tea blends.

PRESERVING THE BOUNTY

At any time of the year, but especially during the summer and fall, you may suddenly find yourself with a huge amount of food which can't possibly be eaten before it spoils. To avoid wasting food, learn to preserve it.

I will deal here only with simple methods for preserving small amounts of food. If you really want to get into preserving food in a big way look over the book list at the end of this chapter and choose a few for closer reading.

DRYING

Drying is the simplest and perhaps the oldest method for preserving foods. All kinds of fruits and vegetables can be dried, but the most easily and frequently used foods for home drying are the various herbs.

Most herbs can be dried for storage by hanging them in a warm, dry, preferably dark room. Wash the herbs first and shake them to remove excess moisture. Tie the herb stems together with strong thread or string and hang them upside down to dry. Depending on the weather, the herbs should be dried in one or two weeks. When dry, strip the leaves from the stems and store the dried leaves in glass jars. Herb seeds, such as coriander and dill, can also be dried on trays or screens placed in a warm, dry room.

Parsley and chives are more easily dried in the oven. Dry parsley on trays in a 400° oven for 5 minutes, turning the herb once to prevent its scorching. Chives are dried between layers of uniodized or sea salt in a 200° oven. "Bake" them for about 20 minutes or until they crumble easily. You can use the salt over and over for drying chives; when you are done you will have onion salt as a by-product.

Once your herbs are dried and stored watch carefully for any sign of moisture condensing on the inside of the jar. If moisture appears the herbs should be discarded as molds or mildew may be growing in the jar. You can avoid this problem by making sure that your herbs are crumbly dry before storing them in glass.

FREEZING

The freezer is one modern convenience that really deserves the name. Put yours to work for you preserving bumper crops from your own or your friends' gardens and storing foods for times when you are too rushed to cook. Finished dishes such as breads and casseroles can be frozen and reheated. You can also cook large amounts of dried legumes or grains and freeze them in small portions for later use.

The trick in freezing is to keep air away from the food. Freezing cold air will dry out the frozen food and give it a funny, although not harmful, taste. Fill plastic bags with the food to be frozen and press the plastic closely up against the food, forcing out all the excess air. Twist the top of the bag tightly and seal with a covered wire twister or rubber band. If the food to be frozen contains liquid (such as fruit frozen in syrup) you must allow a little extra room in the container as the liquid will expand when it freezes. Plastic freezer containers, if you use them, should be packed so that ½ to 1 inch of empty "headspace" remains at the top, again to leave room for expansion.

FREEZING HINTS

Casseroles   Choose a casserole dish or other container which will withstand the effects of freezing temperatures. Place the food in the container and cover it tightly with a plastic bag or foil, squeezing out as much air as possible. Freeze. *Note:* If the casserole contains eggs it should be baked before freezing.

Breads   Use bread which has cooled to room temperature. Unless you want to serve the loaf whole for a specific occasion slice it before freezing. Put each loaf in a separate plastic bag, squeeze all of the air out of the bag and seal it. Freeze.

Cooked Legumes and Grains After cooking drain and cool the food. Freeze in small portions in tightly sealed plastic bags.

Fresh Vegetables Wash and prepare vegetables (chop, peel skins from squash, etc.). Vegetables should be blanched (boiled or steamed for two or three minutes) before freezing. Blanching inactivates enzymes which could interfere with the freezing process. After the prepared vegetables have cooked for about two minutes drain them, plunge them into cold water (to stop the cooking), drain again, and pack the vegetables into plastic bags or freezer containers. Squeeze out as much air as possible. Seal and freeze.

Fruits Wash, skin, and slice fruits. Make a syrup by pouring honey (about 1 T. for every pint of fruit) over the fruit and stirring. Add a little lemon juice to keep the fruit from discoloring. Allow the fruit and honey mixture to sit, stirring occasionally, until the mixture becomes juicy. Pack fruit and syrup into plastic bags or freezer containers leaving a little room for the syrup to expand. Freeze.

CANNING

To prevent food poisoning nearly all canning should be done in a boiling water bath or a pressure canner. If you have a large garden or ready access to a large amount of fresh food in the summer consider investing in one or both of these. It should easily pay for itself in one good season of canning.

Although the experts don't always agree, a few foods may be safely canned without special equipment by using the "open kettle" method. The open kettle method can be used for canning jams and jellies, pickles, and tomatoes. Since tomatoes often come in a flood in September, it's nice to be able to can the extras without making a big investment in equipment. You can also adopt the method for "putting up" your grandmother's favorite pickle, relish, and jelly recipes.

Make sure that all the utensils you use for canning are scrupulously clean. Check your jars to make sure they are not cracked or nicked anywhere, especially around the rim. Read the follow the manufacturer's instructions for the jar lids you are using. Sterilize jars and lids in boiling water and keep them boiling until the *second* you are ready to use them.

To can tomatoes, skin and chop them, discarding any spoiled fruits or bad spots which can cause your whole batch to spoil. Put the chopped tomatoes in a pot and bring them to a boil over medium heat. Boil for 5 minutes, stirring frequently to prevent sticking. Ladle the hot tomatoes into *hot* sterile jars and wipe off the jar rim with a clean, damp cloth. Cap the jar with a *hot* sterile top, following the manufacturer's instructions. Set the jar aside to cool; preferably, the jar should remain undisturbed for 24 hours. Check the cap seal according to the manufacturer's instructions.

The trick with open kettle canning is to get everything as hot as possible (jars, tops, tomatoes), and then to work quickly enough so that nothing will have a chance to cool until the jar is filled and the cap is in place. The jar top will seal as the jar and its contents cool. If the jar *does not* seal, either reprocess the food or use it right away.

For safety's sake, please do not use the open kettle method for any foods other than tomatoes, pickles, jellies, and jams. When you are ready to use the food check it again. If the seal has been broken or if there is any off odor or color to the food discard it *without tasting*.

BOOK LIST

Joy of Cooking, by Irma S. Rombauer and Marion Rombauer Becker (contains several chapters on preserving foods)

Keeping the Harvest, by Nancy Thurber and Gretchen Mead

Stocking Up, edited by Carol Hupping Stoner

Informative booklets on preserving are also available by mail from the Atlas Mason, Ball, and Kerr companies.

GLOSSARY OF NATURAL FOODS

Arrowroot Flour or Starch   This is an ingredient used for thickening sauces. It is used in exactly the same way you would use cornstarch (*see* cornstarch).

Barley   Barley contains fairly high quality protein (NPU of 60). Since it is not particularly high in protein quantity it is generally used interchangeably with brown rice; equal amounts of the two provide about the same number of grams of usable protein. As with other grains, complement the protein in barley with milk products and legumes.

Berries   The whole kernel of a grain is often called a berry. Wheat berries, rye berries, and other whole grains can be prepared in the same way you would prepare rice, although they usually require a little longer cooking time. Wheat and rye berries have a very distinctive and delightful texture, so try to use them when called for in recipes. If you must substitute use bulgar, but expect a change in texture. Complement the protein in whole grains with milk products or legumes.

Bran   Bran is the outer covering of the wheat kernal. It is removed, along with the germ, when the wheat is ground into white flour. Bran is a source of vitamins, minerals, and protein. In addition, it is an excellent source of food fiber. Food fiber has recently come into the limelight in nutritional circles. It has long been known that fiber, or roughage, in the diet is instrumental in regulating elimination. More recent evidence suggests that it may also prevent obesity and various disorders of the digestive system, including cancer.

Bread Crumbs   The bread crumbs in the recipes are whole wheat bread crumbs. Make your own by toasting thin slices of whole wheat bread, cooling, and then buzzing the slices in the blender or crushing them with a rolling pin.

Buckwheat   Buckwheat contains high quality protein (NPU of 65). Buckwheat groats, or kasha, are the whole grain of buckwheat which are cooked and eaten in the same way as rice. Generally the raw groats are sautéed before cooking in water. Buckwheat flour is famous for its use in pancakes; usually you will want to combine it with wheat flour for the best texture. The amino acid makeup of buckwheat is similar to that of wheat, so complement the protein in buckwheat with milk products or legumes.

Bulgar   Bulgar is partially cooked, cracked wheat, which is used extensively in the Middle East. It is a quickly cooked grain, so consider having it for dinner on nights when you are short on cooking time. Complement the protein in bulgar with milk products or legumes. Cracked wheat and steel cut oats are similar to bulgar in protein content and texture. You can substitute them in any recipe which calls for bulgar.

Butter   The use of butter in healthful cooking is controversial. It does have a flavor which hasn't been matched by any other product — but it is high in saturated fats and cholesterol. If you're watching cholesterol you can substitute oil, except in cookie recipes. Good margarines may also be substituted, although these are difficult to find without chemical additives which butter usually doesn't have.

Buttermilk   Buttermilk contains little or no butterfat. It gets its name because it was the residue of churning butter. Today buttermilk is made by introducing friendly bacteria into low fat sweet milk and allowing the bacteria to grow and the milk to clabber (sour and thicken). Buttermilk is used in baking for its rising properties. It also makes a delicious summer drink.

Carob Powder or St. John's Bread   Carob powder is a flour made from ground and roasted carob pods. Its use is recorded in the Bible, so it's been around for a while. Carob powder has a taste similar to chocolate, although fruitier; you can substitute carob in nearly any recipe calling for chocolate. Carob has many advantages over chocolate. It is lower in fat, higher in calcium, and does not contain the oxalic acid present in chocolate which inhibits calcium's absorption in the body. Carob powder can usually be eaten by those who are allergic to chocolate.

Cheese Cheese is an excellent source of protein. One ounce (⅓ c. grated) of most cheeses has about the same number of grams of protein as a cup of milk. The low fat cheeses are higher in protein, ounce for ounce, than the higher fat cheeses such as cream cheese. Try to get natural cheeses if you possibly can — they are better for you. Watch out for things labelled "cheese food" or "cheese food spread." They aren't as high in protein as natural cheeses.

Cornmeal Cornmeal is flour ground from whole, dried corn kernals. (Remember, corn is a grain which we usually eat in its immature state as a vegetable.) Buy *undegerminated* cornmeal as it's higher in protein. White and yellow cornmeal have about the same food value.

Cornstarch Cornstarch is a flour ground from the starchy part of the corn kernal, without the germ or husk. It is used for thickening sauces or puddings. To thicken hot sauces with cornstarch first dissolve the cornstarch in cold water; then, while heating the sauce and constantly stirring, *slowly* drizzle in the cornstarch mixture until the sauce reaches the desired thickness. Cornstarch makes beautiful, transparent sauces. Don't try dissolving cornstarch in hot water or sauce — you'll get lumps instead of thickness. And don't use too much cornstarch, as a very little goes a long way.

Cracked Wheat Cracked wheat is the whole kernal of wheat which has been broken up into small pieces. For the purposes of cooking, cracked wheat is the same as bulgar, and they are interchangeable in the recipes. Since cracked wheat is usually more inexpensive I generally use it instead of bulgar. The nutritional value of the two is the same. Complement cracked wheat with milk products or legumes.

Dried Fruit Dried fruit has had most of its water removed. Eat dried fruits as energy rich snacks or "reconstitute" them by soaking in water overnight. Good for breakfast or for a simple dessert. If you are in a hurry you may simmer dried fruits in water until they are tender. A cooking tip: always keep raisins on hand as they can be tossed into so many dishes for a delightful added touch. Dried fruit from the supermarket has usually had sulfur added to preserve the color. Look for natural food stores or co-ops in your area where you can buy unsulfured fruit and taste its real, natural flavor.

Eggs Eggs have an NPU of 94 — the protein is nearly perfect for human use. Two eggs will provide about one-third of your daily protein need. Get organic eggs if you can, that is eggs laid by chickens which are fed a natural diet and which are not injected with chemicals and hormones to increase laying. Many people are wary of eating eggs because of their high cholesterol count; but eggs are also rich in lecithin, an emulsifier, which logically should counteract the cholesterol, although I don't believe this effect has been proven yet. Avoid eating raw egg whites which can inhibit the body's absorption of one of the B vitamins. Once the egg whites are cooked they lose this undesirable trait.

Egg Replacers   There are two kinds of egg replacers on the market. The frozen liquid type is formulated mainly for people who want to reduce cholesterol intake without giving up eggs. It can be used for scrambling, omelets, baking, custards, and does contain protein. Unfortunately it also contains real egg whites and various chemicals and preservatives.

The powder replacer is basically a binding agent for baking. It contains no egg, animal products, or preservatives, and is good for people with egg allergies. Unfortunately it contains no protein either and can't be used for scrambling. And it doesn't really have the taste of eggs. It is at its best in cakes and quickbreads and does a fair job in custards, soufflés, and grain or bean casseroles. Follow the directions on the package, with a few additional suggestions.

1. Cakes and Quickbreads: use 1 t. replacer and 2 T. water for each egg.
2. Custards and Quiches: use at least 8 t. replacer for each egg in the recipe, mixing the powder directly into the milk or other liquid. Use no additional water, and you may have to increase baking time slightly.
3. Soufflés: use 1 t. replacer and 2 T. water plus ¼ t. baking powder for each egg. Beat the powder into the water very well before adding it to the soufflé.
4. Casseroles: use 1 or more t. replacer and 2 T. water for each egg to bind.

Graham Flour   Graham flour is whole wheat flour. The name graham is not applied very consistently; sometimes it refers to finely ground pastry flour, at other times to a coarser grind than regular whole wheat flour. In most cases this inconsistency won't cause any problem, but if you need pastry flour make sure that is what you are buying.

"Graham" was applied to whole wheat flour in honor of Sylvester Graham, a nineteenth century minister who was one of the earliest advocates of natural foods as a way to good health. Graham travelled throughout the country preaching the Gospel and his own gospel of whole foods for good health. He believed that the Fall of Man occurred when men ". . .began to put asunder what God had joined together," that is, when millers began to remove the bran and germ from the wheat when milling flour.

Honey   Honey is the most healthful agent you can use for sweetening. The sugar in honey is a very simple sugar (like that found in fruits) which is easily digested. The sweetness in honey is so concentrated that you don't need to use as much as you would of white sugar. Honey can be legally sold in the United States without being refined. Its chemical and physical makeup prevent bacteria from growing in honey, so there is really no point in refining it. Buy unheated honey for maximum food value. Try some of the milder honeys for cooking and baking. (Generally the mild honeys are lighter in color than the stronger honeys.) There are connoisseurs of honeys just as there are of wines. The finest is proported to be wild thyme honey from Greece, but there are many others, less rare and expensive, which you might like to try.

Honey has gained the reputation of being a cure-all. I can remember reading a book when I was 7 or 8 which recommended honey for everything from a sore throat to making sure that your dog gives birth to a healthy litter. Check out your local library if you want more information on honey's healing properties.

Kasha   Kasha is another name for buckwheat groats (*see* buckwheat).

Legumes   Beans, peas, and lentils are legumes. In their mature state legumes are rich in protein. To use this protein most efficiently legumes should be complemented with whole grains, seeds, or dairy products. You can buy legumes dried or sometimes fresh or canned. Most dry legumes have a rather bland taste which responds well to herbs and other seasonings. Different legumes are used in different geographical areas — there are long-standing disagreements between areas over which variety makes the tastiest baked beans. Except for soybeans, which have more protein, you can substitute one variety of legume for another and obtain about the same amount of protein. Snap beans and fresh peas are also legumes, but because they are eaten in their immature state they are lower in protein than their mature counterparts.

Milk   Milk and milk products are good sources of high quality protein (NPU of around 80). Besides protein, milk is also our best source of much needed calcium. Be sure to have at least two, preferably four, cups of milk each day. Probably the best milk you can use is certified raw milk. Great care is taken in its handling and it contains vitamins and enzymes which are destroyed in the pasteurization process. If you can't get certified raw milk use regular or lowfat pasteurized milk, milk reconstituted from powdered milk, or diluted, canned evaporated milk. If you have an allergy or intolerance to cow milk try substituting goat milk or soy milk. Milk loses vitamins if exposed to light, especially if exposed to heat and light at the same time. Store the milk in a refrigerator, preferably in containers which keep out light. When cooking with milk, heat the milk in a covered metal saucepan. The protein in milk will complement the protein in most plant foods.

Milk Powder   The milk powder used in the recipes is usually instant milk powder because it is the easiest milk powder to obtain. The non-instant has a smoother texture so use it if you can, especially in creamy foods like icings. When baking with milk powder stir it into the flour before adding it to the liquids. Instant milk powder *may* lump if you add it to a hot liquid, so check your brand before trying to make "instant cocoa." You can substitute non-instant for instant by following the conversion chart:

3 T. non-instant = 4 T. instant
¼ c. non-instant = ⅓ c. instant

Millet   Millet is a small grain which is infrequently used in the United States. Experts disagree as to whether millet contains "complete" protein or is deficient in one amino acid. For safety's sake complement millet with milk products or legumes. Millet has the nutritional advantage over other grains of being fairly high in protein, yet fairly low in starch.

Miso   Miso is fermented soybean paste, similar to, but much thicker than soy sauce. All natural miso is made by using a special culture to ferment the soybeans and sea salt to control the fermentation. *Kome* miso is made from soybeans and rice, *mugi* miso from soybeans and barley, and *hacho* miso from plain soybeans. Miso is less salty than tamari or other soy sauces so it can be used with a freer hand in cooking. If you can't get miso in your area you may substitute tamari, but you may have to adjust the amount of salt in the recipe.

To use miso in cooking dissolve it in a small amount of warm water. (It may be slightly cooled stock from the dish you are cooking.) Add the solution to the other ingredients. For best results do not boil the liquid after adding the miso to it; boiling may destroy many of the friendly microorganisms in the miso. Don't try to add miso directly to a hot dish; the paste will sit in a lump and will never dissolve.

Molasses Molasses is a liquid sugar extracted from sugar cane by boiling. The finest molasses is unsulfured molasses. Sulfured molasses is a by-product of white sugar and its flavor is not as good as unsulfured molasses. Blackstrap molasses was long considered a waste product of sugar production. Although it is not very good tasting it is high in nutrients.

Nuts Nuts are generally high in protein, but unfortunately they are also high in fat. The fat content makes them too caloric to qualify as good protein sources. Do use them occasionally for their flavor.

Oats Oats contain moderate amounts of high quality protein (NPU of 66). The amino acid makeup of oats is similar to that of wheat, so substitute similar oat products for wheat products. If you find yourself without any whole grains and you can't get to your natural food source your best bet is to get rolled oats at the supermarket. Oats cannot be refined because of the kernal structure. To avoid additives and preservatives buy plain rolled oats.

Oils Oils can be pressed from a variety of foods. Buy oils which have been processed as little as possible and keep them in a cool place, especially after you have opened the bottles. Minimally processed oils contain food values which can cause rancidity if the oil is not kept cool. Highly processed oils have had so much food value removed that they will last virtually forever, even at room temperature. One wonders if there can be any food value left.

Be careful when cooking not to let oils get too hot. There are rumors circulating that unsaturated oils will become saturated, or form dangerous substances called "free radicals" if they get too hot. Some nutritionists say that this idea is just nonsense. As I'm not sure what to believe I'd rather play it safe and not let my cooking oils get too hot. Saturated fats, like butter, are considered to be more stable under high heats. Of course, any fat or oil will smoke and burn if you really let it get too hot, so use a medium or low heat. For more about oils see the section on fats in the chapter on nutritoin.

Peanuts Actually a member of the pea family, the peanut is a legume whose "fruit" grows underground. Peanuts can be eaten raw or roasted. Complement peanut protein with milk products, sunflower seeds, and combinations of other foods.

Peanut Butter Peanut butter is made by grinding whole, shelled peanuts, perhaps with a little oil for smoothness. Legally, peanut butter must contain at least 90% peanuts; products such as "imitation" peanut butter contain a smaller percentage. Most commercial peanut butters also contain preservatives and don't contain the germ of the peanut, which is the most healthful part.

If your food store or co-op does not sell freshly ground natural peanut butter, try making it at home in your blender. Start with a little oil and add peanuts a few at a time, processing until smooth. Add salt and honey to taste when the peanut butter is finished.

Pulses Pulse is just another word for legume. You may encounter it in Indian cooking, yoga books, and the Bible — Daniel, Shadrach, Meshach, and Abednego ate pulses and water and were healthier than the King's men, who ate rich meats and wine. An early account of the health benefits of vegetarian eating!

Rice Natural brown rice contains high quality protein (NPU of 70). If you can't get brown rice you may substitute converted rice which is similar in food value. Avoid polished white rice. It's protein quality is much lower (NPU of 57) and many of the vitamins and minerals have been milled away with the outer layer of the rice kernal. Complement the protein in rice with milk products, legumes, seeds, and brewer's yeast.

Rolled Cereals Rolled Cereals are whole grains, usually oats or wheat, which have been flattened under heavy rollers. The flattening makes them cook much more quickly than the natural whole kernal. The recipes call for regular, long-cooking rolled grains. You can substitute "quick" oats (not instant) without too much change in food quality, but expect a certain, often detrimental, change in texture.

Rye   Rye is a strong flavored grain containing slightly less usable protein than wheat (NPU of 58). If you like rye flavor you may substitute rye berries for wheat berries. Rye flour is ground from the whole rye berry. Because of rye's low gluten content, rye flour must be combined with wheat flour for good results in baking. Complement rye as you would wheat, with milk products or legumes. Get dark rye if possible for higher protein quantity.

Sea Salt   Sea water contains minerals in almost exactly the same proportions as human blood. Sea salt contains all the trace minerals found in sea water; so by using sea salt instead of ordinary salt you will be replenishing necessary trace minerals. Ordinary table salt contains chemicals to keep it free-flowing. You can accomplish the same thing without chemicals by adding a grain or two or raw rice to your salt shaker.

Seeds   Certain seeds, such as poppy, caraway, dill, and coriander, are used as seasonings. Others are eaten for their protein content. Among these are sunflower, pumpkin, and squash seeds. Sesame seeds are used for both. Complement the protein in seeds with milk products, legumes, or certain grains. Sunflower seeds can be purchased hulled, which is more convenient for cooking. Buy unhulled sesame seeds if possible for slightly more food value. If you buy these foods in bulk they are really very inexpensive, but if you buy them from the spice counter at the supermarket you'll find about a 300% to 400% markup in price.

To toast seeds (sunflower, sesame, squash, pumpkin) you can use one of two methods. If the seeds are fresh, wash them thoroughly and scrape away any pulp clinging to the seeds. Dry well. Place in a flat pan in a single layer. Bake in a 200° oven until golden brown, stirring every five minutes to insure even toasting. Or you can place the seeds in a dry frying pan and cook over a low heat, stirring constantly until the seeds are toasted. Add salt to taste after cooking.

Sesame Butter or Tahini   Sesame butter has a texture similar to peanut butter. It is made by grinding sesame seeds with a little oil which is the same way peanut butter is made. Sesame butter is made from toasted seeds while tahini is made from raw seeds. Their protein content is the same, so substitute one for the other according to your taste. You can make sesame butter or tahini by following the recipe for peanut butter in the glossary, substituting sesame seeds for peanuts.

Soy Beans   Soy beans are higher in protein quantity and quality than other dried legumes, thus they are considered a separate category in determining complementary relationships. Soybeans provide high quality protein (NPU of 61-65), and they may also be complemented with grains, seeds, and dairy products.

Soy Flour   Soy flour is ground from partially cooked or raw soybeans. It is very high in protein, but is usually high in fat. Buy low fat soy flour if you can. Raw soy flour has a rather bitter taste which disappears during baking. Use soy flour especially for complementing the protein in grain flours when you bake. In addition to grains, you may also complement the protein in soy flour with seeds or dairy products. Being a soybean product, soy flour also has fairly high quality protein (NPU of 61-65).

Soy Grits   Soy grits are raw or partially cooked soybeans which have been cracked into small pieces. Substitute soy grits, in equal quantity, in any recipe calling for soybeans. Soy grits have the advantage of cooking more quickly than soybeans, while giving an equal amount of food value. They are invaluable for complementing the protein in grain dishes without changing the character of the dish. Simply mix the soy grits in with the raw grains in the correct proportions for maximum usable protein (*see* protein charts for proportions).

Steel-Cut Oats   Steel-cut oats are whole oat grains which have been cut into small pieces with steel blades. In appearance, texture, and food quality they are similar to bulgar or cracked wheat. The three can be used interchangeably.

Stock   Stock is vegetable broth. For easy stock, save the water which is left when you steam vegetables. Keep the steaming water in the refrigerator and use it over and over — it will pick up more flavor each time you use it. Use the stock in place of plain water in breads, soups, and stews. For a more flavorful stock use onion skins, potato peelings, celery tops, mid-ribs from lettuce and almost any vegetable matter you can think of. Simmer in water for 30 minutes to one hour and strain. When making stock, avoid using the water from cooking strong tasting vegetables like cabbage and turnips. You may use the water from cooking legumes which makes a rather dark stock rich in minerals. Stock which is prepared and then refrigerated will keep for a week to ten days. You may also keep it indefinitely by freezing it.

Sugar   Sugar includes everything from the simple, healthful sugar found in ripe fruits and honey to nutritionally poor, super-refined white table sugar. All sugar (except honey) legally sold in the United States must be at least partially refined. Since sugarcane fields are usually rat infested there is legitimate reason for this requirement. Still, with refinement comes loss of food value. White sugar contains nothing but pure carbohydrate. The calories are truly empty ones, containing no vitamins or minerals. Aside from being worthless nutritionally, there is some evidence that white sugar may be actively harmful to the system, causing or aggravating conditions such as high blood pressure, hypoglycemia, and diabetes. Brown sugar and turbinado sugar (the so-called raw sugar sold in stores) are not as processed as ordinary white sugar; some of the molasses and nutrients still remain. These forms of sugar are probably not that much better for you than white sugar, but hopefully they are at least not quite as harmful. Use one of them if you must use sugar. A better idea is to substitute honey if you possibly can. In cooking substitute honey for sugar in equal amounts. In baking replace 1 c. sugar with ¾ c. honey and reduce the amount of liquid in the recipe by ¼.

Tamari Soy Sauce   Tamari soy sauce is a naturally fermented sauce made from soy beans, wheat, and sea salt. It is generally aged from 12-18 months before being bottled and sold. If you cannot find tamari in your area get Kikkoman soy sauce, or read the labels to find another brand which is naturally fermented. Many American brands of soy sauce are produced by chemical action rather than by natural fermentation. Chemical types should be avoided as their taste is generally too salty and bitter.

Tisanes or Herb Teas   Tisanes are made in the same way as ordinary tea. Substitute fresh or dried herbs, alone or in combination, for the tea leaves. Tisanes vary in flavor with the herbs used and, with the exception of maté, they contain no caffeine. You can easily grow herbs for tea right on your windowsill. Several companies sell a variety of inexpensive herb teas either in bulk or tea bag form.

Tofu   Tofu is curd or cheese made from soybeans. It is high in protein quantity and quality (NPU of 65). You can purchase tofu at natural food stores and Japanese shops.

Triticale   Triticale is a high protein grain which was developed by crossing hard red winter wheat, durum wheat, and rye. Unlike most hybrids, it does not revert back to the parent stock but remains true triticale, generation after generation. Triticale is not only higher in protein than either wheat or rye, but its amino acid balance is better because it is high in lysine, an E.A.A. usually deficient in grains. A better amino acid balance means a higher quality protein. The N.P.U. of triticale should be at least above 60, the N.P.U. for wheat. Although triticale is higher in protein it does not contain as much gluten as wheat, so when baking bread titicale flour should be combined with wheat flour. Otherwise, you can interchange triticale with similar wheat products in any recipe with excellent results. Like other grains you can complement the protein in triticale with milk products and probably with legumes.

Wheat   Whole wheat contains a moderate amount of fairly high quality protein (NPU of 60). Hard, red, spring wheat contains the largest amount of protein. Wheat is the only grain with an appreciable amount of gluten, a form of protein which is necessary for proper rising of dough; therefore, wheat flour is used, at least in part, in almost all baked goods. Eat wheat in the forms of wheat berries, bulgar, cracked wheat, whole wheat noodles, or baked goods made from whole wheat flour. Complement the protein in wheat with milk products or legumes.

Wheat Germ   Wheat germ is the embryo of the wheat kernal (the part which develops into a plant). The germ contains most of the vitamins, minerals, oil, and protein to be found in the wheat kernal. When wheat germ is called for in the recipes use either raw or toasted wheat germ, depending on your taste preference and what is most easily available. All wheat germ should be kept in the refrigerator to prevent rancidity. To store raw wheat germ for longer than a week, please freeze it. The protein in wheat germ has an NPU of 67, the same as most meats. Raw wheat germ is also an excellent source of the B and E vitamins, but remember that many of these vitamins may be destroyed by the heat required for toasting or by improper handling and storage.

Whole Grain Flours   Whole grain flours are ground from the whole kernal of a grain, including the bran and the germ. Much has been written about the very low nutritional value of white flour. White flour is ground from what is left of the wheat kernal after the germ and bran have been removed. The resulting flour is mostly starch, largely devoid of any vitamins and minerals. Chemical "enrichment" restores only a few of the nutrients which are lost when the germ and bran are removed. I try to avoid white flours like the plague, simply because they are so low in food value. In most recipes you can substitute whole wheat flour for equal amounts of white flour. If you're really afraid of a texture change in substituting, at least use unbleached white flour. In the recipes in this book flour always means whole wheat flour, unless otherwise noted.

For long term storage of whole grain flours refrigerate or freeze them. You can use your blender to grind fresh flour from whole grains, which don't require such careful storage. The blender is especially nice for grinding flours which you use seldom and in small amounts. For instance, I seldom use rye flour. When I need it, I'd much rather grind a half-cup of rye berries into flour than make room in my freezer for a sack of rye flour, which could easily remain there for the better part of a year. Stone ground whole grain flours store better than those ground with steel cutting blades. Stone ground flour seems to store quite well for me at room temperature for about a month. If you use flour less frequently and keep it in the refrigerator or freezer, be sure to let it warm back up to room temperature before adding it to yeast mixtures.

Whole Wheat Pastry Flour This is finely ground whole wheat flour, made from whole kernals of soft wheat rather than the hard wheat usually used for a regular whole wheat flour. Its softness and fine texture make a big difference in pastries and pie crusts. Whole wheat pastry flour is sometimes called graham flour, but make sure you are getting the soft, fine grind if you buy graham flour.

Yeast, Baking Baking yeast is a living organism which is used in breads to make the dough rise. You can buy it in either dry or cake form. Two t. dry yeast (1 pkg.) is equal to ⅔ oz. of cake yeast (usually one cake). Yeast will grow only in a warm, not hot, environment. It feeds on sugars in the flour and honey you use, and as it grows it produces carbon dioxide, which makes the dough rise.

Do not use baking yeast as a nutritional supplement. Live yeast in the system absorbs vitamins for its own use, causing a deficiency in its host. Doughs containing baker's yeast must be baked thoroughly to kill all the yeast so as to avoid the problem of introducing live yeast into the system. See more about yeast in the chapter on baking bread.

Yeast, Brewer's   Brewer's, or nutritional, yeast was originally a by-product of the brewing process. Now it is often grown exclusively for use as a food supplement. In processing, the yeast is killed so it may be eaten without danger of vitamin deficiencies. Brewer's yeast is an excellent source of the B-vitamins and a good source of protein. The protein in brewer's yeast will complement the protein in brown rice.

One problem with brewer's yeast is its taste. Some brands taste pretty good, but some are pretty awful. If you want to take brewer's yeast as a supplement to your diet, and can't find a brand that you like, try stirring the yeast into a little fruit juice and refrigerating the mixture overnight. The change in taste is amazing!

Yogurt   Yogurt is sweet milk into which friendly bacteria are introduced and allowed to grow. Its protein content and quality are the same as the milk from which it is made. Use yogurt to complement the protein in grains, beans, seeds, and vegetables.

SOURCES OF NATURAL FOODS

You may be able to find many natural foods in your local supermarket, if you look. They're often stashed away among the ethnic foods or hidden in the back of the flour shelf. For a larger selection, and the added benefit of getting organically grown foods, find a natural food store or reputable health food store in your area. Food co-ops are another good source of natural foods.

If you come up dry on all these possible sources you can order natural foods through the mail from a number of reputable companies. The following companies sell and ship natural foods. The starred ones are especially quick in answering inquiries.

A & B Natural Foods
2445 Broadway
Ft. Wayne, IN 46807
(219) 744-1413
No catalog, ship UPS, 10% discount on case or bulk items.

Arrowhead Mills
Box 866
Hereford, TX 79045
(806) 364-0370
Wholesale only.

Deer Valley Farm
Guilford, NY 13780
(607) 764-8556

Erewhon Natural Foods
8003 Beverly Blvd.
Los Angeles, CA 90048
(213) 655-5441

Everybody's Store
Van Zandt, WA 98244
Natural and exotic groceries, no catalog. They will ship C.O.D.

The Honey Shop
3150 West Cary St.
Richmond, VA 23221
(804) 358-3943
No catalog, but they do send fliers.

*Jaffe Bros.
P.O. Box 636
Valley Center, CA 92082
(714) 749-1133
Dried and fresh fruits, nuts, seeds, grains, some legumes.

*Natural Sales Company
P.O. Box 25
Pittsburgh, PA 15230
(412) 288-4600
Mostly vitamins and supplements, some grains and legumes, seeds, dried fruit, packaged food.

Rocky Mountain Mail Order
P.O. Box 4073
Boulder, CO 80306
Mail order company for Celestial Seasonings.
Herbs and herb teas, flyer.

Shiloh Farms
Sulphur Springs, AR 72768
(501) 298-3297

*Stern's Natural Food Center
261 Cabot St.
Beverly, MA 01915
(617) 927-4991
Grains, pasta, oils, nuts, herbs, tamari. No catalog.

*Walnut Acres
Penns Creek, PA 17862
(717) 837-6591
Just about everything. Dried fruit, grains, seeds, nuts, legumes, dairy products, pasta, canned goods, cooking equipment.

BIBLIOGRAPHY

COOKBOOKS

Albright, Nancy. *Rodale's Naturally Great Foods Cookbook*. Emmaus: Rodale Press, 1977.

Brooks, Karen. *The Forget About Meat Cookbook*. Emmaus: Rodale Press, 1974.

Day, Avanelle and Stuckey, Lillie. *The Spice Cookbook*. New York: David White Co., 1964.

Ewald, Ellen Buchman. *Recipes for a Small Planet*. New York: Ballantine Books, 1973.

Ford, Frank. *The Simpler Life Cookbook*. Fort Worth: Harvest Press, 1974.

Hewitt, Jean, ed. *The New York Times Natural Foods Cookbook*. New York: Quadrangle Books, 1971.

Lappé, Frances Moore. *Diet for a Small Planet*. New York: Friends of the Earth/Ballantine Books, 1971.

Moyer, Anne, ed. *The Green Thumb Cookbook*. Emmaus: Rodale Press, 1977.

Patten, Marguerite. *The American Everyday Cookbook*. New York: The Hamlyn Publishing Group, 1968.

Rombauer, Irma S. and Becker, Marion Rombauer. *Joy of Cooking*. Indianapolis: Bobbs-Merrill Co., 1931.

Thomas, Anna. *The Vegetarian Epicure*. New York: Alfred A. Knopf, 1972.

NUTRITION

Davis, Adelle. *Let's Eat Right to Keep Fit*. New York: New American Library, 1970.

DeMarco, Toni. *The California Way to Natural Beauty*. New York: Grosset and Dunlap, 1976.

Kloss, Jethro. *Back to Eden*. Coalmont, TN: Longview Publishing House, 1939.

Prevention Magazine. Emmaus: Rodale Press.

Reuben, Dr. David M. *The Save Your Life Diet*. New York: Random House, 1975.

Talking Food Co. *Miso and Tamari, Foods Steeped in Culture*. Charlestown, MA, 1976.

PRESERVING FOOD

Ball Blue Book. Ball Corp., Muncie, IN 47302. 1974.

Bernardin Home Canning Guide. Bernardin, Evansville, IN 47701. 1962.

Kerr Home Canning and Freezing Book. Kerr Glass Manufacturing, Consumer Products Division, Sand Springs, OK 74063. 1950.

Stoner, Carol Hupping, ed. *Stocking Up.* Emmaus: Rodale Press, 1973.

Thurber, Nancy and Mead, Gretchen. *Keeping the Harvest.* Charlotte: Garden Way Publishers, 1976.

HERBS

Foster, Gertrude B. *Herbs for Every Garden.* New York: E.P. Dutton and Co., 1966.

Hylton, William H., ed. *The Rodale Herb Book.* Emmaus: Rodale Press, 1974.

GARDENING

Flanagan, Ted. *Growing Food and Flowers in Containers.* Charlotte: Garden Way Publishers, 1974.

Organic Gardening and Farming Magazine. Emmaus: Rodale Press.

Rodale, Robert, ed. *The Basic Book of Organic Gardening.* New York: Ballantine Books, 1971.

RELATED SUBJECTS

Cadwallader, Sharon. *In Celebration of Small Things.* Boston: Houghton Mifflin Co., 1974.

Rodale, J. I. and staff. *The Organic Directory.* Emmaus: Rodale Books, 1971.

Singer, Peter. *Animal Liberation.* New York: Avon Books, 1975.

INDEX